INDIA AND SAARC ENGAGEMENTS

INDIA AND SAARC ENGAGEMENTS

(In 2 Volumes)

(Volume-2)

Editor
Dr. O.P. Goel

ISHA BOOKS
DELHI-110 033

India and SAARC Engagements

Rs. 1600 (Set)
Rs. 800 (each volume)

ISBN: 81-8205-120-7 (Set)
ISBN: 81-8205-122-3 (Vol. 2)

Published in 2004 in India by
Isha Books, D-43, Prithviraj Road,
Adarsh Nagar, Delhi-110 033

Laser Typesetting at : Shree Vaishnavi Creations, Delhi
Printed at : Chawla Offset Press, Delhi

Contents

14. **Declaration of the Eleventh SAARC Summit, Kathmandu** 303

Regional Cooperation; Cooperation in the Economic Sector; Poverty Alleviation; Cooperation in the Social and Cultural Sector; Women and Children; Education; International Political and Economic Environment; Security of Small States; Terrorism; Report of the Group of Eminent Persons; Enhancing Political Coope-ration; Sub-regional Cooperation; South Asian Development Fund (SADF); Environment; People-to-People Contact; Rationalization and Institutional Issues; SAARC Award; Date and Venue of the Twelfth Summit.

15. **Declaration of the Twelfth SAARC Summit, Islamabad** 325

Regional Cooperation; Poverty Alleviation; Science and Technology; SAARC Award; Information and Communication; SAARC Integrated Programme of Action (SIPA); Sub-Regional Cooperation; Inter-Regional Coope-ration; Enhancing Political Cooperation;

Security of Small States; Thirteenth SAARC Summit.

16. **India and Regional Economic Cooperation** 337
Indo-SAARC Trade Scenario; India's WTO Engagement: Influence of Federalism; Impediments to Economic Cooperation; SAPTA Negotiations.

17. **Potentials of SAARC** 407
Role of SAARC; Future of Cooperation in South Asia; SAARC's Vision for the Future; Centralized SAARC Federal Government.

18. **Democracy and Peace in South Asia** 425
Regional Security Concerns; Security Concern at International Level; India's Security Environment; Security Relationships: Shifting Patterns; Internal Security Issues; Conventional Forces ; Threats of Nuclear Weapons; India's Stand on Nuclear Disarmament ; Energy Security Concerns; Peace Talks; Treaty Between the Republic of India and the Islamic Republic of Pakistan on Measures for Nuclear Risk Reduction; Treaty between the Reublic of India and the Islamic Republic of Pakistan on Notifications of Launches of Balistic Missiles and Space Vehicles; No War Treaty between The Republic of India and the Islamic Republic of Pakistan; Treaty Between the Republic of India and the Islamic Republic of Pakistan on the Establishment of a Demilitarised in the Area of the Siachen Glacier; Agreement between the Republic of India and the Islamic Republic of Pakistan on Easing the the Visa and Travel Restrictions; SAARC's Stand in Kashmir Issue.

19. SAARC LAW **503**
SAARCLAW Charter.

20. Agreement on SAARC Preferential Trading Arrangement (SAPTA) **510**
Preamble; ADDENDUM.

21. SAARC Convention on Preventing and Combating Trafficking in Women and Children For Prostitution on the Member States . **532**

22. SAARC Convention on Regional Arrange ments for the Promotion of Child Welfare in South Asia **542**
Part I - Definitions, Purpose and Guiding Principles; Part II - Regional Priorities and Arrangements; Part III - Relationships and Cooperation.

23. Agreement on Establishing the SAARC Food Security Reserve **553**
Preamble.

24. SAARC Convention on Narcotic Drugs and Psychotropic Substances **561**

25. SAARC Regional Convention on Suppression of Terrorism **582**

26. WIPO Sub-regional Forum for Intellectual Property Cooperation among Member States of the South Asian Association for Regional Cooperation (SAARC) **589**
Forum Statement; Modernization of the Intellectual Property System; Traditional Knowledge, Genetic Resources and Folklore; Intellectual Property and the Digital Environment; Public-Private Sector Partnership Particularly for Small and

Medium-Sized Enterprises (SMEs) and Enforcement; Institutional and Consultative Mechanism; General.

27. **Profile of SAARC Member States** **601**
Bangladesh; Bhutan; India; The Maldives; Nepal; Pakistan; Sri Lanka.

Bibliography 617

Index 619

14

Declaration of the Eleventh SAARC Summit, Kathmandu

The Prime Minister of the People's Republic of Bangladesh, Her Excellency Begum Khaleda Zia; the Prime Minister of the Royal Government of Bhutan, His Excellency Lyonpo Khandu Wangchuk; the Prime Minister of the Republic of India, His Excellency Mr. Atal Behari Vajpayee; the President of the Republic of Maldives, His Excellency Mr. Maumoon Abdul Gayoom; the Prime Minister of the Kingdom of Nepal, Right Honourable Mr. Sher Bahadur Deuba; the President of the Islamic Republic of Pakistan, His Excellency General Pervez Musharraf; and the President of the Democratic Socialist Republic of Sri Lanka, Her Excellency Mrs. Chandrika Bandaranaike Kumaratunga met at the Eleventh Summit meeting of the South Asian Association for Regional Cooperation (SAARC) in Kathmandu, Nepal from 4 to 6 January 2002.

Regional Cooperation

1. The Heads of State or Government reaffirmed their commitment to regional cooperation through SAARC

and underscored the importance of annual Summit meetings in charting common strategies for the realization of the objectives and principles set out in the Charter of the Association. Meeting for the first time at the dawn of the new millennium, they solemnly renewed their pledge to strengthen the Association and make it more cohesive, result oriented, and forward looking, by adopting clearly defined programs and effective implementation strategies in line with popular expectations. To give effect to the shared aspirations for a more prosperous South Asia, the Leaders agreed to the vision of a phased and planned process eventually leading to a South Asian Economic Union.

2. The Heads of State or Government stressed that equitable sharing of the benefits of regional cooperation is essential to achieve and maintain a minimum acceptable level of economic and social development in each Member State. To this end, they expressed their commitment to a speedier process of harmonizing their policies and practices and imbibing regional goals and strategies in their national development programs.

3. The Heads of State or Government expressed their firm determination to fully benefit from the wealth of traditional wisdom, creativity and enterprise in the region. They also pledged to enhance transparency and accountability in governance and to encourage effective participation of the peoples and civil societies in the formulation as well as implementation of the programs of cooperation.

4. Reiterating their resolve to promote South Asian regional identity and to strengthen cooperation at the

international level, the Heads of State or Government also reemphasized the need to evolve common positions on issues of shared interest at the international fora.

Cooperation in the Economic Sector

5. The Heads of State or Government agreed to accelerate cooperation in the core areas of trade, finance and investment to realize the goal of an integrated South Asian economy in a step-by-step manner. They expressed their determination to make full use of regional synergy to maximize the benefits of globalisation and liberalization and to minimize their negative impacts on the region. While recognizing that trade and economic expansion is closely inter-linked, the Leaders made a commitment to widen and deepen the scope of regional networks of activities in trade and financial matters.

6. The Heads of State or Government noted with satisfaction the outcomes of the successive meetings of the SAARC Commerce Ministers aimed at enlarging the scope of cooperation in the core areas. They recognised the importance of achieving a free trade area and reaffirmed that the treaty regime for creating a free trade area must incorporate, inter alia, binding timeframes for freeing trade, measures to facilitate trade and provisions to ensure an equitable distribution of benefits of trade to all states, especially for small and least developed countries, including mechanisms for compensation of revenue loss.

7. Recognising the need to move quickly towards a South Asian Free Trade Area, the Heads of State or Government directed the Council of Ministers to finalize the text of the Draft Treaty Framework by the end of 2002. They also directed that in moving towards the goal of SAFTA, the Member States expedite action to remove tariff and non-tariff barriers and structural impediments to free trade. They also instructed to conclude the meeting of the Inter Governmental Group on Trade Liberalization for the Fourth Round of Trade Negotiations under SAPTA as early as possible as per the decision of the Tenth SAARC Summit in Colombo.

8. The Heads of State or Government renewed their commitment to encourage the participation of the private sector and assured their full support for their socially responsible economic initiatives. While welcoming the practice of holding trade fairs in cooperation with the private sector at the regional level, they appreciated the efforts of the SAARC Chamber of Commerce and Industry to promote regional economic cooperation in the spirit of public and private sector partnership.

9. The Heads of State or Government also decided to instruct the Secretary-General to facilitate the early finalization of a regionally agreed investment framework to meet investment needs of the SAARC Member States.

10. The Heads of State or Government recognized the immense tourism potential of South Asia and underlined the need to take measures to promote South Asia as a common tourist destination through joint efforts in areas such as upgrading of

infrastructure, air linkages, simplification and harmonization of administrative procedures and training and joint marketing.

Poverty Alleviation

11. The Heads of State or Government acknowledged that investment in poverty alleviation programs contributes to social stability, economic progress and overall prosperity. They were of the view that widespread and debilitating poverty continued to be the most formidable developmental challenge for the region. Conscious of the magnitude of poverty in the region, and recalling also the decision of the UN Millennium Summit 2000 to reduce world poverty in half by 2015, and also recalling the commitments made at the five year review of the World Summit for Social Development to reduce poverty through enhanced social mobilization, the Heads of State or Government made a review of the SAARC activities aimed at poverty alleviation and decided to reinvigorate them in the context of the regional and global commitments to poverty reduction.

12. The Heads of State or Government expressed their firm resolve to combat the problem of poverty with a new sense of urgency by actively promoting the synergetic partnership among national governments, international agencies, the private sector, and the civil society. They reaffirmed their pledge to undertake effective and sustained poverty alleviation programs through pro-poor growth strategies and social as well as other policy interventions with specific sectoral targets. The Leaders also agreed to

take immediate steps for the effective implementation of the programs for social mobilization and decentralization, and for strengthening institution building and support mechanisms to ensure participation of the poor, both as stake-holder and beneficiary, in governance and the development process.

13. The Heads of State or Government decided to undertake sustained measures to extend rural micro-credit programs with focus on women and the disadvantaged sections of society. They also stressed the need for widening the opportunities for gainful employment. While highlighting the importance of promoting agriculture, indigenous skills and small scale and cottage industries to address the incidence of rural poverty, they decided to enhance cooperation in agricultural research, extension and adoption. They specifically instructed that the Technical Committees should identify programmes and activities that impact on poverty alleviation. They urged the need to create gainful employment and promote cooperation in vocational training.

14. The Heads of State or Government emphasized the need to promote sharing of the best practices and experiences among the Member States and to this end, instructed the Secretary-General to disseminate such information to the Member States on a regular basis. They directed the Council of Ministers to review, on a continuous basis, the regional poverty profile to be prepared by the Secretary-General with the assistance of the related UN agencies, nodal agencies and independent research institutions specialized in the field.

15. In order to ensure social stability and to protect the vulnerable sections of population from the adverse impacts of globalisation and liberalization, the Heads of State or Government stressed the need to enhance cooperation to create and maintain appropriate safety nets.

16. The Heads of State or Government agreed that a Special Session on poverty alleviation at the Ministerial level should undertake a comprehensive review and evaluation of the status of implementation of poverty eradication policies and programs carried out so far, and to recommend further concrete measures to enhance effective cooperation at the regional level to the Twelfth SAARC Summit. They also directed the Council of Ministers to take necessary steps to fully activate the existing three-tier mechanism for poverty alleviation.

17. The Leaders directed the Council of Ministers to coordinate efforts to integrate poverty alleviation programs into the development strategies of Member States. In this context, they agreed to reconstitute the Independent South Asian Commission on Poverty Alleviation, with Nepal as its Convener and Bangladesh as Co-convenor, for reviewing the progress made in cooperation on poverty alleviation and for suggesting appropriate and effective measures. They instructed the Chairman of the Council of Ministers to seek two nominations from each Member State by end of January 2002 to enable the convening of its first meeting before the proposed Ministerial Meeting on Poverty Alleviation in Pakistan in April 2002.

18. Expressing concern at the region's special vulnerability in the slowdown in world economy and its negative impact on the poor and the marginalized, the Heads of State or Government called for a supportive international environment and an enhanced level of assistance by the international community for poverty alleviation programs in South Asia.

Cooperation in the Social and Cultural Sector

19. The Heads of State or Government reiterated the need for an early finalisation of the SAARC Social Charter and instructed the Inter Governmental Expert Group to expedite their work on the basis of the draft to be submitted by the Secretary-General, as a working paper for its consideration and to complete the draft framework of the Charter as early as possible for consideration at the next meeting of the Council of Ministers. In drawing up the Charter, they also directed the Council of Ministers to include the important areas of poverty eradication, population stabilization, the empowerment of women, youth mobilization, human resources development, the promotion of health and nutrition and the protection of children as decided at the Tenth Summit.

20. The Leaders recognized the debilitating and widespread impact of the HIV/ AIDS, TB and other deadly communicable diseases on the population of South Asia and stressed the need for evolving a regional strategy to combat these diseases. The strategy should include, inter alia, culturally appropriate preventive measures, an affordable

treatment regime and should specially target the vulnerable groups. In this regard, they felt that SAARC should collaborate with the international organizations and civil society. They also emphasized that the SAARC Tuberculosis Centre in Kathmandu should play a coordinating role in the related areas.

21. In accordance with the Colombo Declaration, the Heads of State or Government decided to mandate the Meeting of Ministers of Cultural Affairs in Sri Lanka to finalise the details relating to the establishment of the SAARC Cultural Centre including its financing and to submit its report to the next session of the Council of Ministers.

Women and Children

22. The Heads of State or Government welcomed the signing of the SAARC Convention on Preventing and Combating the Trafficking in Women and Children for Prostitution and expressed their collective resolve to treat the trafficking in women and children for commercial sexual exploitation as a criminal offence of a serious nature. They also welcomed the signing of the SAARC Convention on Regional Arrangements for the Promotion of Child Welfare in South Asia and observed that the Convention reflected their commitment to place the child first in the national and regional programs of the Member States. They instructed the Secretary-General, in consultation with Member States and other specialised agencies, to present a report on measures for the effective implementation of the Conventions to the next meeting of the Council of Ministers.

23. The Heads of State or Government agreed to establish, on the basis of recommendations of the Regional Task Force responsible for the implementation of the provisions of the SAARC Convention on Preventing and Combating Trafficking in Women and Children for Prostitution, a voluntary fund with contributions from Member States, individuals, and donor countries and agencies for the rehabilitation and reintegration of the victims of trafficking.

24. The Leaders recognized the need to form an autonomous advocacy group of prominent women personalities from the Member States with a view to making recommendations to the SAARC bodies on a broad spectrum of gender related issues. They directed the Council of Ministers to take necessary steps to prepare and present, for consideration at their next meeting, the Terms of Reference for the purpose.

25. The Heads of State or Government recognized the need to actively pursue and promote social development through empowerment of women and to achieve their full participation in decision making at all levels. They reaffirmed their commitment to uplift the social status of the people, women and children in particular, in the region and expressed their common resolve to accord the highest priority to promoting social development through specific and targeted programs. The Leaders directed the Council of Ministers to take necessary measures to ensure the enjoyment by women and girl children of their inherent potential. They also directed the Council of Ministers to constitute a Task Force to

review the status of implementation of past decisions related to the social sector and to suggest guidelines for their effective implementation in the future.

26. The Leaders directed the Council of Ministers to take concrete steps to give priority to investing in children as an effective means for poverty reduction in the long run. Reaffirming their commitment to the Colombo Plan of Action and the Rawalpindi Declaration and recalling the declaration of 2001 to 2010 as the SAARC Decade of the Rights of the Child, the Heads of State or Government noted with appreciation the South Asia High-level Meeting on Children held in Kathmandu in May 2001. They reaffirmed their conviction that the children in South Asia deserve urgent and focused attention to enhance the long-term and overall progress of the countries of the region.

27. The Heads of State or Government agreed to mobilize the necessary resources and intensify broad based actions to achieve a set of priority goals related to improving the status of children, such as polio eradication by 2005, protection of children from mother-to-child transmission of HIV/AIDS, and quality basic education to the children within a time-bound period.

Education

28. The Heads of State or Government instructed the concerned Ministries of Governments to devise appropriate strategies for raising the quality of education through the exchange of information among the universities in the region. While

emphasizing the importance of mutual recognition of the educational institutions, they agreed to give the necessary impetus to realize the goal of a common regional educational standard through uniform methods of instruction and teaching aids. They were unanimous in recognizing the benefit of introducing SAARC in the national curricula at appropriate levels of study in order to enhance the awareness about Association's goals and objectives.

29. The Heads of State or Government recognized that access to quality education was an important element for the empowerment of all segments of society, and undertook to develop or strengthen national strategies and action plans to ensure that all children particularly the girl child have access to quality primary education by 2015; and to improve levels of adult literacy by fifty percent by eliminating gender disparities in access to education as envisaged in the Dakar Framework for Action on Education for All adopted by the World Education Forum held at Dakar in April 2000.

International Political and Economic Environment

30. The Heads of State or Government reiterated their firm support for the principles and purposes of the United Nations in order to create a just, balanced and equitable world order. They reaffirmed their commitment to continue working with the NAM and other like-minded countries for the reform and democratisation of the United Nations System with a view to making it an effective and more democratic institution for international peace, security, progress and cooperation.

31. The Heads of State or Government were of the view that stability, peace and security in South Asia should be promoted together with efforts to improve the global security environment. They underscored their commitment to general and complete disarmament including nuclear disarmament on a universal basis, under effective international control. They agreed that global non-proliferation goals could not be achieved in the absence of progress towards nuclear disarmament and in this context called upon all nuclear weapon states, whether party or non-party to the NPT, to engage constructively through a transparent and credible process of negotiations at the Conference on Disarmament. The Leaders also recognized the linkage between disarmament and development.

32. The Leaders emphasized the need to take appropriate measures to make international financial institutions and the global trading regime more responsive to the needs and concerns of the developing countries. They reiterated the call for genuine partnership among the developed and developing countries in international trade and finance and for the reform of the global financial architecture with an enhanced level of resources.

33. The Leaders also called upon the developed countries to facilitate and ensure an unimpeded and enhanced level of market access to products from the developing, the least developed and the land-locked countries.

34. Recognizing the important role that trade can play in advancing the overall development of a country, thus contributing to an equitable and sustainable world

order, the Heads of State or Government also called for an early realization of a rule-based and non-discriminatory world trade regime. In this context, they appreciated the positive elements of the Fourth WTO Ministerial Conference held in Doha and called upon the developed countries to fulfill their commitments to address the particular concerns and needs of the developing and the least developed countries. The Leaders also instructed the forthcoming meeting of the Committee on Economic Cooperation to devote at least half a day for discussions on the evaluation of the decisions of the recently concluded Doha conference in order to evolve better co-ordinated positions among the Member States on all WTO issues. They further stressed the need to intensify coordination among the SAARC missions in Geneva and begin the necessary preparation to advance the common interest of the region in the Fifth WTO Ministerial conference.

35. The Heads of State or Government noted with serious concern the adverse impact of the shrinking Official Development Assistance (ODA) and other concessional financial flows on developing countries in general, and the least developed among them in particular. They further noted with concern the current trend of the global economic slowdown and its adverse effects on these economies. Taking into account the interdependent nature of the global economy, the Leaders urged the developed countries to enhance the level of ODA flows to meet the internationally agreed targets.

36. Recalling the recommendations of the Third United Nations Conference on the Least Developed Countries held in Brussels in May 2001 and the

decisions of the Zanzibar Declaration of July 2001, the Leaders urged the developed countries to adopt more liberal trade and aid policies responsive to the particular needs of the least developed countries. Referring to the forthcoming International Conference on Financing for Development to be held in Mexico in March 2002, the Leaders urged the international community to strengthen cooperation for development by addressing international and systemic issues related to financing for development in the developing and the least developed countries in a holistic manner.

37. The Heads of State or Government welcomed the initiative of the donor countries to relieve the external debt burden of the Highly Indebted Poor Countries. They urged the international donor community and financial institutions to widen the scope and extent of debt relief initiatives to cover all those developing and the least developed countries, which are facing developmental difficulties particularly due to the current global recession. In the context of growing global interdependence, they underlined the importance of forging cooperative partnership between the developed and the developing countries to ensure equitable benefits to all.

38. The Heads of State or Government expressed concern over the continued violence and bloodshed in the Middle East, and the set backs suffered by the peace process. They reaffirmed their support for the achievement of a just, lasting and comprehensive peace based on Security Council Resolution 242 (1967) and Resolution 338 (1973) and the establishment of a sovereign Palestine State under the

leadership of PLO, which could coexist with its neighbours in peace, security and harmony.

Security of Small States

39. The Heads of State or Government recognized that due to their particular vulnerability, small states require special measures for support from the international community for the safeguarding of their sovereign independence and territorial integrity. They reiterated that the real protection of small states should be firmly rooted in the scrupulous adherence to the UN Charter, the rule of law and the strict adherence to universally accepted principles and norms related to sovereign rights and territorial integrity of all states, irrespective of size. This, they stressed, should be ensured by all the countries, either severally or collectively through the pursuit of appropriate action.

Terrorism

40. The Heads of State or Government were convinced that terrorism, in all its forms and manifestations, is a challenge to all states and to all of humanity, and cannot be justified on ideological, political, religious or on any other ground. The Leaders agreed that terrorism violates the fundamental values of the United Nations and the SAARC Charter and constitutes one of the most serious threats to international peace and security in the Twenty-first century.

41. The Heads of State or Government emphasized the need for the urgent conclusion of a Comprehensive Convention on Combating International Terrorism. They also emphasized that international co-operation to combat terrorism should be conducted in conformity with the UN Charter, international law and relevant international conventions.

42. The Heads of State or Government reiterated their support to the United Nations Security Council Resolution 1373 of September 28, 2001 and affirmed their determination to redouble efforts, collectively as well as individually, to prevent and suppress terrorism in all its forms and manifestations, including by increased cooperation and full implementation of the relevant international Conventions relating to terrorism to which they are parties. In this context, they called on all states to prevent and suppress the financing of terrorist acts by criminalizing the collection of funds for such acts and refraining from organizing, instigating, assisting or participating in terrorist acts in states or acquiescing in organized activities within its territory directed towards the commission of such acts. The Leaders reaffirmed that the fight against terrorism in all its forms and manifestations has to be comprehensive and sustained.

43. The Heads of State or Government were unanimous in recognizing the distinct ominous link between terrorism, drug-trafficking, money laundering and other trans-national crimes and emphasized the need to coordinate efforts at the national and regional levels to strengthen the global response to this serious challenge and threat to international security.

They called upon the international community to assist Member States of SAARC to deal effectively with the adverse economic effects of terrorism in general and to meet the rising insurance and security related costs in particular.

44. The Heads of State or Government reaffirmed their commitment to SAARC Regional Convention on Suppression of Terrorism, which, among others, recognizes the seriousness of the problem of terrorism as it affects the security, stability, and development of the region. They also reiterated their firm resolve to accelerate the enactment of enabling legislation within a definite time-frame for the full implementation of the Convention, together with strengthening of SAARC Terrorist Offences Monitoring Desk and the SAARC Drug Offences Monitoring Desk in an effective manner.

Report of the Group of Eminent Persons

45. The Leaders noted with appreciation that the Report of the Group of Eminent Persons (GEP) was an important contribution in the on-going process of introspection into the functioning of the Association as well as in setting out a perspective plan of action for that purpose. They endorsed the report of the Council of Ministers on the implementation of the recommendations of the GEP Report, and directed the Council of Ministers to undertake a review of progress in this regard.

Enhancing Political Cooperation

46. The Heads of State or Government reaffirmed their commitment to the promotion of mutual trust and

understanding and, recognizing that the aims of promoting peace, stability and amity and accelerated socio-economic cooperation may best be achieved by fostering good neighbourly relations, relieving tensions and building confidence, agreed that a process of informal consultations would prove useful in this regard. The Leaders further recognized that this process would contribute to the appreciation of each other's problems and perceptions as well as for decisive action in agreed areas of regional cooperation. They underlined the importance of informal political consultations in promoting mutual understanding and reinforcing the confidence building process among the Member States.

Sub-regional Cooperation

47. The Heads of State or Government reaffirmed the validity of the idea of encouraging the development of specific projects relevant to the individual needs of three or more Member States under the provisions of Articles VII and X of the SAARC Charter.

South Asian Development Fund (SADF)

48. The Heads of State or Government underlined the urgent need to make the South Asian Development Fund operational by making utilization of the existing funds. They also instructed the Secretary-General to submit a proposal for seeking possible assistance from regional and international sources for the implementation of specific regional poverty alleviation priority projects.

Environment

49. The Heads of State or Government noted with satisfaction the growing public awareness on the need for protecting the environment within the framework of regional cooperation. They reiterated their call for the early and effective implementation of the SAARC Environment Plan of Action as endorsed by the SAARC Environment Ministers. They directed their Environment Ministers to take this into account and come up with an agreed position in their forthcoming meeting.

50. The Heads of State or Government also felt a strong need to devise a mechanism for cooperation in the field of the early warning on as well as preparedness and management of natural disasters, along with programs to promote conservation of land and water resources.

51. The Heads of State or Government also stressed the need to develop a cooperative mechanism for the protection, enrichment and utilization of bio-diversity as provided for in the UN Convention on Biological Diversity and to establish a regional bio-diversity database with a view to providing equitable benefits to all Member States. They also underscored the importance of protecting associated knowledge and other indigenous intellectual manifestations for the advancement of the region. They also directed the Council of Ministers to explore the possibility of establishing a SAARC Seed Security Reserve to strengthen cooperation in the field of agriculture and to protect IPRs of the seeds of the Reserve.

People-to-People Contact

52. The Heads of State or Government were unanimous in recognizing the need for further promoting a sense of regional identity amongst the peoples of the region. The Leaders lauded the roles played by intellectuals, professionals and eminent persons in promoting people-to-people contacts within the region and agreed to encourage such endeavours as a healthy sign of regional cohesion and fraternity. In this context, they took note of the activities of the SAARCLAW including other recognized bodies. They also took note of the First Meeting of the Chief Election Commissioners of SAARC Countries held in Kathmandu in February 1999 and appreciated the initiative on free and fair election. The Leaders instructed the Secretary-General to collect on a regular basis study reports and other relevant documents and information from the civil society on matters relating to regional cooperation for dissemination to Member States.

Rationalization and Institutional Issues

53. The Heads of State or Government were in agreement that the Summit and all other meetings of SAARC needed to be made more business-like and result-oriented with focus on programs and activities supported by informed regional inputs from the cross-sections of the society. They directed the Chairman of the Council of Ministers to undertake a review of the functioning and operation of SAARC Secretariat, and to make recommendations to advance the process of rationalisation and to make SAARC

more functional and business-like, to the next meeting of the Council of Ministers.

SAARC Award

54. The Heads of State or Government noted with appreciation the proposal made by Nepal to institute a SAARC Award to honour the outstanding work of individuals and organizations within the region in the fields of peace, development, poverty alleviation and regional cooperation, and requested His Majesty's Government of Nepal to submit a concept paper for consideration by the next session of the Council of Ministers.

Date and Venue of the Twelfth Summit

55. The Heads of State or Government welcomed with appreciation the offer of the Government of the Islamic Republic of Pakistan to host the Twelfth Summit Meeting of the Heads of State or Government of the South Asian Association for the Regional Cooperation (SAARC) in Pakistan in early 2003.

56. The Heads of State or Government of Bangladesh, Bhutan, India, Maldives, Pakistan and Sri Lanka expressed their deep appreciation for the exemplary manner in which the Right Honourable Prime Minister of Nepal conducted the proceedings of the Eleventh SAARC Summit in his capacity as Chairperson. They also expressed their deep gratitude for the generous hospitality extended to them by His Majesty's Government and people of Nepal, and for the excellent arrangements made for the Summit.

15

Declaration of the Twelfth SAARC Summit, Islamabad

We, the Prime Minister of the People's Republic of Bangladesh , Begum Khaleda Zia, the Prime Minister of the Kingdom of Bhutan, Lyonpo Jigmi Yoezer Thinley, the Prime Minister of the Republic of India, Atal Behari Vajpayee, the President of the Republic of Maldives, Maumoon Abdul Gayoom, the Prime Minister of the Kingdom of Nepal, Surya Bahadur Thapa, the Prime Minister of the Islamic Republic of Pakistan, Mir Zafarullah Khan Jamali and the President of the Democratic Socialist Republic of Sri Lanka, Chandrika Bandaranaike Kumaratunga:

Having met at the Twelfth Summit meeting of the South Asian Association for Regional Cooperation (SAARC) in Islamabad, Pakistan, on 4-6 January 2004;

Guided by the vision of a peaceful and prosperous South Asia and proud of its rich culture and traditions;

Deeply conscious of the growing interdependence within and amongst nations and regions in an increasingly globalizing world;

Desirous of promoting peace, stability, amity and progress in the region through strict adherence to the principles of the United Nations Charter and Non-Alignment, particularly respect for the principles of sovereign equality, territorial integrity, national independence, non-use of force and non-interference in the internal affairs of the states and peaceful settlement of all disputes;

Reaffirming the centrality of SAARC for promoting regional cooperation and emphasizing the need to enhance its efficacy;

Strongly reaffirming our commitment to the objectives, principles and provisions of the Charter of the South Asian Association for Regional Cooperation (SAARC);

Declare that:

Regional Cooperation

Economic

1. We renew our commitment to the objectives and principles of SAARC and pledge to reinvigorate cooperation to realize peace, amity, progress and prosperity of all peoples of South Asia.
2. We affirm our determination to create an inclusive, just and equitable partnership for peace, development and prosperity. Satisfactory progress has been made in SAPTA. The signing of the Framework Agreement on SAFTA is a major milestone. It is important to maintain this momentum

and move towards further broadening of economic cooperation and to ensure equitable distribution of benefits of trade and cater to the special needs of the small and LDC Member States by providing them special and differential treatment.

3. We reiterate our commitment made at the 11th SAARC Summit at Kathmandu in January 2002 for the creation of a South Asian Economic Union. In this context, we underline that creation of a suitable political and economic environment would be conducive to the realization of this objective.

4. A study on creating a South Asian Energy Cooperation including the concept of an Energy Ring should be undertaken by the Working Group on Energy.

5. For accelerated and balanced economic growth it is essential to strengthen transportation, transit and communication links across the region.

6. Public and private sector cooperation, particularly joint ventures holds great promise. It is important to move towards Project cooperation under SAARC. Prospects for setting up of a South Asian Development Bank should be examined by the SAARCFINANCE through the council of ministers.

7. Priority attention should also be given to the need for harmonization of standards, simplification of custom procedures, as well as cooperation among the central banks.

8. Development of tourism within South Asia could bring economic, social and cultural dividends. There is a need for increasing cooperation to jointly promote tourism within South Asia as well as to

promote South Asia as a tourism destination inter alia by improved air links. To achieve this and to commemorate the twentieth year of the establishment of SAARC, the year 2005 is designated as "South Asia Tourism Year", for the success of which, each member would individually and jointly organize special events.

9. SAARC members should continue to safeguard their collective interests in multilateral forums by discussing, coordinating and exchanging information with a view to adopting common positions, where appropriate, on various issues.

Poverty Alleviation

10. We recognise poverty alleviation as the greatest challenge facing the peoples of South Asia and declare poverty alleviation as the overarching goal of all SAARC activities. It is imperative to relate regional co-operation to the actual needs of the people.

11. Provision of basic needs, promotion of literacy, and better health care are a regional priority. It is important to undertake effective and sustained poverty reduction programmes through pro-poor growth strategies and other policy interventions with specific sectoral targets.

12. The Plan of Action on Poverty Alleviation, prepared by the meeting of Finance and Planning Ministers in Islamabad in 2002, is hereby approved.

13. The reconstituted Independent South Asian Commission for Poverty Alleviation (ISACPA) has

done commendable work. An effective strategy should be devised to implement suggestions made in its Report "Our Future Our Responsibility". In this context, ISACPA should continue its advocacy role. It should prepare and submit to the next SAARC summit a comprehensive and realistic blue-print setting out SAARC Development Goals for the next five years in the areas of poverty alleviation, education, health and environment giving due regard, among others, to the suggestions made in the ISACPA report.

14. The SAARC Secretariat should periodically update and submit Regional Poverty Profiles.

15. SAARC should continue to collaborate with international organizations and UN agencies in the field of poverty alleviation. Arrangements for SAARC Food Security Reserve should be made more effective. We also recommend the establishment of a Regional Food Bank for which a concept paper should be prepared.

16. Investment in human resources is critical for future development of South Asia. It is, therefore, essential to establish a network of centres of higher learning, training and Skill Development Institutes (SDI) across South Asia. In this context, the role of the SAARC Human Resource Development Centre (SHRDC) is important.

Science and Technology

17. Strengthening of scientific and technological co-operation across the region is fundamental to

accelerating the pace of economic and social development. Sharing of scientific and technological expertise, joint research and development and industrial application of higher technology should be encouraged and facilitated.

Social

18. We hail the signing of the SAARC Social Charter as a historic development, which would have a far-reaching impact on the lives of millions of South Asians. Issues covered under the Charter, such as poverty alleviation, population stabilization, empowerment of women, youth mobilization, human resource development, promotion of health and nutrition and protection of children are key to the welfare and well being of all South Asians.
19. Progress has been made in the constitution of SAARC Autonomous Advocacy Group of Prominent Women Personalities (SAWAG). To enable women to contribute to the socio-economic development, there is a need for SAARC to encourage women entrepreneurs in the region.
20. Member states should move towards an early ratification of the two Conventions on Child Welfare and Trafficking in Women and Children for Prostitution.
21. Easy and affordable health care, prevention and treatment of HIV/AIDS, Tuberculosis and other serious communicable diseases are priorities. The year 2004 is declared as the "SAARC Awareness Year". The SAARC Secretariat should effectively

implement the proposed programmes on the observation of the SAARC Awareness Year and develop a regional strategy through a consultative process and collaborate closely with the Joint UN Programme on HIV/AIDS (UNAIDS) and other international organizations and civil society.

22. The important initiative taken by the Maldives in hosting the Emergency Meeting of the SAARC Health Ministers on SARS epidemic in Male' on 29 April 2003, was a welcome development.

23. As agreed by the SAARC Health Ministers' Conference held recently in New Delhi, a SAARC Health Surveillance Centre and a Rapid Deployment Health Response System should be set up to deal with the emerging and re-emerging diseases as well as to establish a network between various Institutions dealing with malaria and other vector borne diseases in the Member States. Also, documentation of traditional knowledge to safeguard Intellectual Property Rights (IPRs) in medicine needs attention.

24. The importance of cooperation in medical expertise and pharmaceuticals as well as in the field of traditional medicine requires elaboration of a SAARC Plan of Action that should be developed in the shortest possible time.

Cultural

25. We take pride in the rich cultural mosaic of the peoples of South Asia and underline the need for preservation of traditional skills and crafts and promotion of cultural exchanges between nations.

26. We welcome the establishment of a SAARC Cultural Centre in Kandy, which will serve as a symbol of South Asian shared cultural heritage.

Environment

27. It is important to undertake and reinforce regional cooperation in the conservation of our water resources, environment, pollution prevention and control as well as our preparedness to deal with natural calamities. We welcome the early establishment of the Coastal Zone Management Centre in the Maldives.

28. The early and effective implementation of the SAARC Environment Plan of Action is important. We further stressed the early submission of the State of the Environment reports to expedite the preparation of SAARC State of Environment report and the commissioning of the work on drafting a Regional Environment Treaty.

Combating Terrorism

29. We condemn terrorist violence in all its forms and manifestations and note that people of South Asia continue to face a serious threat from terrorism.

30. We are convinced that terrorism, in all its forms and manifestations, is a challenge to all states and to all of humanity, and cannot be justified on any ground, whatsoever. Terrorism violates the fundamental values of the United Nations and the SAARC Charter and constitutes one of the most serious threats to international peace and security. We agree to fully

implement the relevant international conventions to which we are parties.

31. We reaffirm our commitment to SAARC Regional Convention on Suppression of Terrorism, which, among others, recognizes the seriousness of the problem of terrorism as it affects the security, stability, and development of the region.

32. The signing of the Additional Protocol to the SAARC Regional Convention on Combating Terrorism to deal effectively with financing of terrorism is a further manifestation of our determination to eliminate all forms and manifestations of terrorism from South Asia.

SAARC Award

33. We welcome the institution of the SAARC Award on the basis of a concept paper drawn up by His Majesty's Government of Nepal and decide to present the award during the Summits in future. The Award will honour and encourage outstanding individuals and organizations within the region in the fields of peace, development, poverty alleviation, and in other areas of regional cooperation.

Information and Communication

34. We recognize the vital role that information and media can play in the promotion of peace, progress and harmony in South Asia. In this context, the initiatives for introducing regular 'SAARC Roundup' and 'SAARC News' programmes for telecast and broadcast on National TV and Radio Channels,

respectively, in Member Countries is a welcome development. We agree to the establishment of a SAARC Information Centre in Kathmandu.

35. SAARC should endeavour to bring the benefits of information and communications technology to all peoples of the region, bridging the digital divide and assist in the development of knowledge based societies.

SAARC Integrated Programme of Action (SIPA)

36. We note with satisfaction the progress achieved in regional cooperation through SIPA. The commitment to SIPA must be matched by a corresponding allocation of resources for it.

Sub-Regional Cooperation

37. We encourage the development of specific projects relevant to the individual needs of three or more Member States under the provisions of Articles VII and X of the SAARC Charter.

Inter-Regional Cooperation

38. We express our determination to develop mutually beneficial links between SAARC and other regional and international organizations, bodies and entities and agree to establish dialogue partnership with other regional bodies and with states outside the region, interested in SAARC activities.

Enhancing Political Cooperation

39. We envision South Asia to be a peaceful and stable region where each nation is at peace with itself and its neighbours and where conflicts, differences and disputes are addressed through peaceful means and dialogue.

40. Reaffirm our pledge to promote good neighbourly relations on the basis of the principles of sovereign equality, territorial integrity and national independence, non-use of force, non-intervention and non-interference and peaceful settlement of disputes and recognize the importance of informal political consultations in promoting mutual understanding and reinforcing confidence building process among Member States.

Security of Small States

41. We are particularly mindful of the security concerns of small states that arise, inter alia, from their particular vulnerabilities, which should be firmly addressed by scrupulous adherence to the UN Charter, rules of international law and strict adherence to the universally accepted principles and norms related to sovereign rights and territorial integrity of all states. This should be ensured by all, both severally and collectively, through appropriate actions.

42. We endorse the recommendations made by the Council of Ministers at its Twenty-third and Twenty-fourth sessions.

Thirteenth SAARC Summit

43. We appreciate the offer of the People's Republic of Bangladesh to host the Thirteenth SAARC Summit in January 2005.

16

India and Regional Economic Cooperation

SAARC is a manifestation of the determination of the peoples of South Asia to Cooperate regionally and to work together towards finding solutions to their common problems in a spirit of friendship, trust and understanding based on mutual respect, equity and shared benefits.

The SAARC countries account about 21 per cent of the world population and only 3.5 per cent of total land area. However, their share in world output is a mere 1.3 per cent. Further, their share in world merchandise trade is about 1.0 per cent. About half of the World poor inhabit this part of the world. Barring Maldives, all the SAARC countries are low income economies. Their per capita GNP range from US $ 180 (Nepal) to US $ 1000 (Maldives). The per capita GNP of all the members of SAARC taken together was barely about US $ 342 in 1995.

The idea of regional cooperation was first proposed through 'a regional forum' by Bangladesh in 1980, with a view to holding periodic, regional-level consultations among countries in South Asia on matters of mutual interest and possible cooperation in economic, social, cultural and other fields. The rationale was primarily predicated on the premise that regional experiences elsewhere in the globe had been highly successful and that the countries in the South Asian region would benefit enormously from such cooperation as it would strengthen their competitive position, both individually and as a group.

The Bangladesh proposal argued that inherent logic strongly justified regional cooperation, particularly among South Asian countries, because the countries in the region enjoy geographical contiguity, historical, social, cultural and ethnic affinities which would act as centripetal forces and thus, contribute substantively to facilitate coordination and to reducing of transaction costs.

The Foreign Secretaries of the seven South Asian countries accordingly agreed at their first meeting in Colombo (21 - 23 April, 1981) to pursue cooperation in five broad areas, namely agriculture, rural development, telecommunications, meteorology, and health and population services. The Foreign Secretaries also agreed to set up a Committee of the Whole comprising senior officials from the seven countries to identify and report on other areas of possible cooperation. At the first Meeting of this Committee in Colombo (31 August – 2 September 1981), the need to expand economic relations, and the need for cooperation in international economic negotiations were discussed.

In 1983, (24-25 January) the first meeting of the representatives of National Planning Organizations was held in New Delhi. This was in fact, the first 'economic' meeting at a regional level among the South Asian countries. The meeting focussed on three areas viz. first, national planning models and techniques; second, poverty alleviation programmes and third, the global economic situation. The meeting agreed on the need for regular consultations and exchange of information, but more importantly, it called for the systematic exploration of the scope for intra-regional economic cooperation.

The SAARC Charter mentions that among the objectives of the Association shall be acceleration of economic growth, social progress and cultural development in the region, promotion of active collaboration and mutual assistance in the economic, social, cultural, technical and scientific fields and strengthening of cooperation among the Member States in international fora on matters of common interest.

Regional cooperation agreements in other parts of the world identified economic cooperation as constituting the very heart, as it were, of cooperation among the countries, without which the extent and accruant benefits may be severely constrained. However, within the SAARC region a fundamental asymmetry among the Member States, their varied levels of development, including administrative procedures and rules, suggested that economic cooperation, while important, was likely to be a complex and gradual process. Accordingly, the first SAARC Summit in Dhaka (1985) primarily focussed on regional cooperation in areas such as health, population activities and child welfare; culture and sports.

This is not to imply that the Association had decided to leave out economic cooperation. In fact, in 1986, the first Ministerial Meeting on International Economic Issues was held in Islamabad (31 March – 3 April). The

Declaration of this Ministerial Meeting stressed the need for intensifying economic cooperation among SAARC countries and also agreed that SAARC countries should coordinate their positions at the various headquarters of regional and international organizations, as well as in relevant international conferences to further the common objectives of member countries.

In 1987, the representatives of the National Planning Organisations met for the second time in Islamabad (11 - 14 October) and recommended that in view of the adverse international economic situation facing the region, there was a need to pool resources for long-term regional cooperation.

Recognizing asymmetries at the development levels and the fact that the share of SAARC in world trade was relatively small, the Meeting recommended that analytical studies need to be carried out in the first instance to facilitate identification of priority areas for economic cooperation. As a result of this recommendation, a consultant was commissioned to carry out a Study on Trade, Manufactures and Services (TMS) in the South Asian region. Meanwhile, the National Planning Organizations continued to meet and agreed on a series of initiatives which would intensify the consultative process particularly in basic needs programmes and poverty alleviation.

The TMS Study, which was completed in 1991, considered economic cooperation among the countries of the SAARC region as an inevitable imperative for promoting all-round development of the region. In May 1991, the Council of Ministers at their Ninth Session at Malé endorsed the Study and established a high-level Committee known as the Committee on Economic

Cooperation (CEC) comprising Commerce/Trade Secretaries of the SAARC Member States.

The CEC was mandated to formulate and oversee implementation of specific measures, policies and programmes within the SAARC framework to strengthen and enhance intra-regional cooperation in the fields of trade and economic relations. With the creation of the CEC, regional economic cooperation was formally institutionalized. To date, the CEC has held ten meetings.

Over the years, the CEC has emerged as one of the most important groups within the SAARC having a mandate over economic and trade issues. The CEC has provided recommendations and guidance in identifying new areas for cooperation on economic and trade related matters as well as considering reports of constituted groups. In fact, the mandate of the CEC includes monitoring cooperation in areas such as standards and measurement; customs and the harmonization of procedures; preferential trading arrangement; rules of origin; agreements for the promotion and protection of investments within the SAARC Region as also for the avoidance of double taxation; setting up of a SAARC Arbitration Council; sharing information on economic and trade related matters; taking note of special circumstances of Least Developed Countries within the Region; and formulation of joint strategies to be adopted in multilateral negotiating fora. The recommendations of the CEC are submitted to the Standing Committee (of Foreign Secretaries) and through it to higher bodies, namely the Council of Ministers and the Summit.

In December 1991, the Sixth Summit held in Colombo approved the establishment of an Inter-Governmental Group (IGG) to formulate an agreement to establish a SAARC Preferential Trading Arrangement (SAPTA) by 1997. Given the consensus within SAARC, the framework Agreement on SAPTA was finalized in 1993, and formally came into operation in December 1995, well in advance of the date stipulated by the Colombo Summit. The Agreement reflected the desire of the SAARC countries to promote and sustain mutual trade and economic cooperation within the SAARC region through exchange of concessions.

As recommended by the IGG, the Consolidated National Schedules of Concessions agreed to by the SAARC Member States during the First, Second and Third Rounds of Trade Negotiations under SAPTA have been merged by the SAARC Secretariat. You are welcome to access the Merged Consolidated National Schedules of Concessions as approved by the SAARC Member States during the three rounds of trade negotiations under SAPTA.

The table below shows the number of products on which preferential tariff concession has been granted by the Member States in the three rounds put together. The Table have also gives an indication of depth of preferential tariff concession granted by the Member States to LDCs and 1DCs:

Table 1. Number of Products covered and the Depth of Preferential Tariff Concessions agreed to by SAARC Member States in the first three rounds of trade negotiations under SAPTA

Country	*No. of Products*	*Depth of Tariff Conseccions*
Bangladesh	5072	10% and 15%
Bhutan	266	10%, 13%, 15%, 18% and 20%
India	2402	10%, 15%, 20%, 25%, 30%, 40%, 50%, 90% and 100%
Maldives	390	5%, 7.5%, 10% and 15%

Nepal	425	10% and 15%
Pakistan	685	10%, 15%, 20% and 30%
Sri Lanka	211	10%, 15%, 20%, 30%, 50%, 60% and 75%
TOTAL		4951

During the First and Second Round, trade negotiations were conducted on a product-by-product basis. In the Third Round, the negotiations were also conducted chapter-wise. For the Fourth Round, it has been decided that the negotiations would, as far as possible, be conducted on Chapter-wise, Sectoral and Across-the-Board basis. The First Meeting of Inter-Governmental Group on Trade Liberalisation to Initiate the Fourth Round of Trade Negotiations was held at the SAARC Secretariat, with the participation of all SAARC Member States, on 27-28 March 2002 where Member delegations, inter-alia, exchanged request lists.

The Tenth Summit (Colombo 1998) decided that in order to accelerate progress in the next round of SAPTA negotiations, deeper tariff concessions should be extended to products which are being actively traded, or are likely to be traded, among Members; that discriminatory practices and non-tariff barriers should be simultaneously removed on items in respect of which tariff concessions are granted or have been granted earlier. Measures to remove structural impediments should also be taken in order to move speedily towards the goal of a South Asian Free Trade Area (SAFTA). The Summit also directed that the domestic content requirements under SAPTA Rules of Origin be reduced. The Summit affirmed that benefits of the process be equitably shared by all Member States.

One of the core principles of the SAPTA Agreement is that there should be special treatment for Least Developed Countries through the consideration of additional measures. It was accordingly decided in 1999 to reduce the domestic content requirement further under the SAPTA Rules of Origin to enable the smaller and Least Developed Countries to benefit equitably from economic liberalization. This reduction would apply to all products covered so far in the trade negotiations.

Recognizing the important role economic cooperation plays in South Asia, the first meeting of SAARC Commerce Ministers was held in New Delhi (8-9 January, 1996). Since then, two more Ministerial Meetings (29-30 April, 1998 in Islamabad and 2-3 February, 1999 in Dhaka) have been held focussing on enlarging the scope and coverage of regional economic cooperation. Separate meetings of the SAARC Commerce Ministers on WTO issues have also been held.

SAPTA was envisaged primarily as the first step towards the transition to a South Asian Free Trade Area (SAFTA) leading subsequently, towards a Customs Union, Common Market and Economic Union. In 1995, the Sixteenth session of the Council of Ministers held in New Delhi (18-19 December) agreed on the need to strive for the realization of SAFTA and to this end an Inter-Governmental Expert Group (IGEG) was set up in 1996 to identify the necessary steps towards moving into a free trade area.

Recognizing the need to address asymmetries in development and other complexities that may stand in the way of such a tight schedule, the Colombo Summit directed that the text of the regulatory framework for creating a Free Trade Area in the Region should be finalized by 2001. In this connection, a Committee of Experts on Drafting a Comprehensive Treaty Regime on a South Asian Free Trade Area (SAFTA) has been constituted to draft a comprehensive treaty which has, following its first meeting in Kathmandu (July 1999) worked out its broad Terms of Reference.

Eventually, the treaty would incorporate, inter alia, binding time frames for freeing trade, measures to facilitate trade, protection of LDCs including mechanisms for compensation of revenue loss, etc. With the setting up of the Committee of Experts, the IGEG was wound up. At its first Meeting, the Committee directed the Secretariat to prepare the first Working Draft of the SAFTA Treaty. This Working Draft is currently under consideration of the Member States.

The Eleventh SAARC Summit held in Kathmandu on 4-6 January 2002 provided further impetus to the regional economic cooperation. To give effect to the shared aspirations for a more prosperous South Asia, the Leaders agreed to the vision of a phased and planned process eventually leading to a South Asian Economic Union and agreed to accelerate cooperation in the core areas of trade, finance and investment to realize the goal of an integrated South Asian economy in a step-by-step manner. They expressed their determination to make full use of regional synergy to maximize the benefits of globalisation and liberalization and to minimize their negative impacts on the region. While recognizing that trade and economic expansion is closely inter-linked, the Leaders made a commitment to widen and deepen the scope of regional networks of activities in trade and financial matters.

Recognising the need to move quickly towards a South Asian Free Trade Area, the Heads of State or Government directed the Council of Ministers to finalize the text of the Draft Treaty Framework by the end of 2002. They also directed that in moving towards the goal of SAFTA, the Member States expedite action to remove tariff and non-tariff barriers and structural impediments to free trade. They also instructed to conclude the meeting of the Inter Governmental Group on Trade Liberalization for the Fourth Round of Trade Negotiations under SAPTA as early as possible as per the decision of the Tenth SAARC Summit in Colombo.

SAARC has also initiated action on a series of practical measures to facilitate the process of economic integration. A Group on Customs Cooperation was set up in 1996 and so far, has held three meetings. It was inter-alia decided to harmonize HS lines and customs rules and regulations; simplify procedures for intra-regional exports; upgrade infrastructural facilities and provide training facilities.

A Customs Action Plan was drawn up in Islamabad (April 1997) as agreed to by all Member States. A Customs Consultant is also being engaged to prepare a detailed report recommending various measures to be taken on the simplifications and standardisation of customs documents and declarations (for imports and exports); preparation of a commodity description code expanding the 6-digit HS code to accommodate description of goods in vogue within the SAARC region; harmonisation of baggage laws, procedures and allowances; harmonisation of laws, procedure and exemption limits on gifts and postal goods; harmonisation of matters relating to temporary import of vehicles and other goods imported and subsequently re-exported in the same state, etc.

The need to improve the transport infrastructure and transit facilities in the Region was recognized and the 11th Session of the SAARC Council of Ministers in Colombo (8-9 July 1992) directed the CEC to take appropriate steps in this regard. Accordingly a study was commissioned to assess the existing transport infrastructure and transit facilities, including procedural and documental issues in the Region in relation to volume and composition of the existing trade in the Region and to make recommendations for their improvement, with a view to enhancing trade within and outside the SAARC region. The study was completed in 1994 and has made far reaching recommendations.

It is relevant to mention at this stage that the Technical Committee on Transport was established in 1983, covering three major segments of transport, i.e. land transport, divided into railways and roadways; sea transport sub-divided into inland waterways and shipping; and air transport. Seventeen meetings of this Committee have been held. Subsquently, according to new arrangements of the Integrated Programme of Action (IPA), the Technical Committee on Transport has been merged with Communications forming a single Technical Committee on Transport and Communications effective from January 2000.

A draft Regional Agreement on Promotion and Protection of Investment within the SAARC Region is under consideration of the Member States and is meant to create conditions favourable for promoting and protecting investments in Member States by investors from other Member States of the Region. The objective is to finalize the Regional Investment (Promotion and Protection) Agreement prior to the commencement of the implementation of SAFTA.

Linked to the Regional Investment Agreement is the setting up of a SAARC Arbitration Council for which proposals are under examination by Member States. Discussions have also commenced on harmonizing tax laws within the Region to assess the possibility of having a Regional Agreement for the Avoidance of Double Taxation.

Recognizing the importance of standards and measurement, the First Meeting of the SAARC Standing Group on Standards, Quality Control and Measurement was held in New Delhi in June 1999 to identify how national standards may be harmonized and regional standards agreed upon. The Meeting agreed on the Key Elements of the Regional Action Plan on Standards, Quality Control and Measurement.

To review the progress in the implementation of its earlier recommendations, the Standing Group on Standards, Quality Control and Measurement met for the second time in New Delhi on February 4-6, 2002. The meeting considered a proposal for a collaborative arrangement with the German national metrology institute Physikalisch-Technische Bundesanstalt (PTB) and held discussions on subjects related to Mutual Recognition, Conformity Assessment and Accreditation to setting up of a Core Group on the subject of Sanitary and Phytosanitary Standards and concerted attempts on capacity building and human resource development. It was also agreed that India would bring out a series of short films to increase consumer awareness on the importance of standards. The Meeting also decided to meet at least once every year.

In the area of trade and tariff which are critical to individual Member States and to the Region as a whole, particularly those relating to multilateral negotiations in World Trade Organization (WTO), World Customs Organization (WCO), World Intellectual Property Organization (WIPO) etc., regular consultations are held not only at the headquarters of such international organizations, such as Geneva, but also in the Member States themselves, so as to effectively coordinate, project and protect their collective interests. This process of consultations has been intensified so that wherever possible, a regional position may be taken which is compatible with the overall principles of SAARC, and which reflects the needs and requirements of the LDCs in the region through the provision of special and more favourable concessions.

SAARC Commerce Ministers issued a Declaration on the eve of the Second WTO Ministerial Conference (Geneva 1998). A meeting of SAARC Commerce Ministers was also held in Male' in August 1999 with regard to the Third WTO Ministerial Conference held in Seattle (30 November – 3 December 1999) and the SAARC Commerce Ministers issued a preliminary Joint Statement on the issues considered at that Meeting. Positions were also coordinated and a Joint Statement was issued by the SAARC Commerce Ministers (New Delhi, 23 August 2001) for the Fourth WTO Ministerial Conference held at Doha, Qatar on 9-13 November 2001.

At their Eleventh SAARC Summit, recognizing the important role that trade can play in advancing the overall development of a country, thus contributing to an equitable and sustainable world order, the Heads of State or Government called for an early realization of a rule-based and non-discriminatory world trade regime. In this context, they appreciated the positive elements of the Fourth WTO Ministerial Conference held in Doha and called upon the developed countries to fulfil their commitments to address the particular concerns and needs of the developing and the least developed countries. The Leaders also instructed the forthcoming meeting of the Committee on Economic Cooperation to devote at least half a day for discussions on the evaluation of the decisions of the recently concluded Doha conference in order to evolve better co-ordinated positions among the Member States on all WTO issues. They further stressed the need to intensify coordination among the SAARC missions in Geneva and begin the necessary preparation to advance the common interest of the region in the Fifth WTO Ministerial conference. A Meeting of the Secretaries of Commerce is proposed to be held in New Delhi to assess the implications of the Doha Ministerial Declaration and the status of negotiations in Geneva of the various Committees.

The important role played by the Chambers of Commerce and Industry in the Region has been given special emphasis. The SAARC Chamber of Commerce and Industry (SCCI) was set up in 1992 as the first recognized regional Apex Body. SCCI brings together under one umbrella the national chambers of commerce and industry of the Member States and is actively engaged in the promotion of trade and the interaction of the business community within the SAARC region.

SCCI has been involved not only in increasing public awareness through workshops and studies they have been commissioning, including the publication of books and other material, but also through the interactive sessions between government and industry aimed at providing pertinent input to the process of regional economic cooperation. The SCCI also holds regular consultations with the SAARC Secretariat. The SCCI recently brought out a book titled 'SAARC Means Business: Opportunities for Partnership' which highlights sectors of cooperative advantage within the Region.

Indeed, it was in recognition of the positive role played by the SCCI that the Member States decided to wind up the Technical Committee on Tourism (which was set up in 1991) to replace it with SCCI Tourism Council based on inputs from the SAARC Chamber of Commerce and Industry. This Council which represents the private sector perspective towards enhancing and gainfully exploiting the tourism potential of the region would provide policy and other inputs for the consideration of the Committee on Economic Cooperation (CEC).

At their Eleventh SAARC Summit held in Kathmandu on 4-6 January 2002, the Heads of State or Government also recognized the immense tourism potential of South Asia and underlined the need to take measures to promote South Asia as a common tourist destination through joint efforts in areas such as upgrading of infrastructure, air linkages, simplification and harmonization of administrative procedures and training and joint marketing.

The Heads of State or Government at their Eleventh SAARC Summit held in Kathmandu on 4-6 January 2002 renewed their commitment to encourage the participation of the private sector and assured their full support for their socially responsible economic initiatives. While welcoming the practice of holding trade fairs in cooperation with the private sector at the regional level, they appreciated the efforts of the SAARC Chamber of

Commerce and Industry to promote regional economic cooperation in the spirit of public and private sector partnership. A Government-Industry Partnership Affirmation was handed over at the Eleventh SAARC Summit by the SAARC Chamber of Commerce and Industry.

The organizing of SAARC Trade Fairs has become a regular feature since 1996 when the first Trade Fair was held in India. The Second SAARC Trade Fair was held in Colombo 1998. Pakistan hosted the Third SAARC Trade Fair in Karachi on 1-6 September 2001. The Fourth SAARC Trade Fair will be hosted by Nepal in 2002. The Trade Fairs have succeeded not only in projecting the potential of the region but also in promoting the wide variety of products the region produces which match international quality and standards.

At the Colombo Summit, there was consensual recognition of the need to strengthen the individual financial systems of the SAARC countries through the enhancement of their institutional capacity, surveillance mechanism, as well as through closer consultations on, and coordination of, macro-economic policies where appropriate. It was felt that the Region needs to enhance the collective capacity of SAARC in respect of policy analysis with specific emphasis on international financial and monetary, trade and investment issues along with their domestic ramifications.

In this regard, meetings of finance officials of the SAARC countries have been held, including among the Governors of Central Banks to not only put into position early warning mechanisms, but also to coordinate policies to respond to global financial and economic developments that affect the Region. The Meetings of

Governors of SAARC Central Banks, now known as a Group called SAARCFINANCE have been recognized as a formal SAARC body under the framework of SAARC and will report to the SAARC Council of Ministers. The Twenty-second Session of the SAARC Council of Ministers (Kathmandu, 2-3 January 2002) also approved the Terms of Reference of SAARCFINANCE.

It was also agreed at the Colombo Summit in 1998 to establish a SAARC Network of Researchers on Global Financial and Economic Issues comprising members of the private sector, central banks, planning ministries, research institutes and eminent economists nominated by Governments to identify, analyse and help SAARC face up to current global, financial and economic developments affecting the region. Such a network has since been set up and has decided on an immediate and longer-term research agenda which would help identify areas of common concern, as also new areas of cooperation among the Member Countries. The Network also brings out a South Asia Economic Journal and is in the process of bringing out a Directory of Research Institutes in South Asia focussing on global financial and economic issues.

Successive Summits have acknowledged the importance of SAARC pursuing mutually beneficial cooperation with regional, UN and other international organisations on the Association's agreed areas of cooperation.

In terms of external linkages, SAARC and United Nations Conference on Trade and Development (UNCTAD) signed a Memorandum of Understanding in February 1993 on UNCTAD Database on Trade Control Measures and Trade Analysis and Information System

(TRAINS). As envisaged under the MoU, the UNCTAD Database is updated for the SAARC Member States by the SAARC Secretariat. The latest issue of CD-ROM TRAINS (Spring 2001 Version 8.0) contains trade control measures of 119 countries of the world including 44 tariff schedules of 2000 as well as 1999 import data by origin at the Harmonized System 6-digit level for 65 countries. The data in respect of all SAARC countries is available in the CD-ROM TRAINS.

UNCTAD also organised Ad-hoc Expert Group Meeting on Non-Tariff Measures and Trade and Tariff Databases in International Organisations and a Meeting on Trade Analysis and Information System (TRAINS) held in Geneva on 3-7 December 2001 in which SAARC Secretariat participated.

The Meeting was opened by H.E. Mr. Rubens Ricupero, UNCTAD Secretary-General on 3rd December 2001. He inter-alia stated that the convening of this meeting especially after the Doha WTO Ministerial Conference was meant to underscore the importance of accurate information on trade, tariffs and non-tariff measures. As a result, the meeting had brought together different organizations that collect and disseminate trade and tariff data and those that provide related technical and policy advice. He added that a second major objective of the meting was to address the emergence of non-tariff measures related to the implementation of health, safety and environmental standards as such measures could have a major restrictive impact on the export of products from poorer countries.

The participants were drawn from Members of the UNCTAD Inter-Active TRAINS Programme looking after UNCTAD Database in regional organisations like Centre for Central American Integration (SEICA) Latin American Integration Association (ALADI), Inter-American Development Bank (IDB), Islamic Centre for Development of Trade (ICDT) and Common Market for Southern and Eastern Africa (COMESA) and SAARC Secretariat. International and regional organisations also participated such as WTO, ITC, UNIDO, World Bank, OECD, EC, Australian National University and Resident Missions in Geneva.

Similarly, a Framework Cooperation Agreement was signed between SAARC and Economic and Social Commission for Asia and the Pacific (ESCAP) to provide for cooperation on developmental issues through joint studies, workshops and seminars and exchange of information and documentation in poverty alleviation, human resource development, trade promotion, foreign direct investment, environmental protection and prevention of drug trafficking, infrastructure development, etc. ESCAP has also established an institutional mechanism of Consultative Meetings of the Executive Heads of Sub-regional Organisations in Asia and the Pacific (SAARC, Economic Cooperation Organization (ECO), Association of South East Asian Nations (ASEAN), South Pacific Forum) and ESCAP.

A Memorandum of Understanding on Administrative Cooperation between SAARC and the European Commission has been entered into (July 1996). The Secretary-General was authorised by the Twenty-sixth Session of the Council of Ministers in Nuwara Eliya, (18-19 March 1999) to discuss with EC, specific areas of possible cooperation under the MOU. Agreement has been reached on four programmes as follows:

(a) facilitating access into the Single European market;

(b) implementation of the EU-GSP Scheme including cumulative rules of origin;

(c) drawing on the EU experience for the SAFTA process; and

(d) evolving common SAARC standards and harmonisation with international obligations including certification, testing etc.

The first project to be implemented by EC was on EU-GSP Scheme including cumulative rules of origin. Regional cumulation was granted by EC to SAARC Member Countries in October 2000 but due to lack of knowledge of procedural matters on the part of business and trading community in SAARC region no export to EC could take place by the SAARC region under the regional cumulation clause of GSP Scheme of EC. Therefore, in order to increase awareness and understanding of the technical details regarding the GSP Scheme of EC and Regional Cumulation of which SAARC is a beneficiary, the European Commission organised a series of Workshops in the SAARC Member Countries through their consultants and in collaboration with the SAARC Secretariat and the Member Federations of SAARC Chamber of Commerce and Industry (SCCI).

A total of eight Workshops were held as under: -

— Kathmandu 12th February 2002

— New Delhi 19th February 2002

— Mumbai 21st February 2002

— Colombo 26th February 2002

— Malé 3rd March 2002

— Karachi 6th March 2002

— Lahore 9th March 2002

— Dhaka 12 March 2002

The objective behind the Workshops was to go into the details of the GSP Scheme including rules of origin as also benefits arising from regional cumulation. SAARC was accorded this facility by EC in October 2000. The Workshops were attended by representatives from the business community as also from the concerned government Departments such as customs and trade officials. The Workshops were part of the identified projects under the SAARC-EC MOU.

A User Manual on European Union's Generalised Scheme of Preferences, Rules of Origin and Rules of Origin and Regional Cumulation also including 30 Frequently Asked Questions (FAQs) has also been prepared by the Consultants appointed by European Commission.

Since 1998, SAARC has had an informal Ministerial-level dialogue with ASEAN and the European Union on the sidelines of the UN General Assembly in New York.

Among the various areas of cooperation within SAARC, economic cooperation appears to have gained considerable momentum. This is derived to some measure from the changing global economic environment and its apparent unpredictability. The Tenth Summit Declaration expressed serious concern over the severe distortions produced by the process of unrestrained globalization as has been evidenced in the downturn of economies of several Asian states. At the same time, negotiations in the multilateral economic fora appear to disadvantage developing and Least Developed Countries and there is urgent need to not only develop joint positions and strategies but also to find ways and means of protecting natural resources, heritage and knowledge. In addition to both the above compulsions is the recognition within the Region that it is indeed blessed with considerable resources, both natural and human, which not only identifies it as a market but also as a major trading partner provided it is in a position to build on its competitive and comparative advantages.

Recalling the recommendations of the Third United Nations Conference on the Least Developed Countries held in Brussels in May 2001 and the decisions of the Zanzibar Declaration of July 2001, the SAARC Leaders at their Eleventh SAARC Summit urged the developed countries to adopt more liberal trade and aid policies responsive to the particular needs of the least developed countries. Referring to the forthcoming International Conference on Financing for Development to be held in Mexico in March 2002, the Leaders urged the international community to strengthen cooperation for development by addressing international and systemic issues related to financing for development in the developing and the least developed countries in a holistic manner.

Indo-SAARC Trade Scenario

One of the major objectives of SAARC is to promote and strengthen trade among the member countries. However, it took a decade for the SAARC Preferential Trading Agreement to come into being on 7th December 1995. Table 2 depicts some basic facts about SAARC. The performance of all these countries has been shown in the various economic spheres.

Table 2. Some Facts About SAARC Countries

Regional Performance Figure	*Bangladesh*	*Bhutan*	*India*	*Maldives*	*Nepal*	*Pakistan*	*Sri Lanka*
Area 000 Km sq.)	144	47	3288	0.3	147.2	796	66
Population (1996, million)	122	1.65	935	0.26	22.3	131.63	18.2
Annual Population Growth	2.17	2.3	2.14	3.0	2.3	2.82	1.4
Urban Population (1992, %)	18	6	26	26	12	33	22
Life Expectancy (1995, years)	56	49	61	64	54	62	72
Literacy Rate (1995, %)	38.1	27	52.2	52.1	35.7	42.2	89.3
				1		1	1
Per Capita GNP (1995, US$)	245	415	335	1000	180	495	830
Pre Capita GDP, Purchasing Power Parity (1995,US$)	1350	1475	1385	1373	1165	2235	3030
						1	
GDP (1995-96, US$ billion)	31.9	0.3	294.7	0.24	4.7	64.3	16.26
GDP Growth Rate (1995-96 %)	4.7	5.4	7.1	7.2	6.1	6.1	3.7
Rate of Inflation, (1995-96,%)	6.4	7.8	7.6	3.1	8.2	10.3	16.1
Per Capita Exports (1995 US$)	26.1	50.8	33.2	192	15.4	61.4	204.5
Per Capita Imports (1995, US$)	54.1	68.4	37.5	1373	35.3	88.0	324.5
		2		3	3		3
Per Capita Foreign Exchange Excluding Gold (April 1997)	14.5	80.7	23.9	243.7	27.1	6.1	118.2
			3	4	4	3	
Per Capita Foreign DEBT 1995, US$	139.2	55.2	98.6	400	90.9	217.3	353.6
		4	1	5			
FDI (1995-96 US$ million)	915.6	0.98	2587	915	110	1102	272
Currency	TAKA	TRUML	RUPEE	RUFIYAA	RUPEE	RUPEE	RUPEE

1 1996-97, 2. 1995 3. March 4 1992, 5. 1994. Source: World Development Report 1996

It is clear from Table 2 that India has the largest area, population and GDP of all the SAARC countries, whereas Maldives has the smallest area, least population and GDP. About three-fourth of the total population of the SAARC countries inhabits in India. In terms of geographic area, India's share in total SAARC are comes out to be 73.25 per cent. In terms of GDP, India accounts for a little more than three-fourth of the combined GDP of all the SAARC countries. Clearly, India constitutes threefourth of SAARC on these three accounts.

While India has 26 per cent urban population, Bhutan accounted for only 6 per cent for the same in 1992. The per capita exports of Sri Lanka were highest i.e. US $ 204.5 in 1995, whereas Nepal accounted for lowest i.e. US $ 15.4 in the same year. Further, the per capita imports of Maldives were highest i.e. US $ 1373 in 1995, whereas Nepal accounted for only US $ 35.3 in the same year. The per capita foreign debt ranged from US $ 400 (Maldives) and US $ 55.2 (Bhutan).

Though SAARC came into being 1985, yet an attempt has been made to look at India's trade with SAARC countries during the pre and post-SAARC period. During the ten year pre-SAARC period, India's exports increased from US $ 160 million in 1975 to US $ 315 million in 1984. Compared to it, during the ten years post-SAARC period, India's exports increased from US $ 277 million in 1986 to US $ 1532 million in 1995.

As regards the trend, India exports registered an upward trend both in the pre-SAARC and post-SAARC periods. From the export-statistics, it is clear that the institution of SAARC has encouraged India's exports to SAARC countries. Likewise, India's exports to the world during the pre-SAARC and post-SAARC period also witnessed and upward trend.

India's volume of imports from SAARC countries as compared to exports is very less. As is clear from the table, it was just US $ 56 million in 1975 and rose only to US $ 105 million in 1984. During the post-SAARC era, the volume of India's imports from SAARC countries increased from US $ 73 million in 1986 to US $ 182 million in 1995.

While in 1985, the total turnover of India's trade with SAARC was US $ 382 million, it increased to US $ 1714 million in 1995. This increase is satisfactory as compared to the increase in the India's global trade, which increased from US $ 24594 million in 1985 to US $ 64993 million in 1995.

During the pre-SAARC period, the growth rate of India's total trade with SAARC has been lower than that of its global trade. However, during the post-SAARC era, the situation got reversed. Since the inception of SAARC in 1985, the index of India's trade with SAARC countries has increased by about 349 per cent in 1995, whereas the index of her global trade has increased by about 164 per cent during the same period.

The growth of India's trade with SAARC is greater than the growth of her global trade. This is an encouraging trend. Table 3 shows thta India's trade with SAARC has increased from 1.55 per cent in 1985 to 3.12 per cent in 1995, which further exhibits SAARC's increasing contribution to India's global trade. However, it is interesting to note that this share crossed to three per cent level in 1995.

India's share in intra-regional SAARC exports has been higher than imports during 1975-95. Table 4 shows India's share in intra-regional SAARC trade during 1975-95.

Table 3. India's Trade with SAARC and World During 1975-95,* (Value in US$ million)

	Trade With SAARC				Trade With World				
Year	Exports	Imports	Total Trade	(4) As Index 1985=100	Exports	Imports	Total Trade	(8) As Index 1985=100	(4) As Per Cent of 8
(1)	(2)	(3)	(4=2+3)	(5)	(6)	(7)	(8=6+7)	(9)	(10)
1975	161	56	217	57	4364	6198	10562	43	2.05
1976	154	54	208	54	5020	5102	10122	41	2.05
1977	194	50	244	64	6025	6664	12689	52	1.92
1978	263	50	313	82	6627	7820	14447	59	2.17
1979	309	65	374	98	7679	9899	17578	71	2.13
1980	307	141	448	117	7995	13181	21176	86	2.12
1981	197	191	388	102	6827	14550	21377	87	1.82
1982	185	131	316	83	9753	15904	25657	104	1.23
1983	221	110	331	87	9831	15900	25731	105	1.29
1984	315	105	420	110	8231	15115	23346	95	1.80
1985	270	112	382	100	8265	16329	24594	100	1.55
1986	277	73	350	92	9135	15051	24186	98	1.45
1987	306	84	390	102	10798	16841	27639	112	.41
1988	364	92	456	119	13193	19035	32228	131	1.41
1989	379	54	433	113	15839	19297	35136	143	1.23
1990	487	97	584	153	17813	23990	41803	170	1.40
1991	622	95	717	188	17872	19509	37381	152	1.92
1992	717	193	910	238	18498	23227	41725	170	2.18
1993	816	96	912	239	20258	21215	41473	169	2.20
1994	1015	126	1141	299	24195	25477	49672	202	2.30
1995	1532	182	1714	449	30537	34456	64993	264	3.12

**Excluding Bhutan as data were not available,Source: Direction of Trade Statistics Year Books (IMF).*

*Table 4. India's Share In Intra-Regional SAARC**
Trade durin 1975-95 (in Per Cent)

Year	*Exports*	*Imports*	*Total Trade*
1975	49.8	16.0	32.3
1976	48.5	17.8	33.5
1977	49.1	12.6	33.8
1978	57.5	11.5	35.1
1979	53.4	12.3	33.8
1980	48.0	23.4	36.0
1981	34.9	31.3	33.0
1982	36.3	27.3	31.9
1983	47.0	23.2	35.1
1984	51.3	18.7	35.5
1985	45.0	22.1	34.3
1986	50.0	14.2	32.8
1987	49.9	16.1	34.4
1988	45.8	13.8	31.2
1989	54.8	10.1	35.4
1990	56.5	13.4	36.9
1991	61.9	10.6	37.7
1992	58.4	15.5	36.8
1993	69.4	7.8	37.6
1994	71.2	8.8	40.0
1995	76.2	8.3	42.3
Average	53.1	15.9	35.2

**Excluding Bhutan as data were not available, Source : Direction of Trade Statistics Year Book (IMF), (Various Issues 1980 to 1996.)*

India's share in intra-SAARC exports remained between 34.9 per cent (1981) and 57.4 per cent (1978) during the pre-SAARC period of 1975-84. Compared to it, during the post-SAARC period, India's share in intra-SAARC exports ranged between 45.8 per cent (1983) and 76.2 per cent (1995). However, India accounted for 11.5 per cent in intra-SAARC imports in 1978 and 31.3 per cent in 1981 during the pre-SAARC period.

The post-SAARC situation presents a rather discouraging picture from the stand point of regional cooperation. India's share in intra-SAARC imports varied between 7.8 per cent (1993) and 16.1 per cent (1987) during the post-SAARC period. Comparison of India's share in intra-SAARC exports and imports during the post-SAARC era further substantiates the point that India's capacity to meet the import needs of other SAARC members is much greater than the other members capacity to meet India's imports requirements.

During 1975-95. India's share in intra-regional SAARC exports and imports was 53.1 per cent and 15.9 per cent on an average, per annum. She accounted for 35.2 per cent in the intra-regional SAARC trade during this period on an average per annum. From the view point of intra-SAARC trade, India is the major exporter and minor importer as her share in intra-regional SAARC exports is more than three times than that of imports during 1975-95.

Table 5 brings out India's share in global trade of individual SAARC countries during 1975-95. During the pre-SAARC period (1975-84), a major share of Nepal's exports went to India. They varied between 27.9 per cent (1979) and 76.4 per cent (1975). However, during the post-SAARC era (1986-95), the share of India in Nepal's exports started declining at a fast speed. It came down from 29.8 per cent (1986) to a mere 1.6 per cent (1989). Nevertheless, it picked up during the later years.

The same trend is visible in India's share in the global imports of Nepal during this period. The highest share of India in Nepal's imports was 60.6 per cent (1976) and the lowest was 7.6 per cent (1989). However, from 1990 onwards, the trend is upward. Clearly, the share of India in Nepal's trade has decreased in the post-SAARC period as compared to pre-SAARC period. It has much to do with the political relations between the two countries rather than economic rationale.

India's share in the remaining SAARC countries, trade has been very small as compared to Nepal. India accounted for 1.6 per cent of Bangladesh's exports and 5.6 per cent of its imports in 1975. The corresponding figure for the year 1984, however, rose to 2.9 per cent and 3.3 per cent respectively. However, the post-SAARC years witness a falling trend in India's share in Bangladesh's exports till 1993. It started looking up since 1994 and it was 2.9 per cent in 1995.

Contrary to it, India's share in Bangladesh's imports registered an upward trend during post-SAARC period as is clear in table 5. It is interesting to note that India did not import any item from Maldives during the entire period under study. But India accounted for a little more than one-fourth of Maldives imports in 1975 as is evident from table 5. Thereafter, India's share in Maldives imports never rose to this height till 1995.

As compared to Nepal, India's share in Pakistan and Sri Lanka's trade has been a marginal one throughout the period from 1975 to 1995. It is, however, an interesting phenomena that India's share in Pakistan's exports has been higher during the pre-SAARC years than post-SAARC. It is only in 1992 that India accounted for 2 per cent in Pakistan's global exports. The situation is rather discouraging in the case of India's share in Pakistan's imports. It has never crossed 0.7 per cent during 1975-95. In the case of Sri Lanka, India accounted for a higher share of its imports than exports throughout the period.

From 1984-85, India's terms of trade with Bangladesh have been unfavourable whereas from 1989-90, they turned out to be highly favourable. India also experienced favourable terms of trade with Bhutan. With Maldives, India's terms of trade were exceptionally low in 1990-91, followed by 1991-92, 1984-85, 1987-88, 1989-90 and 1992-93. During all other years, India enjoyed favourable terms of trade. The trend of India's terms of trade with Nepal has also been mixed during 1984-85 and 1994-95.

It is interesting to note that India's terms of trade with Sri Lanka have been unfavourable during the first three years of SAARC. However, they have been highly favourable to India during all the latter years of SAARC expect for 1994-95. India enjoyed highly favourable terms of trade with Pakistan except for the year 1992-93 during post-SAARC era.

In the language of gains from trade, India has been a net gainer from its trade with Pakistan, Bangladesh, Bhutan and Nepal during the post-SAARC era. In the case of Maldives and Sri Lanka, the gains between India and these two countries had been by and large evenly distributed. Thus, India had been a net gainer with its trade with SAARC countries.

A comparison of India's overall terms of trade with the whole world, given in table 6, with that of its terms of trade with SAARC reveals that India enjoyed more favourable terms of trade with SAARC countries than that with the world. India's terms of trade with the world had been favourable only during 1986-87 and 1992-95. However, looking at India's meagre proportion of trade with SAARC, the gains in terms of trade is not very large. Nevertheless, India and other SAARC countries can benefit a lot from the intra-SAARC trade in terms of transport and transhipment costs.

Table 5. India's Share In Global Trade of SAARC Countries During 1975-95 (Per cent Share)

Year	Bangladesh		Maldives		Nepal		Pakistan		Sri Lanka	
	Export	Import	Export	Import	Export	Import	Export	Import	Export	Import
1975	1.6	5.6	-	26.7	76.4	54.8	2.1	0.0	0.1	4.0
1976	2.4	6.9	-	6.1	75.2	60.6	0.5	0.2	0.1	5.8
1977	0.2	5.9	-	11.1	34.7	47.7	2.1	0.7	0.1	8.4
1978	0.6	4.1	-	8.8	31.3	43.6	1.7	0.8	0.8	10.8
1979	0.8	5.1	-	16.4	27.9	47.1	1.5	0.3	1.1	8.4
1980	1.5	4.1	-	14.9	33.2	43.4	2.9	0.0	3.1	5.0
1981	1.8	1.8	-	2.6	47.9	37.0	2.6	0.1	5.5	3.4
1982	2.7	1.6	-	1.5	58.5	33.2	2.1	0.1	1.9	3.7
1983	1.1	1.5	-	1.5	51.0	32.8	1.0	0.1	2.9	5.9
1984	2.9	3.3	-	2.8	52.8	35.6	0.8	0.2	1.0	6.3
1985	2.9	4.1	-	1.4	37.1	27.8	1.0	0.2	0.4	3.9
1986	0.9	4.4	-	2.6	29.8	26.1	0.4	0.2	0.9	3.7
1987	1.3	5.3	-	2.0	27.8	15.7	0.6	0.2	0.4	3.6
1992	0.5	9.5	-	4.2	6.5	15.3	2.0	0.6	0.6	6.6
1993	0.6	10.7	-	3.1	5.2	14.2	0.7	0.6	0.6	6.2
1994	1.3	11.4	-	7.2	4.0	14.0	0.6	0.7	1.0	6.7
1995	2.5	14.8	-	3.4	8.2	14.2	0.5	0.6	1.1	6.5
Average	1.4	6.2	0.0	6.2	30.6	29.1	1.2	0.3	1.2	5.5

**Excluding Bhutan as comparable data were not available.*

Source: Direction of Trade Statistics Year Book (IMF), various issues 1980 to 1996

Table 6. India's Commodity Terms of Trade With The Whole World During1984-95 (Base: 1988-89 = 100)

Year (April-March)	Export Unit value index	Import Unit value index	Terms of Trade
1984-85	73.13	87.17	83.89
1985-86	73.56	85.61	85.92
1986-87	77.26	75.15	102.81
1987-88	84.15	86.25	97.57
1988-89	100.00	100.00	100.00
1989-90	119.12	123.13	96.74
1990-91	125.97	144.31	87.29
1991-92	159.13	166.63	95.50
1992-93	181.52	179.73	101.00
1993-94	204.18	176.39	115.75
1994-95	213.01	134.18	150.75

Note: Figures have been readjusted by changing the base period from 1978-79 to 1988-89.Source: Economic Survey, 1991-92. 1994-95 & 1995-96. Government of India, Ministry of Finance, New Delhi.

Given the size and development of Indian economy, India's capacity to fulfil the import needs of other SAARC countries is far more greater than their capacity to meet India's import requirements. As such India's balance of trade with almost all the SAARC countries had been highly favourable except with Pakistan throughout the period under study. It seems to be a matter of great concern to other SAARC members.

The trade delegations from all the SAARC countries expressed their concern regarding their unfavourable balance of trade with India. They, somehow or other wish to have a balanced trade with India though in the era of multilateral trade, such aspects should not be pressed beyond a limit. Any way, given the size of Indian market, India and all other members of SAARC should try to identify more items which India can import from them. They can save a lot in terms of transport and transhipment costs.

Besides the SAARC countries should adopt a short-term and long-term strategy to face the emergent global challenges in the framework of GATT Agreements 1994. Their combined strength and broader mutual understanding is of utmost important for their development. In addition to the exchange of goods, they should concentrate on joint marketing in the global market. Joint ventures is an other very important area, which should be explored and exploited.

The region is very rich in natural resources and they should be exploited to the mutual benefit of all the member countries. Strengthening of mutual economic ties is the guarantee of cordial political relations with each other and in turn is the way to fast economic development and solution to their pressing problems like poverty and unemployment. SAARC Preferential Trading Arrangement (SAPTA) is certainly a quantum jump in the history of SAARC.

The SAARC nations should not be contended with SAPTA only. They should continuously act and move to obtain the higher forms of regional economic cooperation and eventually unite as South Asian Union. However, there is a big catch in it. And that catch is their arrogating matters with each other besides the role of outsiders in the SAARC. The fear-psychosis is another catch which must be removed by the conscience efforts of all the members of SAARC. Nevertheless, India would have to perform a strategic and pivotal role in strengthening the SAARC and carrying it to the ultimate goal-the formation of South Asian Union.

India's WTO Engagement: Influence of Federalism

The World Trade Organization (WTO) has become a potent symbol of at least one dimension of globalization: the multilateralization of national policymaking, a process by which issues that were once purely of domestic concern have become subjected to intergovernmental disciplines. India's engagement with the system of multilateral trade governance negotiated and administered through the WTO is influenced by many factors, including the sectoral composition of the Indian economy and the prevailing international distribution of negotiating power.

The importance of federal institutions for studying the nature of democratic politics is supported by Alfred Stepan's observation that, of 'the total number of people who live in long-standing democracies, the majority of them live in federal systems.' Moreover, he reminds us that among 'relatively long-standing (if often troubled) multinational and multilingual democracies, all the polities that fall most clearly into this category are federal'. For this reason alone it is important to look at the federal dimension of global processes: if we are interested in how democracies respond to these forces, then democracy's tendency towards a federal form makes this a highly relevant analytical parameter. In addition there is a large literature on the response of subnational arenas to global economic and political forces. Much of this has to do with issues of nationalism, but a good deal is focussed on political economy.

The 'extreme globalization theorist' Kenichi Ohmae, for instance, has long touted the benefits of region-states – which are either relatively autonomous provinces from individual nation-states, or an agglomeration of such units from two or more neighbouring nation-states. Ohmae argues that these geographical clusters are in many cases potential engines of huge regional economic growth. Furthermore, the emergence of these informal trans-border economic zones – found, for instance, where Singapore and parts of Malaysia meet – is a reflection of 'natural' economic forces at work, straining at the unnatural constraints posed by national regulations.

There are many points at which globalization and the institutions of federal democracy intersect, both theoretically and in the case of India. One reason why is that both federalism and globalization are terms that denote constantly evolving processes – globalization more obviously so, but federalism as well, in two senses: first, in that federal institutions are under a regime of continuous reform; and second, in the sense that the political relations that underlie centre-state negotiations (often of a partisan nature) produce a systemic bias towards change rather than stasis within intergovernmental bodies. Indeed, this is one of the reasons why federalism has never been a single, clearly definable entity, either in theory or practice. Its animating ideas and legal basis have varied from place to place, and the dominant forms of federalism have differed from one era to the next.

Conceptual distinctions designed to convey key differences between various forms of federalism – from the German 'cooperative' model to the American 'competitive' approach –have inevitably failed to capture the many complex contingencies and historical accidents that have nurtured actually existing federalisms into their messy, contradictory selves. Moreover, federal polities have a habit of changing over time, mutating to adapt to new circumstances.

Oscillation in the United States between enhanced federal regulatory power and the reassertion of states rights has become a regular feature of American politics, and indeed a characteristic of the country's federal system. Other countries have deviated strongly in practice from the principles set forth in their constitutions. Spanish federalism created little room for provincial autonomy under the post-Franco constitution, but has evolved to accommodate regional aspirations, and is now one of the pre-eminent examples of asymmetrical federalism, in which the powers enjoyed by individual subnational units vary from province to province.

Even if, bearing this fluidity in mind, one examines just a small subset of potential globalization-federalism relationships – that is, potential areas of mutual (or unidirectional) impact, in which globalization affects federalism or vice versa – even in such a narrowed field, there are several subspecies that need to be distinguished. Financial integration is one dimension of globalization that has penetrated the core of domestic federal systems.

The role of the International Financial Institutions (IFIs) –the International Monetary Fund, the World Bank, and the smaller regional development banks like the Asian Development Bank – looms large. In late 2001, just months before Argentina's economy and much of its formal political sphere finally went into free fall, the provincial level of the country's dysfunctional system of public finance had the attention of IMF officials.

As part of a short-term IMF bailout package approved in August 2001, Argentina's government, in addition to agreeing to punish tax evaders, promised the

IMF that it would pass legislation to reform provincial finances. On the one hand this episode reflects the growing power of global financial institutions: it demonstrates their ability to penetrate beyond the central state – in fact, to bypass the national level in some cases – and their capacity to demand reforms that affect relations between tiers within domestic constitutional systems.

On the other hand, the very fact that the IFIs had to resort to this level of interference reveals how vulnerable these external interventions are to the vagaries of a federal system, where power is dispersed and policies are affected by multilevel trade-offs. Federal systems, in other words, create additional incentive distortions, which make the political implications of competing policy alternatives even more difficult to predict than they are in the case of unitary political systems.

So the financial aspect of globalization has at least some impact on federalism – even if the nature of this impact is the subject of much debate. IFI programmes can, after all, be either the means by which federal financial agreements favourable to provinces have their terms rebalanced in favour of central authorities, as they have in this example from Argentina (under the regime that the IMF sought to dismantle, Argentina's states were given a guaranteed minimum monthly transfer of 1.35 billion dollars, an entitlement the states were ultimately to lose), or IFIs can serve as a point of leverage pushing for greater decentralisation of decision-making autonomy, as witnessed by many IFI-funded decentralisation programmes.

The prologue to the breakdown of Argentina's economic system also, by implication, reveals that the direction of causality runs in reverse as well. That is, specific features of Argentina's federal institutions – in this case, the rules governing fiscal relations – were also a key factor explaining Argentina's adverse reaction to global financial integration. Arguably, the brittleness of Argentina's federal resource settlement – and the inflexibility of the structures designed to refine it over time – increased Argentina's vulnerability to shifting trends in private and official trans-border capital flows.

Federalism can affect a country's engagement with global processes as much as global institutions and commitments can influence the shape of federal institutions or central-provincial relations. Nothing quite so drastic or direct has taken place in the case of Indian federalism. It is true that international organisations like the World Bank are increasingly orienting their programmes towards the activities, policy processes and reform programmes of state-level governments, as they have in a number of other federal countries. But there is no sense in which IFIs have intervened directly in the redesign of federal structures or resource settlements.

This does not mean that commentators on Indian politics and economics do not often see links between globalization and the federal system. Following the creation, in 2000, of three new states (each carved from one of three much larger existing states), some analysts argued that the new states owed their creation, in greater or lesser measure, to the (paradoxical) decentralising tendencies of globalization. This argument has taken two forms. The first is related to Ohmae's notion of regional economies, where the creation of an economic niche requires control over resources and investment decisions. The second form of the argument maintains that globalization has had an effect – in two of the three new states at least – on the process by which subnational regions have asserted themselves politically.

Tribal groups in the two new (tribal-majority) states of Jharkhand and Chattisgarh have stated their claims for subnational recognition in global non-governmental forums, borrowing inspiration and support from struggles of indigenous people in other countries. Through this sort of international networking among social movements federalism find itself at the receiving end of many intangible incarnations of globalization.

Slightly less tenuous in nature are a number of other connections between the process of global economic integration and facets of Indian federalism. Even these links are not particularly direct. Liberalised rules on inward investment, part of a conscious strategy to increase India's exposure to (and participation in) global economic flows, have placed much de facto decision-making authority in the hands of state governments. As former finance secretary Montek Singh Ahluwalia has argued, '[l]iberalisation has reduced the degree of control exercised by the centre in many areas, leaving much greater scope for state level initiatives. This is particularly true as far as attracting investment is concerned'.

Official clearance from New Delhi is still required for many foreign direct investments, but the relative importance of state governments has increased dramatically since 1991. As a result, states must now compete with one another for private investment, both Indian and foreign. This has been the subject of considerable research, including work that stresses the role of institutional legacies in explaining the differential performance of states, and those based on a more inductive method.

The considerable powers assigned to state governments by the constitution also means that they are often blamed by both Indian and foreign critics for much that is wrong with India's economic performance during the era of liberalisation. In one typical commentary, a leading economics publication argued that state-level incapacity would prevent the government from realising its ambitious plan to create a series of Agri-Export Zones (AEZs). The problem was that 'much of the implementation on the ground, including identification of products via a cluster approach, setting up of the AEZ and development of a comprehensive package of services, will have to be done by the state governments.

At the same time, certain aspects of Indian federalism have helped to facilitate India's integration into the global economy. Three are particularly important. Economically, competition for investment between states can, in theory, drive down regulatory burdens to near-global levels. Administratively, best practice in governance reform can be diffused through demonstration effects.

Politically, divisions between state-level political elites served to lessen the impact of anti-liberalisation constituencies, within and outside the state, disrupting the potential for collective action from key groups, which could thwart reform. These kinds of dynamic effects, typical of multilevel governance, remind us that national policies are not exhausted at the central level but are a combined product of incentives created by central and regional institutions.

Both globalization and the reaction to globalization have, at times, assumed prominent places within state and local political arenas. The new social movements, active at the grass roots of Indian politics for over three decades now are now also locked in conflicts with the institutions and organizations representing the global economic and political power. The global structures have begun to penetrate local spaces without much mediation, either by way of protection or control from the State's centralized institutions of planning and bureaucracy. The result is, local politics has become a variegated scene of conflict and collaboration with global economic structures.

India's engagement with the WTO consists of both its agreement to multilateral rules and its ongoing diplomatic activity within the institution. Its diplomatic activity comprises both the agenda it has sought to advance through negotiating strategies, and its role within other WTO processes such as trade policy reviews, the use of WTO procedures to resolve trade disputes with other member-states, and participation in deliberations on how to improve the fairness of the WTO's structures and operating procedures.

Engagement results in specific legal commitments that narrow government policy options on many tariff and non-tariff issues as well as a domestic political reaction to the government's diplomatic activity. Domestic political activity in India has addressed such questions as whether India should have agreed to existing rules; whether its objectives on issues currently under negotiation are sincere, likely to be effective, or biased towards the interests of certain social groups.

Many factors shape the way in which WTO engagement is 'received' politically in India. The framework of ideas, interests and institutions is useful here. The interplay of ideas about markets, trade, sovereignty, democracy – and a host of other relevant subjects – are important determinants of political reception. So is the configuration of interest groups, however defined. A third factor, institutions, operates in at least two ways. First, domestic political institutions play an important role by shaping the configuration and influence of interest groups. And, second, international institutions can shape the ideological environment in which political and economic ideas can be aired, debated, reformulated and codified.

One domestic institution that has received inadequate attention in understanding the political reaction to the WTO in India is the country's federal system: the constitutionally sanctioned division of responsibilities between the national and subnational tiers of the Indian state. There is much disagreement among experts on how to define Indian federalism, with some constitutional experts referring to India as a quasi-federation or a unitary polity with federal features.

There are three main ways in which federalism shapes the political reception of the WTO in India. The first is the extent to which WTO agreements negotiated and agreed to by the central government in 1994 (under Prime Minister PV Narasimha Rao of the Congress Party) are seen to constrain the rights of state governments to make policy in areas of competence assigned to them under India's constitution. The perceived usurpation of states' rights over agricultural policy in particular has engendered open conflict between political elites operating at the two levels of the federal system.

Some state governments have, in fact, taken the Government of India to court, demanding a reinstatement of the constitutionally mandated division of powers between the central and state governments, in which agriculture is categorised as a state subject. This would, in effect, require the Government of India to renounce its commitments under the WTO's Agreement on Agriculture (AoA), on the grounds that it lacked the authority to ensure their fulfilment. Legally, their case faces almost insurmountable hurdles, Indian jurisprudence having tended towards affirmation of the central government's treaty-making power, partly on the grounds that parliamentary ratification of treaties encompasses state-level representation, both through the territorial electoral constituencies that send delegates from states to the lower house, as well as the direct role of the states in sending representatives to the upper chamber. But politically speaking the states' challenge is less easily dismissed.

Though holding out little chance of success, leading politicians from state-level ruling parties continue to contest the legality of the Government of India's actions at the WTO. Punjab, West Bengal and Tamil Nadu, among others, have pressed on with their litigation. That these legal challenges are driven by partisan electoral considerations – modified by the institutional context of a federal division of powers – can be seen in the political uses to which they have been put.

In late 2001 and early 2002, Punjab's Shiromani Akali Dal (SAD) made anti-WTO rhetoric a mainstay of its re-election campaign in the run up to state assembly elections. Senior ministers and party leaders repeatedly told public rallies of the SAD's intention to pursue further its complaint against the Government of India in the Supreme Court. The motivation behind this and other suits has less to do with state governments' reverence for constitutional norms than it does with their desire to underline, in a classically public way, through a court of law, the 'powerlessness' of state governments in the face of the central government's 'capitulation' to the 'diktats' of the 'IMF-World Bank-WTO combine'.

Politicians operating within India's federal system know that the apportionment of blame for unpopular policies (or negatively perceived outcomes) is an intensely political matter. Whether it is the central government or the state government that incurs the voters' wrath is at least partly determined by the relative success of partisan forces in shaping public opinion. It is not a given. Even when the centre is, objectively speaking, mainly responsible for a policy change, it is often state governments that feel the political backlash for the policy's results, or in some cases its mere enactment. Partly this is because state governments are the only remotely accessible actor for many interest groups. In other cases, state governments manage to blame the centre, whether justifiably or not, for the ills that beset their regions. In those states ruled by parties different from those in power in New Delhi – who in some case are their rivals in state-level elections – there are even more powerful incentives for state-level ruling parties to blame the central government for negative impacts, and vice-versa. Governing elites at both levels must defend against charges that the globalization of the economy is harming ordinary people.

In recent years, state-level ruling parties have become more effective at shifting political blame for various negative economic trends, offloading responsibility to the main party in the central government's multiparty coalition. This is in large part a consequence of changes in India's party system.

The 1990s were characterised by the emergence of the state level as the effective arena of political competition. States were more likely to develop their own idiosyncratic state-level party systems. Regional parties have proliferated. Many are offshoots of all-India parties. Regional parties have become not only more successful at capturing power at the state level through victories in elections to state legislatures; they are also capturing many more parliamentary seats in their home states. Precisely because regional parties have cut into their country-wide seat tallies, national parties now rely on the many small clutches of MPs controlled by regional parties in order to cobble together parliamentary majorities.

The implication of these trends is that even when a regional party supports the national coalition government, regional parties do not necessarily feel constrained in the forms of political rhetoric employed 'back home' in their respective states. Unlike state-level units of centrally managed national parties, the regional parties which now play such a large role in the fluid environment of national coalition politics cannot as easily be silenced. Indeed, the main competing national parties are desperate enough for the parliamentary backing of regional parties that they will countenance even fairly high levels of criticism on contentious issues from their regional allies. The positions staked out by regional parties may involve not only policy differences with the central government on trade and multilateralised sectoral issues, like agriculture, but also outright attacks on the central government's handling of multilateral diplomacy more generally, and even opposition to continued engagement with the WTO at all.

The second way in which India's federal institutional structure influences the politics of its WTO engagement concerns outcomes rather than process. The economic impact of a given WTO rule (or set of rules) can vary significantly from state to state. This is primarily because the rules with the most direct effects are mainly sector-specific. Since certain sectors (and sub-sectors) are concentrated in particular states, representing either a large percentage of a state's economy or a large percentage of total national production in the sector, it is not surprising that how states are affected by WTO agreements or at least how politicians in these states perceived depends chiefly on their regional economic profiles.

The share of the agriculture sector in total economic output varies from state to state in India, as does the crop mix. This has implications for how the impacts of trade, even within this one sector, are experienced. Raw-silk producers in the state of Karnataka, for instance, have at various times been adversely affected by reduced barriers to import competition. Smallscale tea growers in Tamil Nadu have in recent years faced acute price fluctuations as a result of the changing rules governing international trade.

Coconut producers are particularly important in states like Kerala, and have seen their fortunes suffer thanks to India's closer integration into the world economy. Groundnut cultivators in Andhra Pradesh have been hit hard as competing imports from Southeast Asia and elsewhere have driven down prices. As a result, state governments, such as Karnataka's, have felt acute political pressure to take action to cushion producers of locally important crops.

None of these impacts is directly and completely traceable to WTO disciplines, nor even to domestic policy changes introduced to bring India's trade rules into conformity with the provisions of multilateral agreements. Producer groups have been subjected to so many varieties of institutional and policy reform since the current wave of economic liberalisation got underway in 1991 that the independent explanatory power of any single factor is all but obliterated.

But in politics perceptions are crucial. And because these sub-sectoral agricultural interests are often concentrated in certain regions (making local political reverberations proportionately louder), and because federalism affords these regions their own independently constituted tier of elected government, and because agriculture is a classically state subject, agricultural producer groups tend to make their appeals within their own states. Their main strategy, in other words, is to influence political elites whose primary aim is to capture power at the state level, but who also possess a voice in national affairs due to their potential ease of 'exit' from ruling coalitions in New Delhi. The question of motivation is relevant.

Regional parties – or what John Echeverri-Gent has called single-state parties, to distinguish them from the smaller subset of ethnically regionalist parties – such as Andhra Pradesh's Telugu Desam Party (TDP), are more interested in controlling their respective state governments than they are in having cabinet representation in New Delhi. Cabinet representation has, in most instances, been a fortuitous by-product of changes in the national party system. It has also had the added bonus, from the TDP's perspective, of allowing it to trade its MPs' support to the BJP-led national coalition in exchange for (a) a limited amount of influence on national coalition policy (derived from the TDP's credible exit option); and (b) the retention of the TDP's right to complain publicly about any aspect of national government policy out of political convenience.

These are bonuses in that the primary reason the TDP was willing to join hands with the BJP in 1998-99 was its desire to win a majority of state assembly seats, and thereby retain control over the formidable machinery (including most law-and-order matters) of state-level government. What the TDP got for its parliamentary support of the BJP in New Delhi was the BJP's willingness to take political actions back in Andhra Pradesh that would thwart the intention of the main opposition party in Andhra Pradesh, the Congress Party, to oust the TDP from power in the state.

Regionally concentrated agricultural interests do not, of course, always assert themselves through state governments. Especially in sub-sectors where commodity boards have been (or still are) in operation, even spatially dispersed producers tend to generate effective national representation. But even in these cases, there are strong incentives for interest groups to balance their lobbying efforts between trying to affect central government policy and seeking to influence state government implementation. Agricultural producer rely on state governments for many important decisions, concerning land reform (or the lack thereof), the supply of electricity for motorized irrigation pump sets, and so forth.

The representation of regional agricultural interests by regional parties in national trade-policy debates often takes the predictable form of grandstanding in parliament and in the national media. This is a microcosm of the way in which nation-wide discontent with the WTO – as a perceived agent of rich-country domination – drives the public posturing of the Government at India at WTO ministerial meetings in Seattle and Doha.

The political motivation is essentially the same in both instances: to distract from the failure of both levels of government to make use of the considerable number of policy levers over which these authorities still retain control. Nothing in the AoA prevents the Government of India from increasing domestic subsidies from their current levels or pursuing a slower pace of tariff reductions in regionally concentrated crops such as oilseeds.

The government simply chooses to spend public resources and political capital on other priorities. The government fulminates in multilateral discussions about the plight of small farmers, claiming as India's primary WTO negotiating objective a side agreement that will entrench further governments' authority to intervene when vulnerable farmers are threatened – all the while intervening at home less than it could.

State governments are engaged in a parallel process of blame-shifting, complaining of New Delhi's usurpation (through its accession to WTO agreements), while simultaneously failing the use the policy tools at their disposal to help their farmers. To take one example, during 2000-01 the ruling party in Tamil Nadu was eager to demonstrate to small-scale tea growers in that state that it was vigorously pursing their case with the authorities in New Delhi. This imparted a particular shrillness to the state government's public protestations against trade policies that are seen to expose small farmers to excessive international price volatility. For the Tamil Nadu government, making such costless gestures is preferable to cracking down on the cartels of buyers and processors who allegedly manipulate local markets to the detriment of small tea growers.

But state governments can do more than opportunistically champion lost causes. They can, and have, intervened with the central government in more substantial ways, in some cases helping to provide interim relief. For Tamil Nadu's tea growers, the participation of the statelevel ruling party in the national coalition government made the state government an important point of access to national agencies with the authority to arrange compensation. These include the Tea Board, the commerce ministry and the finance ministry.

Tamil Nadu politicians have been involved in mediating – with some small successes in terms of support prices and levels of tariff protection – on behalf of the tea growers with such national authorities. The Union Government ultimately increased tariffs from 15% to 35% for non-SAARC tea, and also agreed to a reduction from 4% to 2% in the central sales tax, and from 8% to 4% in the general sales tax. The importance of regional political considerations is underlined by Tamil Nadu's ruling party's inclination to see the tea price issue not only in terms of how to promote a local industry, but also in terms of the possibility that a further collapse in prices could aggravate local social tensions in the region where the tea is produced.

It is worth briefly mentioning a third way in which the existence of a federal system shapes the political reaction to India's WTO engagement. This concerns the approach taken by state governments to other aspects of economic liberalisation beyond trade – in particular, foreign direct investment.

Before India's economic reform programme got underway in 1991, the central bureaucracy largely determined the spatial distribution of industrial investment. This included both public and private investment, and in the case of the latter, not only investments by Indian firms but also what little foreign capital came into the country. This changed after 1991, as the replacement of 'central planning' with greater reliance on market mechanisms reduced not only the extent of planning, but also the overcentralisation of decision-making. States were suddenly able to court inward investment –from within India and abroad. This naturally generated competition among these sub-national units.

This competition has had other effects as well. The desire to court foreign investors often moderates not only the policy decisions of state governments on issues of direct relevance to investors – taxation, location requirements, labour policy, infrastructure provision – but also state governments' willingness to stake out extreme positions on policy questions that are beyond their own administrative competence, like international trade.

Even on policy positions of no direct relevance to investors contemplating an investment in a particular state – such as WTO rules, or domestic regulatory changes over which states exercise no independent authority – state governments have considerable incentive to refrain from intemperate remarks, lest they alienate the very investors they have taken such pains to lure.

By influencing the domestic political reaction to India's WTO engagement, the existence of a federal system in India can at times indirectly affect the Government of India's multilateral negotiating strategies – including its objectives, its chosen means for achieving them, and the public rationale by which they are justified. All of these, arguably, were affected in the case of the AoA. For instance, the Shiromani Akali Dal (SAD) leader who, as we have seen, made political mileage out of his government's legal action against the central governmentwas also quick to praise the Government of India's diplomatic maneuvers at the Doha WTO ministerial meeting in November 2001. The SAD leader was particularly pleased by the official language, in a provision attached to the Doha declaration, that recognised the need for future multilateral negotiations on agricultural liberalisation to consider not just increased trade, but also such objectives as food security, diversified rural development, and the reduction of inequalities.

But it would be fair to say that the SAD contributed, along with other regional parties, to the creation of a forum within which the multilateralization of policy issues could be debated more openly than they generally have been in India. This is one of two senses in which the federal system has been affected by the way in which the domestic politics of India's WTO engagement has been routed through its federal institutions.It was the pressure exerted by regional parties representing relatively well-off farmers that was instrumental in convincing the central government to conduct a series of federally organised consultations on the WTO's AoA.

In September 2000 a Commerce Ministry-coordinated conference brought together elected officials and civil servants from the central government (representing the ministries of agriculture and food and civil supplies) as well as their counterparts from the state governments. These high-profile meetings, which became the subject of much reportage and commentary in the English and Indian-language press, clarified points of fact (regarding Quantitative Restrictions, for instance) and demonstrated for the first time at a national level (though through state-wise delegations) the nature and extent of opposition to a further multilateralization of policy in this area. Significantly, the discussions produced not just opposition, but also positive suggestions. The most significant were alternative sets of priorities for the ongoing AoA negotiations – in particular, the amendments related to food security and the emphasis on 'implementation issues', or what are perceived to be treaty commitments that developed countries have failed fully to meet.

While state governments have been only marginally influential in shaping India's approach at the WTO, is important to emphasise that federalism itself undergoes a change in the process of mediating the domestic political reaction to globalization. The centre-state consultative forums are set to become a regular feature of India's pre-WTO-ministerial political ritual. The Conference of Chief Ministers and central government ministers in early 2001 – a followup to the September 2000 meeting that was also devoted to achieving greater centre-state consensus on India's multilateral negotiating positions – ensured this by placing this federal consultative forum on a high-level political footing.

The Conference of Chief Ministers received even more press attention than did the meeting of September 2000. Of course, other means for evolving a policy consensus may also emerge. But it appears difficult to imagine any coalition government in New Delhi that included a substantial number of single-state parties – and this appears likely to remain, for the foreseeable future, the winning formula in India's parliamentary politics – not convening such meetings, on a federal basis, as WTO negotiations reach critical junctures in the years ahead.

Despite the absence of formal decision-making authority, informal arrangements such as these, because of their representative nature, signify an incremental contribution to a larger phenomenon: the thickening of the Indian polity's federal institutional structure. If 'thickening' is the process of elaborating on a social system's basic rules and assumptions, then what is happening to India's federal political system would seem to offer a prime example. In Michael Walzer's formulation, 'with thickness comes qualification, compromise, complexity, and disagreement'.

All four characteristics could equally describe India's evolving federal order, which has emerged from a period of great institutional rigidity – manifested in the high rates at which state governments were dismissed by the central government under a constitutional provision known as President's Rule – to a new phase, beginning in the early 1990s, in which a more diverse set of institutional linkages between the central and state levels of India's political system is creating the basis for more imaginative compromises. That this does not always translate into recognisably greater influence for states does not make it any less significant an institutional shift.

That India's federal political system is becoming elaborated through an accretion of quasiformal institutions – and that these are at least partly a result of India's encounter with the WTO – is supported by organisational changes taking place in the states themselves. Numerous state governments – Punjab, Gujarat and others – have constituted expert committees to examine the impact of WTO agreements on key sectors in their respective regions. A few – Karnataka and Andhra Pradesh among them – have gone to the extent of creating divisions within their state bureaucracies to institutionalise this process of assessing potential impacts and making policy recommendations. The Andhra Pradesh government's interdepartmental 'WTO Cell' came into being following the recommendations of an expert panel, which argued that the central government 'did not do much to anticipate, analyse and act quickly to face the adverse fall out and implications of the agreement [AoA] on the farming community'. Andhra Pradesh's farmers were then hit by 'the crash in international price, 'low rates of tariff applied on imports of commodities like edible oils, sugar, etc.', and 'the removal of quantitative restrictions'. The justification for setting up Andhra Pradesh's WTO Cell went beyond the need to monitor the impacts of past agreements; the intention was to establish a means of adapting state government policies to changing events and, crucially, of influencing future government negotiating positions:

'Now a new round of negotiations has been launched, which will deal with agriculture as well as a number of other areas. As the international trade in agricultural commodities is likely to be liberalised further, a greater preparedness is required to face and prepare for competition in the international market. Andhra Pradesh, being one of the major agricultural states of the country, needs to set up a WTO cell in the state, which will access and analyse trade and price information and provide policy advice to the State Government on matters related to WTO and international trade'.

The proliferation of these state-level units does not break the hegemony of the central government over foreign commercial relations. But it does change the nature of bilateral relations between individual states and the central government by dismantling informational monopolies (or duopolies, in those cases where the knowledge of private-sector actors is relevant). Moreover, as more states have established WTO-oriented bureaucratic entities, the networking among them has grown, creating greater countervailing power vis a vis the analogous central agencies, and shifting the boundaries of traditional balance-of-power federalism.

The second way in which federalism is affected as a result of its role as a channel for mediating the domestic political reaction to WTO processes concerns the fiscal dimension of federalism. Fiscal federalism is in many ways the heart of the centre-state relationship, in India as in most other federal systems. Politicians fight over money as much as over any matters of policy or principle. The elaborate arrangements for regulating this point of interface testify to its centrality.

The work undertaken by the Planning and Finance Commissions, which determine (according to complicated and ever-evolving formulae) the distribution of resources, is inherently political. Much of this is partisan politics: ruling parties in New Delhi are often accused of favouring states controlled by the same party (or one of its allies). But the ideological dimension of politics is important as well. The rhetorical forms through which centre-state financial relationship is conducted reveal a host of moral claims, concerning 'fiscal rectitude', 'profligacy', 'step-motherly treatment by the centre', and the needs of the poor. All of these discourses have become mainstays of centrestate financial diplomacy during the 1990s.

If the terms in which centre-state financial diplomacy matter, then there is significance to the shifting discourse in the negotiations between the central and state governments over federally shared resources. In the newly emerging discourse, in which references to the WTO play an increasingly central role, states are to work as 'facilitators' of 'sectoral adjustment to globalization'.

For instance, Y.S. Alagh, a leading Indian planner, has argued that in negotiating for their share of funds in the various institutions of fiscal federalism, states should demand 'adjustment funds' that could be used to encourage crop diversification and to promote exports of agro-based products. Alagh's proposal is that 'such a fund should be utilised for preparing farmers for global competition and taking on the new challenges to be faced as a result of the World Trade Organization'.

It may or may not make technical sense to have state governments, rather than the central government, performing this facilitating role. But the legitimacy of regional political leaders' claim on any such resources has been enhanced by the nature of political conflict between the centre and the states on WTO issues. In particular, the tendency for state governments to cast themselves publicly as defenders of India's farmers – a role that stems from both the constitutional division of power and the political incentives arising from the simultaneous emergence of national coalition politics and the regionalization of the party system – has increased the negotiating leverage of state governments.

India's federal political system has had a significant impact on the way in which domestic political forces have reacted to the 'multilateralization' of key areas of policy-making, most notably with respect to the agriculture sector. Policy parameters that had previously been a matter for domestic political negotiation between domestic interest groups, as well as between the central and state governments, have been subjected to WTO disciplines. State-level political elites face strong incentives to view WTO-related matters through regional lenses, and to cast their political responses in federal terms.

The Government of India's agreement to WTO disciplines generates grievances by state-level politicians, who regard WTO treaties on such matters as agriculture as trespassing on the constitutional prerogatives of state governments. Many state-level politicians object to the impact of new 'WTO-compliant' domestic policies, blaming them for a variety of ills that beset their respective states. In short, the multilateralization of policy via India's accession to WTO agreements is perceived by many states (and advocates of states' rights) as likely to have an adverse impact on the share of political burdens that will have to be shouldered by the states.

In the process of influencing the form taken by the domestic politics of India's WTO engagement, Indian federalism itself is subjected to certain, sometimes contradictory, changes. On the one hand, the tendency for states to feel aggrieved by the Government of India's agreement to WTO provisions increases the level of confrontation between centre and states, placing federal institutions under even greater strain than they otherwise are. On the other hand, the casting of political conflicts in centre-state terms also spurs the demand for quasi-formal consultative forums that recognise the federal division of powers.

These kinds of informal institutions serve to 'thicken' the federal system in ways that affect future rounds of centre-state interaction, and thus the nature of federalism itself. They also provide a platform for states to give voice to certain region-specific interests and, indirectly, to influence India's multilateral negotiating strategy. That performing its mediating role allows India's federal political structure to influence –even to a very limited degree – an important aspect of globalization, with federalism itself getting affected in the process, raises questions of the relationship between democratic representation and the institutional and policy convergence taking place throughout much of the developing and developed world.

Impediments to Economic Cooperation

South Asia was slow to take up the issue of regional economic cooperation. Although SAARC was established in 1985, the South Asian Preferential Trade Agreement (SAPTA) was accepted only in 1993 and came into operation with the ratification of the first round of negotiations only in December 1995. Developments in the global trading system undoubtedly exerted their own influence on South Asian policymakers.

South Asia was increasingly being marginalized as a region – Europe, North America, Latin America and East Asia were all moving either in the direction of forming new regional trade arrangements or strengthening existing ones.

For South Asian countries, in the absence of an entry point into a more dynamic regional body, the second best option appeared to be to cooperate amongst themselves in the hope that it would generate political goodwill, if not actual economic benefits in the medium to longer term. The first round of trade negotiations covered only 226 products, largely of little relevance to the actual trade that was taking place amongst the member countries.But it was sufficient to build enough confidence amongst the regional partners to actually initiate a dialogue of taking South Asia from a preferential agreement to a more intense level of integration in the form of a regional free trade area. In principle, the concept was accepted by member states in 1996 and a date of 2000 but not later than 2005 was proposed for the establishment of SAFTA.

Thereafter, at the 1997 Summit in Male, the date was inexplicably brought forward to 2001. However, in the following year – voicing concerns of some member states – the Eminent Persons Group proposed a longer timeframe of 2008. But the constant reversals of dates did not help in instilling confidence that SAARC had carefully thought out its agenda. Rather, it appeared far too hasty in setting itself an ambitious timeframe for the establishment of SAFTA, without due consideration to overcome the problems and challenges it was likely to face.

SAPTA Negotiations

An analysis of the SAPTA negotiations underlines the constraints that South Asia faces in attempting to integrate as a regional entity. There have been 3 rounds of negotiations under SAPTA; with the conclusion of the third and final round in November 1998, over 5000 tariff lines of a total of 6500 have been covered by preferences to member countries.

India has offered the largest number of concessions followed by Bangladesh and Pakistan. The LDC member states within SAARC have also been offered a larger share of such concessions *vis-à-vis* the non-LDC states.

Table 7. SAPTA Preferences

	LDC	*Non-LDC*	*Total*
Bangladesh	44	558	602
Bhutan	122	68	190
India	2412	484	2896
Maldives	369	19	388
Nepal	177	252	429
Pakistan	242	284	526
Sri Lanka	52	144	196
SAARC	3418	1809	5227

There are inherent problems of using preferential trade concessions as a means of increasing trade volume within any given regional framework. Countries can appear very generous simply on the basis of the number of concessions given, but what is more relevant is the actual trade coverage of those preferences. Similarly, the depth of tariff cuts offered under a preferential agreement can again be limiting.

The South Asian Preferential Trade Agreement suffers from both these factors.Looking purely at the examples of India and Sri Lanka and their concessions offered under SAPTA illustrates the point clearly. Sri

Lanka's major exports to India are in agricultural related exports, base metals, plastics and rubber, textiles and paper products, but the number of concessions of actual trade interest to Sri Lanka on these items are minimal under SAPTA. India has offered concessions on a total of nearly 2900 products, of which non-LDC members like Sri Lanka are eligible for concessions under 484 products. In terms of the trade that is taking place between Sri Lanka and India, only 30 items of that 484 are of actual trade interest to Sri Lanka.

Similarly, while India's major exports to Sri Lanka are again in agricultural products, textiles, transport goods, machinery and base metals, Sri Lanka has offered concessions on 11 items of animal products which account for 1 per cent of total Indian exports to the country. The only item on which Sri Lanka appears to have offered significant concessions is in base metals where India has an export interest. In total, of the 144 items offered by Sri Lanka to non-LDCs, only 63 items are of actual trade interest to India.

The bilateral example of India and Sri Lanka illustrates the irrelevance of much of the goods on which South Asian countries have offered concessions to each other under the SAPTA process. And this is true for other countries within SAPTA as well. Sri Lanka's exports to South Asia as a percentage of its total exports was 2.5 per cent in 1995; it declined in the following year to 2.2 per cent before recording an increase to 2.8 per cent in 1999.

The percentage of such exports falling under SAPTA concessions in the meantime has indicated a steady decline from 33.9 per cent in 1997 to 24.6 per cent in 1999. What it appears to suggest is that exporters are taking advantage of the SAPTA preferences, but that those preferences are too limited in both the depth of tariff cuts and coverage of traded items to have any impact in actually increasing the volume of Sri Lankan exports to the rest of South Asia.

Table 8. Distribution of Traded Goods Eligible for Concessions under SAPTA

	Indian Concessions to SL		SL Concessions to India	
	Of trade interest	Composition of SL exports to India	Of trade interest	Composition of Indian exports to SL
Animals/animal products		2.2	11	1.0
Vegetable products	6	38.8	3	19.3
Animals/vegetable fats&oils	7.3		0.1	
Prepared foodstuffs	4	0.8		3.8
Mineral products	2	0.2		0.8
Chemical products	6	1.0	7	9.6
Plastics & rubber	4	11.3	1	3.1
Leather products		0.2	2	0.1
Wood products	3	0.1		0.4
Paper products	2	9.6		3.8
Textile articles	10.9		6	18.7
Footwear	1	0.2		0.1
Stone, plaster, cement		1.0		1.8
Pearls		0.3		0.4
Base metal	1	14.0	23	10.3
Machinery/mechanical goods		1.7	6	11.4
Transport equipment	1	0.0	4	13.7
Optical, photographic equip.	0.1		0.7	
Arms & ammunition		0.0		0.0
Misc. manufactured articles		0.2		0.8
Works of art		0.0		0.0
Total	30	100.0	63	100.0

In terms of SAPTA's impact on imports, Sri Lanka's imports from South Asia as a share of its total imports have declined marginally from 11.8 per cent in 1997 to 11.7 per cent in 1999. The percentage of such imports falling under SAPTA concessions have again shown a decline from 12.4 per cent in 1997 to 11.7 per cent in 1999. Therefore, as in the case of exports, there has been no change in the share of imports originating from South Asia as a result of concessions offered under SAPTA.

Hence, it is very clear that despite the rhetoric on strengthening trade links between SAARC countries, the reality is that very little by way of benefits has emerged. For the most part, intra-SAARC trade as a percentage of South Asia trade with the rest of the world has stagnated at around 4 per cent in the latter half of the 1990s.

The question the experience of SAPTA negotiations raise is whether South Asian countries are genuinely committed to regional trade liberalization or whether it is merely a confidence building exercise that is being pursued as a means of easing political tensions in the region. Some take the argument further to insist that economic cooperation will inevitably lead to greater political cohesion in the region and therefore should be pursued even if initial trade related benefits of SAPTA prove very limited. Is this argument valid for South Asia? Are South Asian interests best served by pursuing economic cooperation? Or are the political obstacles too deeply ingrained to justify the costs of negotiating, administering and implementing a regional trade arrangement?

Some political economists have drawn what seems to be an inevitable conclusion that the most likely scenario for South Asia is that it will remain locked in an unstable situation. Their argument is that given the Indo-centric nature of the region, any change will require that India becomes more accommodating, but that India may regard accommodation as unnecessary given that it considers itself powerful enough to cope with any tension in the subcontinent.Such reluctance will then serve to strengthen anti-Indian hawks in Pakistan and as a consequence, South Asia may never benefit from a spirit of regionalism. These arguments have been taken even further.

There are those who argue that in the case of India, for example, even with increase in trade within SAARC, it will not fulfill the needs of the Indian economy. In the case of Pakistan, it is suggested that a real integration with SAARC that has India as the dominant member can threaten to blur Pakistan's political and strategic identity and, therefore, will not be fully acceptable. And these sentiments are largely true of the South Asian political landscape.

No doubt SAARC may have a useful role to play in easing tensions in the region by at least getting its major actors together. But a regional trade agenda that is being dictated to by political expedience is unlikely to generate the benefits that will build support for it amongst the South Asian people. The agenda for SAARC economic cooperation remains very much a discussion between government officials, researchers and limited participants from the private sector. If economic imperatives are to put pressure on the political process, then wider participation of civil society and stakeholders are no doubt essential. But that will come only with proven benefits of economic cooperation – a factor that is unfortunately missing in South Asia's experience with the SAPTA process to date.

The political constraints to economic cooperation is most clearly evident from the recent experience where the SAARC agenda has come to a virtual standstill since the nuclear test explosions of early 1998. A resultant development of that stand-off has been the shift in focus to bilateral trade agreements between SAARC member countries. It is not an exaggeration to suggest that the sudden decision to sign the Indo-Lanka Free Trade Agreement (ILFTA) in December 1998 was driven by political considerations on the part of India.

For Sri Lanka, the driving imperative was in terms of first mover access to the Indian market. Bilateral free trade agreements have been far more generous in freeing trade between South Asian economies.So far, bilateral arrangements have been confined to three specific trade agreements, that of the free trade agreements India has signed with Bhutan, Nepal and Sri Lanka. But all the signs are that the trend is catching on; Sri Lanka and Pakistan are currently holding talks on a bilateral free trade agreement and there is speculation that India also may consider a bilateral arrangement of some sort with Bangladesh at some not too distant date.

What then are the implications of pursuing an essentially bilateral agenda in the context of efforts to promote economic cooperation at a regional level? There is very little evidence of similar trends in other regional groups; the vast majority of regional blocs have started from an agreed base on the intensity or degree of cooperation and have progressed from there, taking collective decisions with regard to either the speed of integration or admission of new entrants to the bloc. In those situations, the members of the regional grouping set specific guidelines and time frames within which potential members have to meet targets in order to qualify for membership. This is clearly the path that has been followed by the more successful regional groupings such as the European Union and ASEAN member countries.

But South Asia is currently faced with the spectre of countries within an existing regional trade arrangement moving ahead to form bilateral agreements that are far more liberal and substantial than anything under the regional framework. The concept of some countries within SAARC forging ahead with liberalization on a fast-track basis has been discussed for sometime. The idea behind was to allow, say for example, the non-LDC members of SAARC to implement SAFTA at a quicker pace and allow LDC countries a longer period of adjustment. But this has now been overtaken by the conversion to bilateral agreements that are effectively outside the SAARC process itself.

But where does this take us in the context of SAFTA? First and foremost, bilateral arrangements can undermine broad support for the formation of a South Asian Free Trade Area. In the case of Sri Lanka, for example, its support for SAFTA was prompted largely by the desire to gain access to the Indian market. Having already achieved that under the ILFTA – with the prospect of signing a similar agreement with Pakistan, Sri Lanka's other major trading partner in South Asia – there is a real danger that SAFTA will become marginal to its trade interests. And this is not only true of Sri Lanka, it is likely to be the case for other South Asian economies as more such bilateral agreements are entered into.

Secondly, it raises the issue of how these bilateral agreements are to be treated *vis-à-vis* SAFTA negotiations? Will they be incorporated into the SAFTA process or will they stand as separate bilateral trade agreements? If they are to be incorporated, then they will have to be used as the starting base from which to begin negotiations. If not, they will then exist as parallel trade agreements. The Indo-Nepal FTA, however, offers far more liberal terms to Nepal than does the Indo-Lanka FTA. It effectively has no negative list safeguards – what it has is a very minimal negative list – and this is unlikely to be acceptable to a majority of the SAARC countries.

There are important lessons to be learnt from the bilateral negotiating process. There was little discussion prior to the signing of the Indo-Lanka FTA. This has been defended on the grounds that were it to have been made public, then interest group pressure may have led to lengthy negotiations or that opposition could have ultimately killed off the agreement altogether. Even with this backdrop, it took more than a year after the agreement was signed for India and Sri Lanka to agree on a negative list that was at least partially acceptable to both countries.

The compromise solution arrived at compelled Sri Lanka to accept some form of quantitative restrictions on its exports of tea and garments into India under the ILFTA. Now that this process is multiplied to include all seven countries of SAARC, the task of agreeing to a formula with regard to negative lists is going to involve intense negotiations. Are negative lists to be worked out after signing the bare skeletons of the agreement such as under the ILFTA or will they be worked out before the agreement is signed? Whatever the procedure adopted, it will mean that SAARC countries have to show a greater commitment to open their markets to other member countries than has been the case under the SAPTA process. Whether such a commitment will be forthcoming given the political backdrop to the SAARC process, is debatable.

Alternatively, if bilateral agreements are to continue alongside the SAFTA process, this will mean that countries will have to contend with a multitude of bilateral and regional agreements – what some economists have referred to as a 'spaghetti bowl' of overlapping trade agreements. Whether South Asian interests will be best served by such arrangements is again questionable; it will mean a greater administrative burden, as well as less cohesion in marketing South Asia as a region to foreign investors. Do the customs authorities have the capacity or should they even be called upon to deal with multiple trade agreements?

Even in the case of SAPTA and the ILFTA, there are instances where Sri Lankan exporters are eligible for tariff concessions under SAPTA but where those same items fall within the Indian negative list under the ILFTA. Multiple trade agreements will only serve to confuse exporters and investors alike. Hence any potential benefits of bilateral agreements have to be weighed against the political fallout in a wider South Asian context.

Not only is there the real danger that bilateral agreements may undermine commitment to a greater South Asian economic area, but there is a far greater danger of alienating key players even further. For the moment at least, it appears that both India and Pakistan are intent on signing agreements with their smaller South Asian partners.

To some extent this is driven by the political imperatives that drive the SAARC process, but such a strategy will only serve to widen rather than bridge, existing differences between these two key players. It is undoubtedly time for SAARC to clearly determine the future path of economic integration in South Asia. Inaction will mean that more and more countries will seek the bilateral path to serve their own national interests. If more bilateral agreements come into play – and all indications are that there will be a few more – then the situation becomes highly complex.

To complicate matters further, most South Asian countries are not confining themselves to South Asia alone. They are also seeking membership of other regional bodies and trade blocs, both within Asia and outside. Unless SAARC wakes up and takes the initiative, it may find itself redundant in the whole process of regional integration of South Asian economies.

17

Potentials of SAARC

South Asia is one of the poorest regions of the world. With 22 per cent of the world population and that too with high rate of density. It is plagued by high level of illiteracy, prevalence of poor health conditions and above all, a poor degree of gross national product. Historically, the region has been the profitable hinterland for several colonial powers which perhaps remained as a major reasons for backwardness in all sectors from education to health, from agriculture to industries, etc.

On the other side of the coin, the potentials in the region are not too bad. In fact, the region is rich in terms of natural resources which, if harmessed appropriately, could perhaps change the entire scenario. However, this is the particular area where there is tremendous flaw despite the known facts of the opportunities.

It is true that there is great amount of disparity in the distribution of economic resources in the region. It is also true that all the countries in the region are striving to accumulate as much physical and human capital to achieve and accelerate their economic development.

Against this backdrop and particularly in the face of growing competition in global trade, economy and investment, concerted cooperation among the countries of the region has become imperative.

The process of globalisation has also spearheaded the concept and practice of interdependence. Economic and trade liberalisation policies enforce stronger bilateral and multilateral cooperation. This has infused the trend for regional and sub-regional cooperation in many parts of the world and, as we have been seeing, such moots resulted in substantial benefits. The case in point could be the Asean, EU, Nafta, etc.

There have also been several attempts in the region to stage such cooperative endeavours. Not one but many. But regrettably nothing has worked well so far and the situation tends to remain as dim as ever. The need for a strong regional or more specifically sub-regional cooperation has always been orchestrated well. Unfortunately, the real work has never surfaced.

Formation of regional or sub regional cooperative endeavours is indeed imperative when resources are shared by the concerned countries and more so, when opportuntities for accumulating common benefits are in place. While we should not ignore the possibilities of benefit from such cooperation, we must also ensure that these endeavours are based on natural and due advantages for each and every participating country.

For accelerated economic development, sub-regional efforts should encompass some pragmatic steps. It includes mainly simplification of tariff and taxation, and, of course, waiving of non-tariff barriers. let it be known clearly that discriminatory practices and lack of reciprocity, where it is applicable, shall never bring any tangible result to the endeavours for any kind of cooperation. To make sub-regional cooperation in the region comprising Bangladesh, India, Nepal and Bhutan meaningful, a wide array of current perspectives have to be taken into account.

There are good possibilities for developing a workable economic interaction in the region which can ensure a massive uplift of the socio-economic facade of the teeming millions here. But these possibilities are being overshadowed by huge trade imbalances between the countries in the region. To cite an example, there is a trade imbalance between India and Bangladesh, the annual trade deficit being over US$800 million in the recent year. Similar situation remains between India and Nepal as well as between India and Bhutan.

Because of its own economic strength fuelled by its geographical size and availability of resource capital, India does obviously have the comparative advantage over its smaller and weaker neighbours. Once again to give an overview in this case, we may see the share of India, Bangladesh, nepal and Bhutan in the regional trade.

While India's share is over 90 per cent, Bangladesh has 8.16 per cent, Nepal 1.03 per cent and Bhutan 0.10 percent. In spite of all such big differences, we can work out a strategy for enhanced possibilities for equitable sharing of benefits which ultimately will go for strengthening economic potentials of the region under discussion. We may take the case of European Union which shows how very large and very samll countries can mutually benefit from economic integration. Whether it is a rich and big country like Germany or France or a small and relatively weaker one like Portugal or Spain, each member of the Union has equal benefit. Their cooperation is beased on reality. They have waived non-tariff barriers in their trade and expanded their market accessibility.

In the context of a sustainable sub-regional economic cooperation, there are certain important aspects which have to be taken into serious consideration at the outset. To boost sub-regional economic cooperation in trade, the first and foremost thrust has to be given to the development of the entire network of infrastructural facilities which mainly entail transportation, telecommunication and banking. The physical constraints existing in missing linkages in road and railway network will have to be overecome. Then comes the transit facilities which have to be drawn and respected in govemmance of an individual country's economic sovereignty.

The perception of sub-regional economic cooperation should definitely merit a lot of appreciation and understanding. But to make it worthwhile, the precondition must absolutely be on the basis of equality. There cannot be cooperation if it is tracked one way. The pros and cons of the opportunities and problems of both parties should be taken in full cognisance, say, in the case of India's desire to improt natural gas from Bangladesh, it would perhaps be worthwhile if India imports fertiliser and other products produced by using the gas. This will help Bangladesh develop in industrial infrastructure.

Moreover, to make sub-regional cooperation fruitful, the intentions and commitments have to be given the topmost priority, how can we foresee the good effects of such cooperation when we find that there are continuous attempts to obliterate such intentions? To cite an example, jute exporters in Bangladesh are now finding problems with their export of jute to India following New Delhi's latest move to levy surcharge. Another example would be India's refusal to allow import of rubber and tea from Sri Lanka though both the countries have recently locked themselves into zero-tariff trading facility.

The conception of sub-regional economic cooperation still looks possible with all opportunties of benefit. It is working well in several parts of the globe and why shouldn't it be so in our case. The greatest output of such a cooperation would not only be the development of the concerned economics alone but it could contribute substantially to the proper balance of global trade as a whole.

Role of SAARC

The international situation of South Asia in the Post Cold War period has changed dramatically with the nuclear tests by India and Pakistan in 1998. As two nations belonged to the same area and the neighboring countries that hold dispute in Kashmir for the last half-century turned into a nuclear power. The international tensions in this area are increasing as the highest degree.The anti-terrorism and U.S. led international front had made after the major incidents in 9.11 of 2001 at the United States.

However, between India and Pakistan, it is stopped by the civil aviation way as of March 2003, mutual banishment of a diplomat continues, and it has become one of the areas where tensions are the highest degree in the world. Carrying out a deer Peace agreement with the government and the anti-government organization in Sri

Lanka which was also very important dispute for the past 16 years are reached the peace making agreement in the last year. And also, anti-government organization agrees with the negotiation start with the government in Nepal.

There are some lights to provide peace and stability is appearing to be seen. In fields other than international relations, economical liberalization of this area, especially in India is progressing at remarkable tempo, and is also increasing the direct investment from a foreign company or an abroad India system company. But in South Asia, economic development of this regional power India is a rare example, and the problem on which South Asia area each country should still tackle infrastructure maintenance, educational spread, export promotion, etc. has accumulated.

The South Asia area was constituted in seven nations, and The South Asian Association for Regional Cooperation (following, SAARC) held the 1st Summit meeting in 1985. In SAARC, its' standing secretariat is installed in Katmandu of Nepal, on the principle of mutual respect as each country are equal, and in order to aim at cooperation promotion within the area in fields, such as economy, society, culture, technology, and science, activity is continued. Furthermore, in SAARC, the various kinds of intra-regional meetings such as a summit meeting, foreign minister deliberations, and minister class deliberations. In these talks were offered periodically, and activity in symposium or a committee is also developed. However, it must be said that the activity result of old SAARC is very scarce.

The cause is the shadow of Indo-Pakistan dispute, and is because SAARC is brandished by the intention of hostility nuclear power India in an area, and Pakistan. Even if it becomes constant and a talk is held, adjournment of a fixed summit meeting serves as top news of media because the leaders of India and Pakistan united the face, and has contributed to neither substantial cooperation formation nor trust brew.

Moreover, as opposed to such a situation, the disappointment to SAARC is openly told from five countries. However, there is meaning with important advancing the measure for the social economy problem on which a political and religious confrontation is overcome and the countries in the same area are common. Moreover, it should serve as significant trust also in the relation of confrontation countries.

Future of Cooperation in South Asia

Today, more than a decade later, the world is attempting to decide which direction its future should follow. The world political and economic theatre has perhaps never found itself in such a precarious and uncertain position as it finds itself today. The terrorist attacks on September 11th, 2001 revealed to the world the economic and physical dangers of geo-political extremism. The global economy has entered into a widespread contraction and jobs are being lost worldwide at an increasingly fast pace. Nuclear proliferation is on the rise and urgent environmental concerns are increasingly being put on the back burner.Things seem to be taking an all around turn for the worse rather than for the better.

Clearly changes need to be made to the underlying fabric of global structure in order to bring about greater peace, prosperity and worldwide harmony. The exact nature and structure of these changes, however, are in great dispute. The current US administration of George W. Bush is in the process of proposing and, much more importantly, undertaking its own transformational "solution" to the current geopolitical structure.

The policies of the Bush administration (e.g. abandonment of the Kyoto Protocols, a massive military buildup, annulment of numerous missile treaties with Russia, a re-imposition of domestic tariffs etc.) suggest the current US government has, however tacitly, endorsed just such an international policy and is prepared to impose "Pax Americana" on the geo-political theatre.In this idealized world, the US will impose its will on any and all international problems and in doing so, bring about an era of US led global peace and prosperity. This misguided policy will lead to a global dark age, which shall consist of widespread anti-Americanism, global unrest, potential trade wars, environmental degradation, possible arms' races etc. This shall mark an overall step backwards in the process of the global integration, which was started with the founding of the United Nations in the post World War II era.

In the 21century and beyond the global power matrix will consist of several autonomous yet mutually dependent geographical blocs of nations growing out of already extant trade organizations such as the North American Free Trade Agreement nations (NAFTA), the European Union (EU) and the South Asian Association for Regional Cooperation (SAARC).These geographical blocs of nations, due to their mutual international trading needs, will be forced to negotiate with each other on a variety of issues (e.g. trade, defense, politics etc.) and will most probably do so in the arena of the United Nations.

Not only will these blocs, through their mutual dependencies, transform international relations beyond their respective blocs, but they will also do so within them. Instead of contending with the nationalistic rivalries that arise within nearby nations, bloc-member states shall be forced, due to their mutual trade dependencies, to "partner up" with their neighbors and live together in a federal member-state structure under the general governing authority of the bloc organization.

The various blocs also will be forced to settle their differences with each other in the United Nations in a peaceful manner instead of risking an economically fatal trade embargo and/or trade war. Any member state or bloc that turns "rogue" will face the full and united economic and military force of all the combined member blocs. Just the threat of this, however, will prevent any member state from breaking with international norms. Thus, this structure will allow for global peace, harmony and prosperity to reign and will usher in a new era for humanity.

The neo-conservatives of today often advocate their "Pax Americana" policies as a "compassionate" way of promoting US interests in the face of the very real and dangerous geo-political problems facing the world today. They are very quick to point out that, in the Middle East, the conflict between the sovereign state of Israel, presently led by the conservative Likud party, and various Palestinian groups has reached a fevered pitch. They also point out how Sub- Saharan Africa, with some very notable exceptions, has emerged from the cold war as a land that is being ravaged by internal strife, repressive governments, diseases, and economic turmoil.

Since the role of the Taliban regime in Afghanistan in the terrorist attacks of September 11th 2001 became revealed, however, few regions have garnered as much attention in the neo-conservative agenda as sub-continental South Asia (i.e. Afghanistan, India, Pakistan, Bangladesh, Sri Lanka, Bhutan, Nepal and Maldives).The neo-conservatives seem to have found no better place to begin to lay the foundation for a global "Pax Americana" than in this historically divided and volatile region.

Already, thousands of American troops have formed a quasipermanent base in Afghanistan and the current Bush regime, while publicly affirming its commitment to the development of Afghani democracy, makes no secret of its financial and military support of various ex-Taliban warlords.Also, the Bush administration has publicly given great military and financial support to the military dictatorship of President Pervez Musharraf of Pakistan and has tacitly ceased to attempt to eliminate the presence of nuclear weapons on the Indian subcontinent.

The uplifting of trade sanctions on India and Pakistan evidences this.Also, while building up Pakistan and Afghanistan, the US government has also recently warmed up to the conservative led Indian government and has begun cultivating that nation as a potential rival to combat the increasing clout of China in that region. In short, the Bush doctrine in South Asia, as elsewhere, seems to not focus on building unity and peace in volatile regions, but on promoting US interests by further aggravating/arming regional rivals and inserting itself as a mutually necessary "middle-man." In doing this, the current US regime continues an age-old "divide and rule" strategy that is the first step towards establishing a global "Pax Americana." Fortunately, however, nations of sub-continental South Asia are countering this US effort through the establishment and cultivation of SAARC.

SAARC's Vision for the Future

SAARC's formation evolved from the Declaration of South Asian Regional Cooperation (SARC) in 1983, which was preceded by a historical meeting of the foreign ministers/secretaries of the seven countries in 1980.The heads of state, in 1985, clearly stated SAARC's purpose as being:

"To promote the well-being of the populations of [sub-continental] South Asia and improve their standard of living; to speed up economic growth, social progress and cultural development; to reinforce links between the countries of this area; and, lastly, to promote mutual collaboration and assistance in the economic, social, cultural, technical and scientific fields.xvi A grand vision, such as the one outlined above, required that a structure be set up that increased collaboration and communication between the various SAARC members."

In order to realize this vision of increased collaboration and interdependency in the realms of culture, society, and economics, SAARC's institutional structure entails international government cooperation on various levels. The heads of state of the seven SAARC members meet on an annual basis, with a few historical exceptions, in order to maintain and build upon the organization's initial goals and ties.

The foreign ministers of each government constitute the Council of Ministers and are involved in the actual formulation of the policies. The foreign ministers also jointly constitute SAARC's Standing Committee, which ensures the implementation of these programs and policies by mobilizing financial and political support for them from their respective nations. Once this is done, these committees begin to oversee the programs' overall coordination.

The day-to-day responsibilities of the implementation of SAARC programs, however, is divided into and undertaken by the seven Technical Committees, which consists of members from all the seven member states. These Technical committees consist of experts in the following seven areas:

— Agriculture and Rural Development

— Communications and Transport

— Social Development

— Environment, Meteorology and Forestry

— Human Resources Development

— Energy

— Science and Technology

After a few years, however, SAARC member states realized that the progress made in each of these areas is completely dependent on the overall economic development of the region, and for this reason the Committee on Economic Cooperation (CEC) was established in 1991. It contended with issues ranging from "standards and measurement to customs cooperation and most importantly preferential trading arrangements. The idea of preferential trade agreements between these geographically linked nations greatly excited the member states and, in order to provide the institutional framework for such economic collaboration, the SAARC Preferential Trading Agreement (SAPTA) was passed in 1993.

SAPTA called for trade liberalization among the SAARC member countries and urged member states to make previously unimaginable tariff concessions, while trading amongst each other. The success of this program was so notable that SAARC members are in the process of drafting an even more elaborate comprehensive treaty system that shall allow for the development of a free trade area, entitled the South Asian Free Trade Area (SAFTA), within the SAARC region.Since 1985, SAARC has been able to accomplish a lot in this bitterly divided region, however it has unfortunately also been held back greatly in its quest to establish a prosperous and united sub-continental South Asia.

In order for an organization such as SAARC to succeed, the governments of the member states must feel as if their interests and voices are being fairly represented in the organization. Certainly, dominant members will emerge and those members will certainly be afforded additional privileges and responsibilities, but these members must treat their smaller counterparts with respect.

Unfortunately, India, which accounts for "76% of the total [SAARC] population and 77% of the regional GNP," has not lived up to its responsibility and must do so if it wishes for regional trade liberalization to continue. Pakistan, which is SAARC's second largest member, must similarly not attempt to dominate the organization. Only when both nations become more committed to promoting regional unity and balance can SAARC, in its current structural form, achieve its grand ambitions.

Another reason for the slow growth of interdependency among SAARC nations is that India currently opposes the use of multilateral approaches to solving regional, often bilateral, problems. India must be willing to sacrifice its regional hegemony in order to achieve the greater good not only for other SAARC states, but also for its own future. The cost of not utilizing the international apparatus to find the most effective solutions to longstanding problems far outweighs any possible benefit.

Several regional issues, including the hotly contested state of Kashmir, Indus river/valley water rights and cross-border terrorism, can be settled through the UN and any opposition to this only prolongs the conflict and greatly hinders the development of SAARC into a powerful and united geo-political bloc.

SAARC, as it exists today is a great first step towards the building of a powerful regional bloc. Its current problems are certainly not impossible to overcome and, given time and a change in governments will most probably be solved. There do, however, exist certain structural changes that need to be made to SAARC in order to allow it to fully develop into the geopolitical regional power bloc. The very existence of such a bloc in such a historically divided region, provides strong support to the belief that this bloc structure is going to become the next great power matrix.

In order for SAARC to develop into a notable geo-political power bloc, SAARC member states, especially India and Pakistan, will have to make revolutionary changes to the organization and the manner in which they deal with each other. Though there are myriad potential changes that will need to be made to the

SAARC structure (e.g. a new constitution, increased trade liberalization, more independent judicial offices, fairer regional elections etc.).

One of the reasons why sub-continental South Asia (i.e. SAARC member states) is considered to be one of the most dangerous places on Earth is simply because several of SAARC member states have built up excessive defense forces and are in engaged in some form of either immediate or potential conflict. If SAARC is to be developed into a geo-political power bloc, then these hostilities must end and the surest way to force the respective parties to the negotiating table is to remove their armed forces.

Certainly, each member state can and should retain a minimal defense force to deal with any emergency, but those national defense forces should be extremely small compared to their current sizes. Any conflict can then be solved at the SAARC negotiating table and/or through the UN apparatus. Furthermore, once these nations stop building their defense forces, they will find themselves with ample financial resources to contend with regional and domestic needs.

The current governments of India and Pakistan, the largest SAARC states, are not presently following this doctrine. To the contrary, these governments are engaged in an economically and potentially physically mutually disastrous arms race. India has deployed the 150 km range Prithvi I SRBM missile and is in the process of creating a longer-range missile force named the Agni series.India also has an ambitious nuclear program, having built up a stock of approximately 40-90 weapons.

Pakistan, meanwhile, has deployed the 1300-1500 km range Ghauri missile series and is also reportedly building a longer range (approximately 2500 km) force named the Shaheen series.The Pakistani nuclear program is also substantial, with the Carnegie Endowment estimating that it has enough weapons grade uranium to stockpile approximately 25 bombs.The attached graphs on the following pages reveal the extent of this arms race. In building these arms, India has spent 2.5% of its GDP on military expenditures in 2002,while Pakistan has spent approximately 4.6% of its GDP on military consumption.

According to Stockholm International Peace Research Institute (SIPRI) Yearbook, India has spent 28% of its government funding for science on military research and development – only the U.S surpasses this astounding figure. When nuclear and missile research and development is included, the percentage of government science funding devoted to the military jumps to 68%.These expenditures could be utilized for economic and infrastructure development instead of in an arms race that makes the sub-continent a more dangerous place and inhibits the growth of SAARC into a regionally powerful and peaceful geo-political bloc.

The abolishment of these large regional defense forces is an economically wise and politically necessary step in the development of SAARC. As mentioned above, any international or intra-national military crisis can be dealt although Pakistan is the second largest country in SAARC, it was until 1995 only the fourth largest source for Indian exports, behind Bangladesh, Sri Lanka and Nepal. These numbers will shoot up once peace reigns within the bloc, and the implications of increased trade among the SAARC region are numerous.

The increased collaboration among the countries will lead to a gradual diminishing of nationalistic feelings, which will in turn lead to a large -scale decrease in hostility between Muslim dominated Pakistan and Hindu dominated India on a religious level, providing a common basis for future collaboration on a myriad of cultural and social endeavors that is currently unforeseeable because of the religious vitriol currently spewed by both parties. The artificial boundaries created by the British colonialist empire will be knocked down permanently, opening unlimited avenues for cooperation in the Indian Subcontinent.

For the positive benefits of this economic awakening to be maximized, however, the SAARC nations must speed up the process of trade liberalization and remove protective trade tariffs as quickly as possible. To that end, SAARC has already begun work on SAFTA and hopefully will be able to put it into practice in the near future.

Centralized SAARC Federal Government

The goals outlined above are extremely ambitious ones and in order to realize them, SAARC must institute a centralized federal government, which supersedes that of the various member-states. This centralized government should be modeled after the United Nations, but should be given control of all critical regional external affairs (e.g. defense, foreign policy, trade policy etc.), while also acting as a forum for mediation between any SAARC member states. Such a government be based on a strictly democratic model with each member nation getting a vote with veto power given, due to their disproportionately large populations, to both Pakistan and India. Moreover, this government should be based on neutral territory given by a member state to the federal government in order to emphasize its neutrality in intra-bloc disagreements. This system of centralized regional government will have many positive implications.

Firstly, this centralized government will prevent SAARC members from making international decisions based solely on their personal interests. It will force the member-states into a structure where decisions are made only if they are mutually beneficial. This solidarity will serve to increase the bloc's international and economic standing and will allow it to negotiate more aggressively with other nations and/or blocs. In fact, the very existence and formation of a powerful SAARC bloc will encourage other nations to join together in similar blocs.

Secondly, the increased political and economic integration of SAARC member states will allow for the restoration of the semi-autonomy enjoyed by pre-British regional sub-cultures. Instead of having regions in India, Pakistan or Sri Lanka fighting civil wars with the central government for greater autonomy, these regions will increasingly begin to view themselves as part of a greater geographical whole.

The economic benefits of SAARC integration will provide these regions with the incentive to stay in the SAARC union. Furthermore, the now weakened central governments will be more than happy to grant these regions their long sought for semi-autonomy by relinquishing some, if not all, of the day-to-day operational control to these local governments. In short, SAARC integration will "solve" the growing problems associated with regionalism and nationalism in one swift stroke.

18

Democracy and Peace in South Asia

South Asia can surely be regarded as a region where the benefits of democratic peace would be more than desirable. South Asia's image as a region of chronic instability was only to be seconded by U.S. President Clinton's remarks in March 2000 that the Line of Control (LoC) in Kashmir is the 'most dangerous place in the world'. Besides the well-known conventional and nuclear security risks, South Asia is also among the poorest and least developed regions in the world according to international social and economic indicators. Despite these developments there are remarkable traditions of democratic rule at the same time.

During most of the 1990s, South Asia was the biggest democratic region after the transition from authoritarian rule in Pakistan, Nepal and Bangladesh. Moreover, South Asia is the only region where western political institutions go hand in hand with a variety of nonwestern civilisations and where religion plays an active role in current politics. The only forms of Hindu and Islamic democracies are to be found in Nepal and Bangladesh, and Buddhism received a foremost place in the Sri Lanka constitution.

In contrast to other Asian regions there is a strong commitment by South Asian countries to follow the development model that is included in the democratic peace debate. There is a great consensus for democracy and economic liberalisation. The constitutions of South Asian countries promote individual rights in contrast to community rights that created the debate on "Asian values" in parts of East and Southeast Asia some years ago.

The ambivalent picture of conflict, poverty, and democracy offers an interesting test case for the theoretical assumptions of the democratic peace debate. In a discipline like international relations that is characterized by various disputes the debate seems to have an exceptional place because it is regarded as 'the closest thing we have to an empirical law in the study of international relations.'

The argument that democracies do not go to war with each other is a powerful challenge for basic assumptions of the realist school of international relations. Here the external behaviour of states is either explained by the anarchic structure of the international system and the self-help behaviour of states or by their quest for power and their capabilities. The starting point of the democratic peace debate is Immanuel Kant's small volume "Zum ewigen Frieden". Already in 1795 he laid down two conditions for the peaceful coexistence of states: First, all states should become republics. Secondly, they should form a "peace union". This international institution, to use a contemporary term, should promote the peaceful coexistence and should prevent wars.

Kant's arguments have established a sophisticated debate that can be differentiated into a monadic and a dyadic level. The monadic level focuses on the internal structure of the state and can be differentiate in two arguments. The first argument emphasizes the norms of the democratic state. In contrast to autocratic regimes, political decisions are reached by compromise and consensus. The second argument emphasizes the institutional structure of democratic states. Political decision making in democracies is very complex and influenced by many interests groups. This guarantees that any decision for war has to pass various checks and balances. Moreover, democratic rulers are more accountable towards their citizens who have to pay the price for any warlike intervention by their governments. Because democratic governments can be replaced by elections their willingness to engage in war is only very limited. Kant has already mentioned the hardships of war among which the citizens have to decide themselves.

In the dyadic view the interaction between democracies comes to the fore. The starting point is that democracies are not more peaceful than non-democratic regimes, but that they have not fought wars against each other up to now. The reasons for this cannot be found in their internal structure but in their bilateral relationship.

Risse-Kappen has pointed to the importance of interaction and communcation. According to him, democracies share a "presumption of innocence" among each other and feel less threatened by other democracies. If domestic conflicts are solved by peaceful means, then decision makers tend to apply these norms in their relations with other democracies. Moreover, public opinion plays a much bigger role in the decision making on foreign policy. A similar argument looks not so much at the perception but at the shared values in order to explain democratic peace. The argument is that the recognition of freedom rights in a democracy is also awarded by citizens of other democracies. This creates a respect for political independence of these states and an abandonment of any form of violent intervention in their internal affairs.

The most sophisticated approach includes a triadic argument and was developed by Russett/Oneal. They demonstrated that democracy, economic interdependence and the membership in international institutions explain the peaceful coexistence of democracies in the international system. Their focus is not so much on the well-known vicious circles of anarchy that come from the realist tradition. Instead of this, they promote a virtuous circle that consists of democracy, interdependence and international institutions in order to secure peace in the international system.

A theoretical debate opens up a number of interesting questions for South Asia. Let us look at the different arguments and assumptions of the theoretical debate of the different approaches (monadic, dyadic, and triadic) and ask for their relevance for South Asia. The three approaches correspond to a domestic level (monadic approach), and a regional level (dyadic approach). The triadic approach takes into account effects of foreign direct investment (FDI) and the role of international organisations.

South Asia is an interesting laboratory. In no other region the interplay between western political institutions and religious traditions like Hinduism, Islam, Buddhism has developed a similar variance of democracies with different cultural backgrounds from the West. The definition of democracy mostly follows minimalist criteria as formulated by Diamond, Linz and Lipset.

Democracy is as a political system that meets at least three conditions: first, there is competition among organized groups and individuals over government power on a regular basis and without the use of force; second, it allows for political participation through regular free elections that should not exclude defined social groups; and third, it offers a certain level of civil and political rights that ensures competition and participation.

The state of democracy in South Asia is difficult to evaluate. Looking at the electoral records of South Asian countries we can at least conclude, that the foremost function of democracy, the exchange of power by electoral means is achieved. Bangladesh, India, Nepal, Pakistan, and Sri Lanka have an impressive electoral record under their democratic governments.

In contrast to popular views, incumbent governments are not approved but are mostly voted out of power in elections. But the picture gets marred if democracy is regarded as a set of institutions for peaceful conflict mediation. All democratic governments in South Asia have to cope with violent conflicts that threaten the integrity of their statehood showing the failure of democratic institutions to deal with these challenges.

Unfortunately, democratic governance is also not positively correlated with the rule of law or positive human development. Despite the empirical problems involved there is ample evidence by the reports from the media, as well as national and international human rights organisations that the assurance of constitutional rights is hardly met in most countries. Figures from Freedom House illustrate this ambivalence in democratic performance. It is especially noteworthy that figures for civil liberties that include constitutional rights are worse than the respective country figures for political rights. Even if all countries enjoyed an institutional democratic setup, Kant would hardly be satisfied with the way in which they work.

One of the main arguments is that citizens in a democracy value their basic rights and freedom and are willing to share these norms with citizens from other democracies. These shared norms on a societal as well as on a leadership level are regarded as a strong protection against war. Whether this kind of public democratic culture does have roots in South Asia is an interesting research question.

At least the conclusion seems valid, that it is hardly applied to neighbouring countries. Even if democratic norms are shared, widespread popular mistrust against neighbouring countries is still the dominant feature. The persistence of negative images and stereotypes in most obvious in Indo-Pakistan relations. The endeavours of the BJP-government in India to give a Hindu religious complexion to the educational system in accordance with the Hindutva-ideology is only one piece of this puzzle.

The debate about text books and the type of collective images they promote is another aspect of this development. The relations with India are an important part of the bilateral relations and the domestic debate not only in Pakistan but also in Sri Lanka, Bangladesh, and Nepal.

But India's negative image in the neighbouring countries due to the various bilateral conflicts persisted even after their democratic transition. The far reaching changes that India undertook in her regional policy with the Gujral doctrine in the mid-1990s, did not seem to have altered the perception of India as a regional hegemon.

The remarks of Bangladesh home minister Altaf Hossain Chowdhury in March 2002 about India's still expansionist designs can be regarded as representative for the perception of many intellectuals and political decisionmakers in the neighbouring countries.

Despite the deplorable state of democracy in South Asia, what are its repercussion on foreign policy? It is one argument in the debate, that the transparent political process of democracies prevents leaders from going to war with each other. South Asian countries are, like many western countries, characterized by the fact that, first, there is a great consensus on foreign policy.

Secondly, South Asia also equals most developed countries in the fact that foreign policy issues do not have a high priority on the electoral agenda. Kashmir may be the most pressing bilateral problem for India and Pakistan but given the socioeconomic situation it is hardly astonishing that the Kashmir issue figures not very high on the voter's agenda. The relative unimportance of foreign policy issues for elections was elaborated for India, but there is some evidence that this holds true for the other countries as well.

Various studies especially from the U.S. have highlighted the impact of institutional and organisational structures on foreign policy decision making. The famous dictum "where you stand depend on where you sit" from Allison's study on American foreign policy decision during the Cuban crisis revealed the constraints involved. In contrast to this, there is a lot of evidence that foreign policy decision making in South Asian countries in crisis situations, like war, is limited to small circles, be they hand-picked ministers, advisors or members of kitchen cabinets. Nehru's dominance of India's foreign policy is as well known as the kitchen cabinet decisions of his daughter.

The role of Parliament in foreign policy matters was reduced, so that democratic checks and balances did not work. The political decision for the nuclear tests in May 1998 by the newly elected BJP-government was also limited to a very small group of persons within the government. In Sri Lanka the UNP-government held secret negotiations to bargain the Indo-Sri Lanka treaty of 1987 that was followed by a massive employment of Indian troops on the island. In Pakistan the military has the last word in security and foreign policy matters thereby curtailing the sovereignty of elected governments.

One of the rare examples of an effective democratic control of foreign policy issues is Nepal where the founding fathers of the 1991 constitution included a paragraph that parliament has to give its consent to treaties that relate among other things to foreign affairs or boundaries questions of the with a two third majority. This reflects the past bitter experience of Nepalese governments in their dealings with India.

Higher democratic participation in foreign policy matters can be expected when the process of economic liberalisation will continue as the Indian case illustrates. In contrast to the period of mixed economy, liberalisation will make it necessary for the different interest groups like companies and trade unions from the agricultural, industrial, and service sector to aggregate their political interests and articulate their demands towards the government.

The growing world market integration will also increase the importance of other ministries in foreign policy decision making. The finance, commerce or trade ministries will emphasize their different interests compared to the national security issues. Liberalisation has also increased the foreign engagement of the chief ministers of Indian states in their search for foreign investment.

The slow pace of SAARC can also be explained, besides Indo-Pakistani rivalries, by the institutional framework in which it is embedded. Regional co-operation is mainly dealt with in the ministries of foreign affairs were perceptions of national security normally dominate political decision making. Widening the SAARC process to respective ministries, like finance, labour, transport, would probably also give the SAARC process a much greater importance domestic importance.

That greater participation as an indicator of democracy can have an impact on foreign policy is illustrated by the increasing importance of NGO. The debate about the Narmada project has demonstrated the growing impact of NGOs on government policies in India. Such examples underline the liberal argument about the rising importance of non-state actors in foreign policy decisions. But when it comes to security concerns, the decision making still seems to be limited to a small group of people.

Regional Security Concerns

Regional relations in South Asia are still dominated by India's security concerns on the one hand and the apprehensions of her smaller neighbours against it on the other hand. The long democratic tradition of India's political system and her political elites did not seem to have an impact on her foreign policy towards the smaller neighbours. The promotion of democracy could be used when it deemed necessary but could also be neglected when security concerns were touched.

India's intervention in Nepal in the early 1950s and in Bangladesh in 1971 can be used to demonstrate a certain interest of Indian governments to promote democracy in neighbouring countries. But the argument cannot be taken too far. India's security interest against China in Nepal and her interest to defeat Jinnah's two nation theory with the separation of East Pakistan can be regarded as equally strong motivations for India's intervention. That security concerns dominate democratic principles became most obvious in the case of Sri Lanka.

The training and support of Tamil militant groups in the 1980s in their fight against a democratically elected government in Colombo can only be understood in the light of Indira Gandhi's security doctrine and her hegemonic ambitions in South Asia. This kind of covert action of democracies against each other is not a new phenomenon. The U.S. intervention in Guatemala in 1954, Chile in 1973 and against the Sandinista government in Nicaragua in the 1980s can be cited as other examples. Some authors see these covert action as an affirmation of the democratic peace argument as "covert action [...] would usually be perceived as illegitimate by citizens of the intervening power."

But the discovery of India's covert actions against Sri Lanka did not rose similar protests like in the U.S. That democracy hardly made a difference in bilateral relations became most obvious in Indo-Pakistan relations during the 1990s when both countries were ruled by democratic governments. Despite free and fair elections and changes of governments their relations turned even worse.

The Kashmir conflict saw a new escalation of violence during the 1990s, with the numbers of victims going up steadily. The nuclear factor was already a threat before the tests of 1998 like the crisis of 1990 illustrated. The nuclear tests of 1998 demonstrated the will of both democratic governments in India and Pakistan to pursue the military logic to achieve their foreign policy goals.

The Kargil war of summer 1999 deserves special attention.The Kargil episode seemed to be one of the rare instances when two democracies have fought a war with each other. 'War' normally includes military activities with more than 1.000 deaths in a battle. In summer 1999 India and Pakistan could be regarded as democratic countries. The elections in India brought the BJP-coalition to power in spring 1998, and the February elections of 1997 in Pakistan saw the return of Nawaz Sharif to the government.

It is not astonishing, that Indian and Pakistan media reports differed in the number of casualties. Pakistani sources claimed that up to 1.700 Indians have been killed, whereas the Indian Defence Minister George Fernandes admitted that the Indian army lost 519 men. General Malik who led the Indian operation in Kargil said that around 1.350 men had been killed, two thirds of them from Pakistan. Pakistan's Information Minister Mushahid Hussain did not hestitate to call the Kargil episode "a de facto fourth Indo-Pak war".

Some authors still question that Kargil was an interstate war because the incursion was undertaken mainly by Islamic guerrillas. In contrast to this, Indian army officials have identified various parts of the Pakistani armed forces like the Northern Light Infantry, Special Services Group and Chitral Scouts who participated in the fighting. Think Tanks like RAND have confirmed the involvement of regular military forces in the fighting and conflict researchers have classified Kargil as a 'war'. This shatters the democratic peace argument and it remains open to argument whether this episode will be the exception that may confirm the rule. At the same time Kargil also contested the assertion that nuclear powers do not go to war with each other.

The contradictions of the Kargil episode point to various problems in the assumptions of the democratic peace argument. Knowing about the role of the military in Pakistan political decision-making, especially in security and foreign policy matters, it is quite obvious that Kargil was intended to thwart the Lahore process of the political leadership that was initiated in February 1999. Therefore it would be easy to qualify Pakistan simply as a non-democratic state. This would save the democratic peace argument but would be a delicate blow to the process of democratic transformation in the country.

The limits of the democratic peace become clearer when looking at democratic dyads like India and Sri Lanka. Of course, both countries did not go to war with each other and bilateral relations were good for most of the time since independence. The Indian intervention of 1987 took place after a formal accord and the official invitation of the Sri Lankan government. Nevertheless, Indo-Sri Lankan relations illustrate at least two shortcomings of the democratic peace debate. First, democratic peace seem to offer an alternative model that followed liberalinstitutionalist lines rather than neo-realist assumptions of power and national selfinterest.

Unfortunately, the democratic traditions could not overrule neo-realist security interests permanently. On the other hand, this does not mean, that neorealist assumptions have always shaped bilateral relations. But it seems that democracy alone will not prevent democratic states to pursue a hegemonic policy against other democracies. Secondly, democratic peace protagonists put their emphasis on classical interstate war. Unfortunately, most violent conflicts are inner-state conflicts since the end of the Cold War. Whether democracies are more immune against civil wars is a different research question. The experiences of most South Asian countries demonstrate, that democratic institutions *per se* are not sufficient to prevent violent conflicts.

South Asia offers various examples for democratic governments supporting militant movements in neighbouring democratic countries. Again, India and Pakistan could be cited as case studies. There are various claims that both countries supported militant movement in the other countries and again, democracies did not seem to make a decisive difference. The Indian training for Tamil militants is again a good case if this kind of modern, indirect warfare that can also occur between democracies. Although it is difficult to evaluate it empirically, there is some evidence that more than 1.000 people were killed in the fighting between the Sri Lankan army and Indian trained Tamil militant troops even before the Indian intervention in 1987.

Security Concerns at International Level

The democratic transitions in Bangladesh, Nepal and Pakistan between 1988 and 1991 and the economic liberalisation in India after 1991 brought an unprecedented correspondence of political systems and economic policies in South Asia. Until the military coup in Pakistan in October 1999, all states had democratic regimes and they are still pursuing a policy of economic liberalisation and world market integration. Compared to its population, the share of South Asia in world trade is still marginal. Being the second largest country and the eleventh largest national economy in the world, India's share in the world market is less than one percent.

The proportional figures for other countries may be better because they have a longer tradition liberal economic policies. But even countries like Sri Lanka or Pakistan are far away from the export/trade figures of Southeast Asian countries. The attractiveness of South Asia for foreign investment is still limited. The chronic instability of the region has prevented a large influx of foreign direct investment.

India is by far the most attractive market for foreign investors, and received considerable FDI compared to the pre-1991 period. But in the international comparison on FDI, India is only on rank 16 together with a country like Peru. The hesitation of international investors can be traced back to regional and/or domestic political problems, like Indo-Pakistan relations, political turmoil in Bangladesh or the civil war in Sri Lanka.

Economic interdependence on the regional level is even worse. Economic interdependence is highest among developed countries most of them being democracies. Comparative studies from economists have shown the limits of regional cooperation between developing countries. So it is not astonishing that regional groupings like SAARC are not able to reach similar intra-regional trade figures like the EU.

Intra-regional trade in the South Asian Association for Regional Cooperation (SAARC) is therefore only about 3 to 4 percent despite new agreements like SAARC Preferential Trading Arrangement (SAPTA) to extend regional trade links. The missing complementarities between the national economies are a major structural constraint that prevents the improvement of economic relations. The lack of infrastructure is another variable of the political problems in the region that have averted better economic development up to now. India and Pakistan as the two largest economies only have one border station and Pakistan is still hesitant to grant India the Most-Favoured Nation (MFN) Status according to WTO rules.

In regard to the role of international organizations, democratic peace research has shown that shared membership in international organizations (intergovernmental organizations, IGO) reduces the risk of interstate wars. According to Russett/Oneal IGO fulfil several functions like coercing norm breakers, mediating among conflicting parties, reducing uncertainty by providing information, establish expectations for gains and congruence of interests and socialisation and shaping norms. Their indicator is the number of shared organizations to which a pair of states do belong.

Although India and Pakistan, as the most war-prone dyad in South Asia, are members of various IGO, "they shared membership in just thirteen IGOs, as compared with an average of thirty one for contiguous states."That the benefits of shared membership do not work in South Asia is illustrated by the examples of UN and SAARC. Both countries belong to the UN this has not helped to bring about a resolution to the Kashmir conflict. Despite various UN resolutions, India is insisting on a bilateral approach following the Simla treaty of 1972 with Pakistan.

On the regional level, the SAARC Charter has excluded all contentious issues from the agenda. Nevertheless, the organization turned into the only forum for confidence-building measures of the region in recent years.

This is not to say that there would not be benefits from regional cooperation. Various studies have demonstrated that there are enough areas of cooperation in which all the countries involved could reach considerable gains for their national development. A look at international social and economic statistics reveals immediately the necessity for all countries in the region for closer cooperation in order to overcome their domestic problems.

India's Security Environment

During the Cold War peropd, Soviet Union was a pivotal actor that influenced India's formulation and conduct of its security policies. India had established security and military ties with the Soviet Union in the mid-1960s following wars with China in 1962 and Pakistan in 1965. The growing collaboration was highlighted in September 1971 by the Indo-Soviet Treaty of Peace and Friendship which was signed at the height of the East Pakistan secessionist movement. With Sino-American "rapprochement" also in progress at the same time, the treaty with the Soviet Union enabled India to resolve the "Bangladesh" issue by force in December 1971.India waged war with Pakistan without much fear of military intervention by Pakistan's then allies, China and the United States.

However, even before 1991, India's security problems were not directly related to Cold War politics. The primary sources of Indian security fears were regional, not global, although these fears were compounded by great power intrusions into the region emanating from the politics of the Cold War. Rivalry between the United States and the Soviet Union, and China and the Soviet Union, enabled Pakistan to obtain American and Chinese military assistance to counter Indian military capabilities. Meanwhile, India had turned increasingly to the Soviet Union for weapons to counter or preempt Pakistani arms procurement. During this period there were constant pressures on the part of both India and Pakistan to become nuclear weapons states. Two underlying characteristics may be noted about the covert or latent nuclear arms race in South Asia, one perpetual and the other a relatively new situation.

First, Pakistan's propulsion towards nuclear weapons arose mainly from strategic imperatives, namely, the threat from India. The nuclear energy rationalization put forward by Pakistan later was an afterthought. The Pakistani program may be viewed, therefore, as a "Security-to-Energy" driven phenomenon. India, on the other hand, perceived nuclear energy programs as critical for meeting anticipated shortfalls in the country's overall energy needs. Thereafter, various security rationalizations for nuclear weapons, such as the Chinese nuclear threat, tended to be spinoffs from the technological capability generated by the energy program. The Indian program, therefore, may be seen as an "Energy-to-Security" driven phenomenon. This analytical distinction is important when attempting to prevent proliferation in South Asia. In the case of Pakistan, it is more critical to address its security concerns, real or imagined. In the case of India, it may be more meaningful to watch its nuclear energy and space programs. These may be for genuine civilian development purposes, but they could be diverted to the making of nuclear weapons and missile delivery systems.

The second characteristic of the South Asian nuclear situation was the change in the direction of India's primary nuclear threat perceptions. As before, India still insists on maintaining its "nuclear option," i.e., it will neither acquire the bomb nor sign the Nuclear Non-proliferation Treaty (NPT) for the present. But, India also proclaims the right to acquire nuclear weapons in the future if its security warranted such a move. However, the same "option" policy now exists in a radically different setting.

Before the 1974 Indian atomic test, India's nuclear option policy was directed solely at China's perceived nuclear threat, but conditioned by Pakistan's expected reaction. But, as Pakistan proceeded headlong towards acquiring the bomb after the 1974 Indian test, there followed a decade of ambiguity and uncertainty in India about the direction from which it faced a nuclear threat. Was it China or was it Pakistan? By the early to mid 1980s, Indian analysts were convinced that Pakistan had put together an effective nuclear weapons program. Thereafter, India's nuclear option policy was directed primarily at the Pakistani nuclear threat.

This change in the orientation and direction of India's perceived nuclear threats continues into the 1990s. It also marks a significant change in India's ability to control the nuclear situation in South Asia. At one time, India had the "luxury," as it were, of deciding whether or not South Asia would become nuclearized. Now Pakistan determines whether South Asia will become nuclearized—while India can only respond. Meanwhile, India's internal security problems, to include violent secessionist movements and communal (mainly Hindu-Muslim) rioting, have become perennial since independence. Only the extent and intensity of these problems have varied.

Until the early 1980s, the separatist movements were largely confined to the tribes of the northeast: Nagas, Mizos, Gharos, Khasis and others. Following long bouts of insurgency and counterinsurgency, carving out three mini-states from the state of Assam (Nagaland, Mizoram, and Meghalaya) mainly resolved these pressures. Violent separatist movements in the major states of Punjab, Assam and Kashmir commenced only after 1984. Hindu-Muslim rioting remained sporadic, occurring mainly in Uttar Pradesh, Bihar, Gujerat, and Maharashtra.

By rank order, Indian policymakers during the period 1960-90 judged threats in Southern Asia from China and Pakistan to be of paramount concern, followed by the policies of the United States and the Soviet Union. The "nuclear option" continued to be an important part of the security debate among policymakers, analysts, and the attentive Indian public. While separatist movements in the northeast and Hindu-Muslim tensions were of concern, by Indian standards, at least, political life went on "as usual."

Whether gradual or sudden, substantial alterations have taken place in the India's security environment. The strategic relationships among India, Pakistan, and China at the regional level, and China, Russia and the United States at the global level, continue to define the security framework of India, although the nature of these relationships has shifted, and the intensity has declined.

Certain specific post-Cold War global political, economic, and social trends—democratization, marketization, increasing concerns about human rights violations, regional integration—further define the evolving Indian strategic environment. These constant or changing regional and global interstate relationships directly or indirectly affect the three basic levels of India's security concerns: internal security, conventional military security, and nuclear security.

Each of these three basic levels demands new priorities in policymaking. Considerable interaction takes place among them. Internal security problems at the first level include domestic violence and proxy wars conducted by India's neighbors across national boundaries in support of Indian secessionist movements. India alleges that Kashmiri and Sikh insurgents operate out of Pakistan with Pakistani support. Before the Indian Peacekeeping Forces went into Sri Lanka, many Tamil insurgents in Sri Lanka allegedly operated from India.

Before the creation of Bangladesh in 1971, both China and Pakistan supported the Naga and Mizo separatist movements in Northeast India. Secessionist violence continues to rise and fall in Sindh in Pakistan, and Assam in India. India could fuel the neighboring Sindhi separatist movement, and Bangladesh could do the same with the Assamese and Mizo separatist movements. Burma could support separatist violence in Nagaland and Mizoram if it chose to do so.

During the height of these tribal insurgencies in the 1960s and 1970s, Naga and Mizo guerillas moved freely across the uncontrolled Indo-Burmese frontiers and received small arms from across the Burmese-Chinese border. Insurgency in Tibet in the 1950s led to war between India and China in 1962. Despite improved relations between India and China today, repression or instability in Tibet generates domestic debate in India regarding its relations with China.

India is directly or indirectly involved or concerned about all such "internal" security issues both within its own borders and those of its neighbors. Security pressures at the second level concern the continuing conventional arms race and the prospects for a conventional war between India and Pakistan. The conventional arms race needs to be examined in the context of internal security problems and nuclear weapons capabilities in the region.

The interaction of domestic and unconventional security problems (insurgency, terrorism, and large-scale civilian violence) with conventional external security problems (traditional inter-state wars) complicates and muddles the role of the armed forces. Should the regular armed forces be used to address both problems of security since they impinge upon each other? The Indian armed forces have resisted this idea, claiming that they are not trained to deal with internal security and that such a role would also undermine their effectiveness in dealing with external security threats.

Security concerns at the third level may be found in the potential nuclearization of South Asia and its likely impact on regional and global stability. Is South Asia already nuclearized? Should we attempt to create a nuclear weapons- free zone in South Asia, or a nuclear weapons-safe zone? Is it possible for India and Pakistan to develop and deploy nuclear weapons without test detonations? Would a "nuclearized" South Asia be stable or unstable? Needless to say, nuclear developments in South Asia affect proliferation elsewhere, and conversely, proliferation elsewhere affects nuclear strategies in South Asia.

All three security levels are interrelated, perhaps as a possible scenario of conflict escalation. Conflict may begin with secessionist violence within a state, which may then spill across international frontiers by a proxy war, sparking a regional conventional war. This may further escalate into a regional nuclear war, then a strategic nuclear conflict as allies are drawn in. This scenario of three-stage escalation applies to Indo-Pakistani confrontations only. However, the first stage of war in South Asia—namely, spillover wars through proxies—could apply to all the major countries of South Asia.

The three levels of security and conflict reflect the origin, sequence, and probability of occurrence. Thus, secessionist or separatist violence, as in the case of Indian Kashmir and Punjab, in Pakistan's Sindh province, and in Sri Lanka's Tamil areas, is most frequent and perpetual. From such internal insurgencies, conventional inter-state war may occur, especially between India and Pakistan. This could escalate to nuclear levels since both India and Pakistan possess the ability to convert their nuclear resources and technology to weapons capabilities at short notice. Indeed, they may already possess covert nuclear weapons stockpiles.

Contrary to some speculation, there is little evidence that a covert or mutant "Cuban Missile Crisis"-type situation occurred between India and Pakistan during the intensity of the 1993 Kashmir crisis.Indeed, this scenario's worst-case last stage of escalation—nuclear war—is mentioned here to prompt methods to prevent it from happening.

Security pressures and violent conflict, or the prospect for such conflict, at each of the three levels are modified or magnified by several emerging conditions and trends, to include greater privatization and democratization; the decline of the non-aligned movement; improvements in Sino-Indian relations; shifting patterns in security relationships; and the general erosion of state sovereignty.

Privatization and democratization

The trends towards greater privatization and democratization in South Asia may alleviate these security problems. All the countries of South Asia are now democratic except Bhutan, which represents less than one percent of the population of South Asia. If the recent observation made by Bruce Russett and other political scientists carries merit, namely that democracies have not gone to war against each other over the last 50 years, then it could be argued that the avoidance of war between India and Pakistan throughout the Kashmir crisis was due to prevailing democracies in both countries.

The growth of market economies and democracy may minimize or soften security problems among neighboring countries which possess the same economic and political values. This growth may lead to greater regional economic integration, a trend that may imitate and parallel the one-time warring member states of the European Union and of Association of Southeast Asian Nations, or ASEAN. But this potential in South Asia remains doubtful.

The South Asian Association for Regional Cooperation (SAARC) has not been doing so well.Even cricket matches between India and Pakistan, which were expected to serve as confidence-building measures, usually turn out to be a sort of non-shooting war by proxy.Kashmiri Muslims, and indeed probably many Indian Muslims elsewhere, usually cheer Pakistani cricket teams against India. This is not a laughing matter because many Hindu nationalists point to this phenomenon as proof that most Indian Muslims are really "Pakistanis" at heart.

Nonalignment, the onetime fulcrum of India's foreign and security policy, has become irrelevant, whether it still exists in some other reincarnation or not.With no competing global power blocs, it may be important for India to take into account that the West is militarily and economically dominant. Russia can be of no assistance in countering any pro-Pakistani stance that the United States may take up.

At present both India and Pakistan are wooing the United States and the West as possible quasi-allies. Indeed, at the end of the Cold War there was a sudden Indian rush towards embracing the United States. New Delhi sought greater military cooperation with the United States, but soon ran into several roadblocks.

India's refusal to protect American pharmaceutical patents, its decision to buy from Russia cryogenic engines for its rocket program, and the testing of the Prithvi missile in defiance of American warnings, have cooled U.S. interest to establish closer military ties, and provoked growing suspicions in India about American friendship.However, it is important to note that while Indo-American military ties have not progressed as well as India would desire, economic ties have been booming as never before.

The United States was always India's main trading partner, but now leading American corporations have rushed into India with investment capital following New Delhi's economic liberalization.Correspondingly, while it has become clear that Russia has few economic benefits to offer India, the sudden break in Indo-Soviet military collaboration following the end of the Cold War is now being mended.

Much of this change stems from India's desire to purchase or manufacture under license Russian weapons, especially the MiG-29 and the Sukhoi-30 combat aircraft.Indeed, proponents in both India and Russia push the creation of a new triangular defence relationship between India, Russia, and China.

Security Relationships: Shifting Patterns

Sino-Indian relations have recently shown considerable improvement, possibly to Pakistan's security detriment.A de facto solution to the Sino-Indian border dispute has taken effect.Relations at the official level have displayed increasing cooperation, although various Indian analysts have pointed out the potential for future disputes and military rivalry.A basic and underlying rivalry still remains, especially since the Chinese conventional and nuclear arms buildup continues unabated.

India's development of the Agni Intermediate Range Ballistic Missile (IRBM) and the conversion of Polar Satellite Launch Vehicles to match the capability of an Intercontinental Ballistic Missile (ICBM) appear "targeted" against China, not Pakistan. A growing Sino-Indian naval rivalry is possible in the future. The Chinese Navy has been active around the Spratly and Paracell Islands, and there have been reports that China is aiding Burma to build a naval base at Rangoon. Since India's maritime territorial jurisdiction extends from the Lakshwadeep Islands in the Arabian Sea, to the Andaman and Nicobar Islands in the Bay of Bengal, stretching up to the Straits of Malacca, the possibility increases of Sino-Indian naval confrontation.

India and Pakistan are looking now in different directions to define the central aspects of their foreign and security policies.Pakistan is looking west towards the Islamic world (Central Asia, Iran, and Turkey) to foster closer political, economic, and perhaps military ties. Pakistan has been at the forefront of promoting the enlarged Economic Cooperative Organization (ECO), a kind of successor to the Pakistan-Iran-Turkey Regional Cooperation for Development (RCD) which emerged from the old Central Treaty Organization (CENTO) defense pact.The ECO consists of these three states, joined by all six of the Muslim republics of the former Soviet Union,plus Afghanistan. But the ECO is not working all that well.Afghanistan as a functioning country barely exists anymore.

An on-and-off civil war continues in Tajikistan. Iran and Turkey are pursuing their own political agendas in the Central Asian republics. At the same time, India is looking eastward towards Southeast Asia and East Asia for economic ties, and inwards to deal with its numerous internal security problems.

However, state sovereignty is generally eroding, especially where human rights violations are taking place. This erosion affects India, Pakistan, and Sri Lanka's handling of its internal security problems, especially in the Kashmir, Punjab, Assam, Sindh, and Tamil regions. Serious human rights violations now often result in international intervention, as in the cases of Cambodia, Iraq, Bosnia, and Rwanda. Undoubtedly, it is much more difficult to threaten to intervene in the case of states as big and powerful as China (in Tibet), Russia (in Chechnya), or India (in Kashmir), but they could face international economic sanctions.

Internal Security Issues

The most serious threats to the states of South Asia are internal conflict and the potential for state disintegration.Two successful secessionist movements have already taken place on the subcontinent: the creation of Pakistan out of British India in 1947 and the creation of Bangladesh out of Pakistan in 1971. The creation of these two states was preceded by bloody communal conflict, followed by Indo-Pakistani wars. Similarly, within Europe the breakups of the Soviet Union and Yugoslavia in the early 1990s were extremely violent, as was, after a bloody 10-year African war, Eritrea's 1993 break from Ethiopia. The basic dilemma underlying secessionist conflict is whether to recognize the right to national self-determination of various ethnic groups who feel that their future is best served by carving out their own independent states or to support the right of the state to maintain its sovereignty and territorial integrity as it sees fit because it is sovereign and independent. Except for the creations of Pakistan and Bangladesh, all nationalist-secessionist movements in South Asia have been crushed or simply dissipated through a combination of military pressure and political negotiations.

The Baluchi and Pashtun separatist movements have melted away, while the Sindh separatist movement may also hopefully go the same way. In India, the Dravidastan separatist movement among the Tamils simply dissipated after the DMK gained power in Tamil Nadu in the mid 1960s. The Naga, Mizo, and Khasi/Gharo secessionist movements were resolved through a combination of military force and political concessions, mainly by allowing new mini-states to be formed within the Indian Union. A combination of military force and political concessions short of conceding independence resolved the Sikh and Assamese separatist movements. Thus, the three main problem areas remaining are Kashmir (in India), the Tamil Ealam movement (in Sri Lanka), and the Sindhi-Mohajir question (in Pakistan).

The Kashmir situation somewhat differs from the other separatist movements because it involves a dispute between India and Pakistan that dates back to partition in 1947, when the Muslim province remained a part of India. For Pakistan, the Kashmir question is the unfinished business of partition.

As far as India is concerned, the Kashmir problem is an internal problem; it considers the accession by the Maharaja of Kashmir legal and final.After the separation of East Pakistan in 1971, the Kashmir issue seemed finally settled. Pakistan no longer appeared to represent the Muslims of the subcontinent, especially given the Mohajir situation in Sindh and Islamabad's internal war with Sindhi Muslims. Pakistan rarely made serious claims to Kashmir after 1971 until the revolt erupted in Indian Kashmir following the rigged elections of 1987.

Unlike past crises over Kashmir that provoked conventional wars between India and Pakistan, this crisis involves terrorism, insurgency, a proxy war, and a fundamental and qualitative shift in the nature of the crisis itself. Past differences between India and Pakistan concerned the acceptance and validity of the "two-nation theory" of Hindu and Muslim nations in an undivided India.

The current Kashmir crisis is far more "international" and "Islamic" in character. Various Kashmiri insurgent groups have accepted the Islamic fundamentalist beliefs of Iran, adopted the insurgency tactics of the mujaheddin struggle in Afghanistan during the Soviet occupation, and assumed the style and approach of the Palestinian Intifada.

Under the present conditions of Muslim alienation from India in Kashmir, if a two-way plebiscite (a choice between India or Pakistan) were to be held in Kashmir today, in all likelihood India would lose the plebiscite, and the majority of Muslim Kashmiris would vote to join Pakistan. However, if a third option, of independence, were offered, the majority of Kashmiris would probably choose independence. Ultimately, India's power will prevail, affirming its international legal right to rule in Kashmir whether or not it earns the political legitimacy bestowed by the consent of the governed.

Nevertheless, it would appear more advisable to maintain the territorial status quo in South Asia whatever India's legal and moral rights in Kashmir. There are more Muslims in India than in Pakistan or Bangladesh, and sending Kashmir to Pakistan could set Indian Muslims back to the bloody strife of 1947. Some extreme Hindu nationalists have declared that if Kashmir is ceded to Pakistan, Pakistan should be prepared to save the remaining 120 million Indian Muslims as well.

Perhaps there may be a growing feeling among moderate Hindus that hanging on to Kashmir has become counterproductive, not unlike the feeling of some in Great Britain about hanging on to Northern Ireland. Let Kashmir go to Pakistan and let Northern Ireland go to Ireland as they probably should have when Pakistan was created in 1947 and Ireland in 1921. But, the difference is the probable consequences for 120 million Indian Muslims if Kashmir is transferred to Pakistan. Besides, whether Northern Ireland is part of Great Britain or Ireland may make little difference now, since Great Britain and Ireland are now both members of the European Union which maintains open borders among the member states. South Asia has not yet reached that stage.

As regards Tamil demands for an independent Tamil Ealam carved out of Sri Lanka, and Sindhi demands for a free Sindhudesh independent of Pakistan, it appears doubtful if either of these demands will be conceded. Prospects for Tamil Ealam are now even more distant, with India supporting Sri Lanka to maintain its territorial integrity against the Liberation Tigers of Tamil Ealam (LTTE). India has thrown a naval cordon around Sri Lanka to prevent the smuggling of arms to the Tamil Tigers.

Much of the official Indian anger towards the Tamil Tigers began with the bloody involvement of the Indian Peace-Keeping Forces (IPKF) with the Tamil insurgents whom the IPKF had gone to protect. India's withdrawal of support for the Tamil cause (although this was always short of Tamil independence) followed the assassination of then Indian prime minister, Rajiv Gandhi, by a Tamil Tiger suicide killer. Indeed, this event alienated much of ethnic Tamil support within India's Tamil Nadu for the Tamil Ealam movement in Sri Lanka.

Within Pakistan's Sindh province, Mohajir demands for their own state within Pakistan pits them against the Sindhis, the sons of the soil, who believe they have already been dispossessed by the Indian emigre Muslim population. Sindhis want an independent Sindhudesh. Mohajirs talk about creating their own province within Pakistan out of its Sindh province linking the main cities of Karachi, Hyderabad, and Sukkur through corridors, or just creating a state south of the 26th parallel. This would leave an impoverished and rump Sindh province with virtually no resources.

India's position on this issue has remained ambiguous, wavering between sympathy for both the Sindhi separatists and the Indian Muslim emigres. The Sindh separatist movement and the opposing Mohajir's violent struggle against the Sindhis undermines Pakistan's moral claims to Kashmir. Although India appears to be less involved, if at all, in the violent struggle taking place in Pakistan's Sindh province, instability in Sindh counterbalances instability in Kashmir.

Pakistan's ability to undermine India by playing the "Kashmir" card, can be countered by India's ability to undermine Pakistan by playing the "Sindh" card. Meanwhile, through Indian application of armed force and political concessions, the Assamese and Sikh separatist movements were fizzling out in the early 1990s, although there is some revival of the United Liberation Front of Assam (ULFA) which spearheaded the Assamese independence movement.There is a similar revival of the Naga independence movement. There are other demands in India for new mini-states within India such as Gurkhaland and Bodoland in the northeast, and the carving out of a large new state for the Adivasis out of Bihar, Madhya Pradesh and Orissa to be called Jharkand.

The fact is, with the exception of Bangladesh which has a minor tribal separatist movement in the Chittagong Hill Tracts, India, Pakistan, and Sri Lanka are all vulnerable. The threat to the territorial integrity of these states comes mainly from within. Successful internal security management will determine the survival of these states in their present form.

Conventional Forces

In the past, the conventional arms race and the balance of conventional forces in South Asia were usually considered crucial in understanding the probabilities of war occurrence and war outcome in South Asia. The conventional military balance now appears relatively less deterministic about such probabilities compared to the earlier decades. Any war between India and Pakistan in the future must take into account each side's ability to conduct wars of proxy concurrently, and the threat to escalate the war to nuclear levels. They constitute complicating or supplementary factors in devising strategies of conventional wars in South Asia.

In South Asia, land forces remain crucial to the conduct of wars, and while some global technological advances will have been absorbed by the armed forces, technological levels do not equal those found in the United States and the West. Efforts by South Asian countries to upgrade their weapons systems with advancing military technology (such as precision guided missiles) for all the Services will not radically change their military strategy; doctrine continues to give the primary combat role to ground forces, with air and naval forces providing mainly supporting roles.

Following the 1962 Sino-Indian War, India's defense against China has rested on the 10 to 11 lightly-armed mountain/infantry divisions raised in the 1960s, which supposedly act as a "tripwire." But, there is really no fall-back conventional defense measure short of demonstrating an Indian nuclear deterrent based on IRBMs tipped with nuclear warheads. This is precisely what the Indian Agni missile and covert nuclear weapons programs are intended to serve.

Against Pakistan, India's battle scenarios do not look fundamentally different from the those fought in 1965 and 1971. In the 1965 war, the armies and air forces of India and Pakistan fought independent and separate battles with limited close air support. For the greater part, the Indian Air Force and the Pakistan Air Force conducted their own separate interdiction campaigns, targeting ammunition dumps and air bases. The navies of the two countries were not involved.

During the 1971 war, all three services were engaged, but there was not much synchronization except for the Indian naval attack on Karachi harbor, which was coordinated with an Indian air attack on the city to draw away the Pakistan Air Force. For the rest, the air forces and navies on either side conducted their own wars with limited ground support provided in certain battles.

Military legacies and traditions change slowly in South Asia. Not even the major shock of 1971 losses provoked a change to Pakistani military strategy which continues to emphasize land forces. There is an effort to obtain advanced aircraft from the West (including unsuccessful efforts to obtain F-16s from the United States), and there has been a modest build up of the Pakistan Navy with the acquisition of short-range Augusto and Daphne- class submarines and a few frigates.

The Pakistan Army remains the backbone of the Pakistani military. India has adjusted better, with the army now drawing only 60 percent of the defense budget (down from a high of almost 80 percent in the 1950s). India paid greater attention to its air force and navy. But even here the lessons of the Gulf War and Bosnia highlighting high-tech, precision-guided weapons have not been incorporated in Indian strategic thinking, force structure, and equipment.The failure to copy Western military strategy based on the supremacy of high-tech air power may result from India's inability to procure or pay for such technology. Also, direct Western military intervention in another war in South Asia, which would upset the regional military balance, is not expected. Recall that India conducted a proxy war in East Pakistan throughout 1971 before a two-front conventional war broke out between India and East and West Pakistan.

The insurgency in East Pakistan speeded up the Indian military victory in the east. In the west there was a stalemate. The conduct of another India-Pakistan war must take into account Pakistan's ability to simultaneously feed the Kashmiri insurgents, and India's potential to fuel unrest in Sindh. In that respect, Kashmir is India's "Bangladesh."In a similar vein, Sindhi nationalists in Hyderabad and London told me that they had made a mistake when they failed to seize the opportunity to carve out a "Sindhudesh" in 1971 with the help of the Indian armed forces while they were "liberating" Bangladesh. Thus, if India loses Kashmir in another Indo-Pakistani war (although quite unlikely), Pakistan could also lose Sindh. The loss of Kashmir or the loss of Sindh could completely unravel both India and Pakistan into several independent states, as happened in the former Soviet Union and Yugoslavia.

A future Indo-Pakistani war could be messy, with aspects of the Vietnam/Afghanistan syndrome coming into play. Along the Himalayan frontiers, in the less likely event of another conventional Sino-Indian war, India could stir up insurgents in Tibet, while China could do the same in Kashmir, Assam, and the other mini-states of Northeast India. India still deploys its ten mountain divisions ready to fight the last war of 1962 again. Sino-Indian tensions would only occur in the event of another Tibetan uprising which seems unlikely at present. This is in part because—through migrations and settlements—Han Chinese have become the majority in Greater Tibet. Hindu Nationalists advocate a similar resettlement policy and solution for Kashmir as well. Indeed, three million Kashmiri Muslims could easily have been overwhelmed decades ago through Hindu and Sikh settlements in Kashmir. This India has not done.

Despite the renewed, but mellowed, wave of "Hindi-Chini Bhai-Bhai" (Indians and Chinese are Brothers), voices within India are cautious regarding the growth of Chinese military capabilities.China's aggressive policies toward Hong Kong, the Paracell and Spratly Islands, and Taiwan, have produced periodic criticism in the Indian parliament and press regarding the current Congress government's rush towards embracing China without serious qualifications.In early 1996, former chiefs of the Indian armed forces urged the Congress government to bolster its military capability and focus on China's long-term plans in South Asia.

According to the assessment of Lieutenant General K.K. Hazari, "Pakistan is not a military threat, but we have to work out a long-term perspective on capability vis-a-vis China, say after 15 or 20 years."According to retired Vice Admiral R.B. Suri, "China is making inroads into the Indian Ocean by building up a navy that in the next 10-15 years could interfere with our interests in the region."However, Indian concerns about the growth of Chinese conventional and nuclear military power and its aggressive territorial claims to the Spratly Islands and Taiwan are countered by those who argue that Indian political—if not military—cooperation with China and Russia is essential to counter the military, economic, and political dominance of a U.S.-led West.Indeed, it may not be too farfetched to say that while the Defense Ministry is warning about Chinese threats, the External Affairs Ministry is seeking to promote Sino-Indian and Indo-Russian cooperation.

Chinese military modernization has targeted air and naval forces. In early 1996, China contracted with Russia to purchase 72 Su-27 multi-role fighters to replace some of its aging 4,000 indigenously built aircraft based on 1950s Soviet technology.The Chinese have claimed that these purchases were to counter Taiwanese purchases of American F-16s and French Mirage-2000s.

The size of China's land and air forces is numerically overwhelming, although the qualitative standards of some of its equipment may be inferior to that of India. As in the growth of the Indian Navy in 1980s, it is the growth of the Chinese Navy in the 1990s that may be of greater concern to the Southeast Asian countries. Neither India nor China have "blue water" navies;they can be better described as "brown water" navies. Whereas India has two ex-British aging aircraft carriers, China has none. On the other hand, whereas India's naval expansion has slowed down or even halted, the Chinese Navy has begun to expand. In 1995, China arranged for the purchase of four submarines from Moscow at a cost of $4 billion.The purchase of another six submarines is being negotiated, with the purchase of yet another 12 by the end of the decade.

The purchase of 22 submarines in 5 years suggests that China is moving well beyond a coastal defense role and towards an offensive naval capability. Both India and

China sought to buy from Ukraine a former Soviet aircraft carrier, now rusting in a Ukrainian harbor, but the quality and price proved unacceptable. Both India and China are attempting to promote and establish indigenous naval technologies. Although India's recent efforts to produce its own submarines in collaboration with a German firm has been abandoned, India's indigenous Godavari-class frigate development program, an extension of the construction of the Leander-class frigates in Bombay in collaboration with a British firm, has been a major success.

Any major expansion of the Indian Navy into a blue water capability has always raised the possibility, albeit remote, of a naval response from Indonesia, Pakistan, and Iran, the three major Muslim countries of Asia. However remote this may now appear, it could potentially create a virtual Islamic naval triangle around India. In the 1960s, the Indonesian Navy under Sukarno attempted to expand, and likewise, the Shah of Iran sought to build up a significant Iranian naval force during the 1970s.

Meanwhile, Pakistan, in response to India's naval buildup, has acquired nine submarines and 11 combat ships. Similarly, any major expansion of the Chinese Navy may invite an Indian naval response and also trigger naval purchases in Indonesia, Malaysia, and the Philippines.The Asian security dilemma at sea may interlock naval rivalries among the littoral states of the Arabian Sea, Bay of Bengal, and the South China Sea.

In any future Indo-Pakistani or Sino-Indian conventional war, the nuclear factor must be taken into account, quite unlike the past, when all wars in South Asia were strictly among conventional powers. China tested its first bomb in 1964, two years after the 1962 Sino-Indian War. India tested its first bomb in 1974, about two years after the December 1971 Indo-Pakistani War. No wars between India and its traditional antagonists have occurred since these wars in the decade between 1962 and 1971.

The present conditions for another conventional war are now under the shadow of nuclear capabilities in China, India, and Pakistan. A "nuclear India" could deploy IRBMs capable of reaching the industrial cities of south China. India now possesses a second-strike capability against China. Both India and Pakistan possess aircraft capable of dropping nuclear weapons. Mutual retaliatory strike capability exists between India and Pakistan. All of this affects conventional war strategy in South Asia. The threatened use of nuclear weapons in South Asia may be seen as a strategy of conventional war deterrence, or, if war did break out, of conventional war termination.

Since the end of the Cold War, the conventional arms race in South Asia has slowed down considerably.No major new weapons acquisitions have taken place. Pakistan is trying to obtain the F-16 fighters whose purchase from the United States was halted by the Pressler Amendment, or get its money back; India is trying to obtain from Russia a few more MiG-29 fighters and some T-72 tanks. Indigenous design, development, and production of weapons systems continue as before in India, but successes have been limited to certain parts and sections of weapons systems.

Development of the Light Combat aircraft has floundered, while several prototypes of the Main Battle Tank have not met the expectations of the Indian Army and have proven very costly. However, a variety of aircraft, tanks, frigates and submarines have been produced in India through technology transfers from overseas manufacturers. Although India's naval capabilities are quite modest, its navy still appears overwhelming compared to that of Pakistan.

However, much of India's Soviet-vintage submarine fleet is being taken out of commission. Efforts failed to obtain a third carrier, but two old British carriers remain in service. Conventional weapons purchases in South Asia have been relatively quiet despite the availability of weapons from the ex-Soviet republics at bargain basement prices. The size of the Indian Army has actually declined from about 1.2 million uniformed personnel at its peak in the 1970s to just under 1 million in the mid-1990s.

Size alone is an inaccurate tool to evaluate ground forces. Indian force capabilities dwarf those of Pakistan, but the force deployment throughout the various regions, especially in the north and east, produces local parity. India argues that raw numbers of men and equipment, without an assessment of their comparative technological sophistication, are insufficient to determine military advantage.

Terrain and duration also play a role. India claims to have the disadvantage in fighting wars against Pakistan and China in Kashmir and along the Himalayan frontiers, respectively, and in wars that last barely a month, quantitative superiority in weapons is less decisive than the effectiveness of frontline equipment that can be deployed immediately.

India justifies this naval expansion since it was never really tied to Pakistani naval capabilities but to India's large coastline, its island territories, the increasing seaborne trade, and so on. The power of the Chinese Navy and claims to the Spratly Islands and Paracell Islands suggest a future possible Sino-Indian naval arms race as China extends its naval reach to the Straits of Malacca. However, as with the other two services, Indian naval policy has been largely that of force maintenance and sustenance rather than expansion.

Economic reforms in India and Pakistan, especially the process of marketization and privatization, affect weapons procurement. In India, "privatization" unleashed the private sector and opened up the Indian market to foreign investments. Public sector undertakings, to include defense, have not benefitted; rather, they are just being allowed to wither away slowly.

It is unclear what the government intends to do about public sector defense production; the government may neglect industries such as Hindustan Aeronautics, Mazagon Docks, Bharat Electronics, and so forth, or replace them with private sector contracting for defense goods. Indeed, it is unknown whether these defense public sector undertakings will be sustained. In other words, India's privatization may not apply to defense production, at least in the short run.

The fact that future conventional wars in South Asia will possibly involve concurrent domestic low-intensity conflicts raises the question of the use of conventional forces to deal with internal conflict and security. The militaries of India, Pakistan, and Sri Lanka have been used to crush secessionist movements at various times: in the northeast tribal belt, in Assam, Punjab, and Kashmir by the Indian Army; in East Pakistan (unsuccessfully), in Baluchistan, the Northwest Frontier Province and Sindh by the Pakistan Army; and in the Tamil areas of the Northern and Eastern provinces by the Sri Lankan Army.

Until the Indian Army's assault on the Sikh's Golden Temple in Punjab in 1984, the military was viewed by much of the Indian population as a symbol of national unity. To most Indians, the military was, and still is, the trusted friend of the people. Indeed, the Indian military sees itself as the defender of the nation and as an important symbol of national unity, and it would like to keep things that way.

The military acts as an integrating force in its national recruitment efforts; its role as the defender of the nation against external aggression; and, its role in providing disaster relief and other assistance to the civilian authorities during natural calamities. The recruitment policy and composition of the Indian military are largely responsible for the stability of India's democracy; the absence of such pressure may provide clues, on the other hand, to why democracy in Pakistan failed, even though Pakistan inherited one-third of the British Indian military services.

Perceptions of the regular armed forces as symbols of national unity and integrity began to decline following the 1984 assault on the Sikh's Golden Temple in Amritsar. Its prestige fell further as a result of its reluctant role in the maintenance of internal security. Controversy over the use of force to quell domestic insurgencies, of course, surrounds both the paramilitary forces and the armed forces.

In the case of the paramilitary forces, the issue is not whether they have a role to play in the maintenance of internal security; they were, after all, raised for that purpose. The issue is whether such special internal security forces could be misused by the government in power. Arguably, the greater the size of paramilitary forces, the greater the probability that democratic processes and the freedom of the citizens are likely to be undermined. On the other hand, in the case of the regular armed forces, the question is whether such forces should be used at all in the maintenance of internal order.

The Indian military, unhappy about this role, has protested that the use of the military to deal with internal conflicts could lead to military demoralization, increasing politicization of the military, and to the breakdown of civilian controlled democracies. The use of the Indian Army to attack the Sikh's Golden Temple nearly led to a mutiny by some Sikh soldiers of the Indian Army, and it destroyed civilian-military confidence in Punjab.

The military argues that to use the armed services "against their own people" would not only produce a breakdown in the military-civilian trust that has been built up over several decades, but also—if the army were deployed on domestic security missions in the border provinces such as Punjab, Kashmir, and Assam—would undermine its own ability to fight a conventional war because of the alienation of the people living in those regions.

The military would eventually be seen as the enemy of the people, a situation already found in Pakistan and several other developing countries in Asia, Africa, and Latin America. However, these military misgivings have not stopped the civilian authorities from ordering the armed forces to deal with internal security; the military is resigned to the situation given the growing threats to the security and sovereignty of the Indian state from within.

The Indian civilian authorities' response has been to build up the paramilitary forces under the Home Ministry. But this has had its own problems. The Indian paramilitary forces, especially the Central Reserve Police Force and the Provincial Armed Constabulary, are not very disciplined.

The growth of such forces to nearly half a million potentially threatens civilian authorities. They often get caught up in the emotions of Hindu-Muslim or Hindu-Sikh conflict and take sides. The Provincial Armed Constabulary and the Central Reserve Police Force have been notorious in getting involved in communal conflict against Muslims in Uttar Pradesh and Gujerat. Allegations of human rights violations in Kashmir have been mainly directed at paramilitary forces such as the Border Security Force.

India has one advantage over Pakistan and Sri Lanka in the deployment of armed forces to deal with internal conflicts; it is capable of introducing a "neutral" force in the old imperial military tradition of British India. For example, the Indian government could send Gurkhas to Kashmir, Madras regiments to Punjab, the Maratha Light Infantry or Sikh regiments to Assam, Dogra regiments to Nagaland or Mizoram, and so on. On the other hand, because of Punjabi-Pashtun domination of the military in Pakistan and the exclusive Sinhalese composition of the Sri Lanka armed forces, the use of "neutral" forces becomes less possible in these countries. Arguably, Punjabi-Pashtun intervention between Sindhis and Mohajirs constitutes intervention by a neutral force, but it may deteriorate into a three-way ethnic conflict. It does little for Pakistan's national integration and may only reinforce the image of Punjabi military domination. Similarly, when the Sri Lankan army is sent to crush Tamil separatism, it aggravates the Sinhalese-Tamil divide.

Threats of Nuclear Weapons

The recent NPT renewal conference in April 1995 went better than expected.Virtually everybody signed except

India, Pakistan, and Israel. Israel says it will sign when all the problems revolving around the Israeli-PLO Peace Accords are settled. That would leave only India and Pakistan as the significant "hold-out" states. Shortly after the Cold War, Thomas Graham of the Rockefeller Foundation declared that the United States must not think just about "coping" with proliferation, but with "winning" the struggle against proliferation.

The renewal of the NPT in 1995 would indicate trends in that direction. With the 1974 Biological Weapons Convention (BWC) and the 1993 Chemical Weapons Convention (CWC) also in effect, it would appear that the world is now becoming safer from dangerous unconventional weapons. However, whereas the BWC and CWC are non-discriminatory universal treaties,the problem with the NPT is that it remains a discriminatory non-universal treaty. So long as China has nuclear weapons, India is reluctant to sign the NPT; if India does not sign, Pakistan will not sign as well. Fortunately, the chain appears to end here.

There are still two other general problems. First, nuclear proliferation in the future, especially among NPT signatories, is likely to be either latent or covert where nuclear weapons technology (short of putting the bomb together) will be maintained. Little difference exists between India's peaceful nuclear energy program and that of Japan. Indeed, Japan stockpiles or has access to greater levels of plutonium and enriched uranium than India. The American determination of who is a potential proliferator or not is based on motivations rather than technological capabilities. Thus, for instance, Pakistan is considered a more likely proliferator than India, and India a more likely proliferator than Japan.

Secondly, verification will remain difficult. Iraqi and North Korean nuclear weapons development were discovered quite late.Because India, Pakistan, and Israel (with suspected development programs) have not signed the renewed NPT, attention is constantly focused on them; therefore, they are more readily monitored and illicit activity detected. Verification is even more difficult when attempting to detect clandestine production of chemical weapons. The CWC is a very large document of over 200 pages, much of it dealing with verification; the NPT is only about two or three pages long—with little said about verification and compliance enforcement. So long as there is no technological "fix" to trace the shift from a peaceful nuclear energy program to a nuclear weapons program, reliable verification will prove elusive.

India and Pakistan are probably de facto nuclear weapons states if conversion to nuclear capability at short notice is considered the criterion. Some Indian and Pakistani strategists have argued that since India, Pakistan, and Israel are virtually nuclear weapons powers anyway, the nuclear club should be opened to them—then closed again with eight members. Iran, Egypt, North Korea, South Korea, or even Japan, are not likely to accept this arrangement. Many states would invoke Article 10 and withdraw from the NPT if the nuclear club was going to be opened to new membership.

The standard interpretation argues that nuclear proliferation is dangerous and could lead to nuclear war.The more the number of nuclear weapons states, the greater the chances of nuclear war. Opponents contend that a few more nuclear powers such as India, Pakistan, Israel, and Japan may actually generate greater nuclear stability through conditions of regional and multiple nuclear deterrence.Non-proliferation prevents nuclear war among potential new nuclear weapons states through denial.

Deployment of nuclear weapons and the threat of counter-attack would deter war among new nuclear weapons states. For example, nuclear deterrence may have prevented a conventional war between India and Pakistan during the 1991 Kashmir crisis because both either possessed clandestine nuclear weapons or were on the brink of such capability.

The argument that nuclear weapons in South Asia (implying a legal increase in the number of members) could actually support stability has been put forward in India by K. Subrahmanyam and General K. Sundarji.Indian and Pakistani strategists have argued that instead of attempting to create a Nuclear Weapons Free Zone in South Asia, the international community should focus on establishing a Nuclear Weapons Safe Zone in South Asia. There is some limited merit to the nuclear deterrence argument, provided nuclear weapons do not spread beyond the eight powers. If it is possible to have a stable nuclear relationship among the United States, the Soviet Union, and China during the Cold War, then why not a stable relationship among China, India, and Pakistan? On the other hand, there are four composite and standard arguments supporting the thesis that proliferation in South Asia would be dangerous: Emotional Intensity, Geographical Proximity, Sudden Change, and Frequent Wars.Each argument has its own strengths and weaknesses.

The "Emotional Intensity" argument suggests that religiousbased antagonism between India and Pakistan is more dangerous than more secular-based antagonism among the five nuclear powers. Rationality under stress would be difficult for either power to maintain. However, this is not borne out in reality. Indian and Pakistani decisionmakers have always been quite rational when on the brink of war or during the conduct of war. Indeed, Indo-Pakistani wars have been essentially gentlemanly wars. As former Army Chief, General K. Sundarji noted: "India and China are Not Crazy States. They share a civilization going back 5,000 years. During the three wars fought against each other, they have displayed enormous restraint in targeting civilian industry or infrastructure.

"The "Geographical Proximity" argument suggests that weapons of mass destruction across common frontiers in each other's backyards could lead to greater paranoia and nuclear preemption. After all, there would be no warning time. The counter to this argument is that nuclear attacks on each other could produce fall-out in the territory of the attacking country, since India and Pakistan are contiguous states. Therefore, there exists a mutual built-in deterrent system between India and Pakistan.

The "Sudden Change" argument suggests that nuclearization in South Asia would occur overnight with little or no learning time. Therefore, this could prove destabilizing. However, this is not necessarily so, because India and Pakistan already understand the logic of nuclear strategy as played out by the nuclear powers during the Cold War. They understand the conditions of nuclear stability and instability.

The "Frequent Wars" in South Asia argument suggests that nuclearization of South Asia would imply greater chances of nuclear war. However, the situation has actually proved to be the opposite. A nuclear India or Pakistan would not even dare engage in conventional wars for fear of escalation to nuclear levels. We should keep in mind that the existing nuclear powers never engaged in direct conventional wars with each other although there were two major wars conducted against each other, by the Soviet Union and the United States through their proxies in Vietnam and Afghanistan.

Similarly, Pakistan is conducting a war against India through its Muslim proxies in Kashmir. But there appears to be no imminent danger of a conventional war between India and Pakistan over Kashmir, let alone a nuclear war. This situation may exist because latent nuclear weapons capabilities in India and Pakistan have now paralyzed military action at the conventional and nuclear levels. However, the avoidance of wars under the logic of nuclear deterrence implies a restricted number of nuclear weapons states locked especially in a two-way or three-way relationship. Nuclear relationships that were four-way or more, or several two-way and three-way nuclear relationships sugggest instability. Nuclear deterrence might create nuclear stability between India and Pakistan, but it might not be relevant if nuclear weapons were to spread to Iran, Iraq, Syria, Egypt, the Koreas, Japan, and Taiwan.There were fears in early 1996 that India, following the examples of France and China, was about to conduct a series of nuclear tests before the Comprehensive Test Ban Treaty (CTBT) was finalized.

A similar Indian pro-bomb lobby had advocated that India test atomic weapons before the finalization of the NPT in 1968 in order to classify itself as one of the "haves" in the treaty and thereby become exempt from the nuclear weapons ban on the "have-nots." The fear at present is that once the CTBT, which India has always advocated and supported, is "opened for signature,"India would be forever prevented from testing nuclear weapons.

Creation of a nuclear device without test detonations is considered technologically difficult for India; to accede to the CTBT before such extensive tests would, in effect, take away India's nuclear option. These considerations have led to Indian demands in early 1996 that the CTBT be accompanied by a firm timetable for the elimination of all nuclear weapons by the existing nuclear "haves" as a for Indian abstinence from weapons testing.

India and Pakistan have been developing their ballistic missile capabilities as well. India, which performed a nuclear test in 1974 and has material for 20 to 50 bombs, has developed surface-to-surface missile (SSM) and IRBM missile systems. The SSM Prithvi-150 has a range of 90 miles, while the improved Prithvi-250 can travel 150 miles. The IRBM Agni has a range of 1,500 miles. Pakistan has never tested a nuclear device, but analysts suggest that it has material for 6 to 15 bombs. Its two missile systems, both SSMs, include the indigenous Haft-1 (range 48 miles) and Haft-2 (range 180 miles), and the M-11 (range 180 miles) purchased from China.

Clearly, India does not have unrestricted access to foreign nuclear weapons and missile technology given the restraints imposed by the NPT and the Missile Technology Control Regime (MTCR). However, the expected technological sophistication of indigenous nuclear weapons and missiles need not match the quality of those found in the United States, Great Britain or France. The minimum expected requirement at present of such weapons is that bombs must detonate when launched, and missiles must reach their designated targets.

Technological parity with existing nuclear weapons states, including China, is not considered important, although this attitude may change if India decides to embark on an overt nuclear and missile arms buildup to rival that of the "medium" nuclear powers. However, India must be reasonably assured that its missiles meet predefined and projected range, payload, accuracy, and other operational requirements. In the case of the Army's short-range tactical missiles, Indian military expectations are that such missiles must match the technological level available to India's adversaries.

Medium and intermediate range missiles intended for strategic deterrence need meet less stringent requirements since they serve a somewhat more flexible and ambiguous purpose. Whether or not the civilian nuclear energy program is economically viable, and whether or not the program is intended primarily to maintain India's nuclear weapons option, the program has acquired considerable resources and "technological selfsufficiency." India has about 50,000 tonnes of uranium deposits; it is also almost self-sufficient in the basic raw materials needed to conduct the nuclear program. India also has: developed and constructed a self-sufficient nuclear fuel cycle, with uranium mines and mills, a uranium purification UO2 plant, fuel fabrication plants, plutonium reprocessing plants, nuclear power reactors and research reactors. In addition, it has a small uranium conversion UF6 plant, a pilot uraniumenrichment plant, and heavy-water production plants.

India is experimenting with gas centrifuges for the enrichment of uranium.The civilian nuclear program has run into severe technological snags and breakdowns. India's projected goal of attaining 10,000 megawatts of electricity by the year 2000 is likely to produce in reality only 5,770. However, India's ability to siphon off a nuclear weapons program from its energy program is not in doubt. The gestation period of converting civilian programs to weapons programs at one time almost reached 2 years—the period needed to test the first atomic device at Pokharan in Rajasthan in May 1974. Today, however, the period may be as short as 4-6 weeks. By the end of 1995, India's stock of weapons-grade plutonium was estimated at nearly 420 kilograms, enough for about 85 nuclear weapons.Much of this plutonium came from the Dhruva Research Reactor, which is not under international safeguards. Further progress on India's Fast Breeder Reactor (FBR) programwill provide India with more plutonium for bombs.

Meanwhile, India's civilian space rocket and satellite development programs indirectly support the military Agni and Prithvi missile programs.The MTCR does not carry the same legal constraints as the NPT, which is a multilateral and nearuniversal treaty. The MTCR is an American-initiated, informal agreement among the G-7 industrialized countries not to transfer missile and rocket technology to those countries aspiring to develop missiles. The MTCR does not prohibit an overt program to acquire missile technology; signatories agree merely to take all measures to prevent the transfer of such technology. Similarly, New Delhi has also embarked on the indigenous development of nuclear powered submarines, which India agrees falls within a grey area not covered by the NPT. The development of the submarine program at Mazagon Docks in Bombay ran into political problems involving alleged kickbacks and had to be cancelled. However, the development of the reactor and its containment vessel has been progressing at a satisfactory pace.

These security issues discussed impinge upon each other. Internal security problems complicate the conduct of external conventional wars and raise the question of whether conventional armed forces should be used to crush domestic insurgencies. Concepts of nuclear deterrence, conventional war escalation control, and threatened nuclear utilization to terminate conventional war overshadow conventional military strategies. On the other hand, democratization and marketization tend to mellow these security concerns. Wars appear increasingly less worthwhile. Another conventional war would likely be a stalemate, while a nuclear war would be catastrophic and unacceptable. In conclusion, we may ask whether political pressures arising from security problems affect democratic processes in South Asia, and whether marketization and privatization trends reduce security pressures.The experience in South Asia has been that internal security pressures tend to corrupt democratic practices through the introduction of draconian laws restricting individuals' rights. Such pressures increase the levels of human rights violations, and they politicize the armed forces when they are used to deal with domestic violence. However, the emphasis on economic reforms and development issues in South Asia tend to counter these trends to produce a greater level of strategic stability in the region.

India's Stand on Nuclear Disarmament

India has been consistent in its commitment to the elimination of weapons of mass destruction and to global nuclear disarmament on a universal and non-discriminatory basis. At the same time, India's legitimate national security requirements cannot be overlooked, especially in view of the developments in this region. In this context, as a non-aligned country, India has always maintained that it would not be a party to any discriminatory non-proliferation system.

The principal plank of our nuclear policy has not changed and we continue to believe that a nuclear weapon free world would enhance India's security along with the security of all other nations. Moreover, our nuclear policy has also been marked by restraint and openness.

As a nuclear weapon state, we are even more conscious of our responsibility in this regard. In the past, we have undertaken a number of initiatives in pursuance of global nuclear disarmament. India would continue to take such initiatives both individually and collectively. We are committed to co-operating with like-minded States to ensure that the emerging world order will rest on the principles of universality, democracy and non-discrimination.

The circumstances under which India was obliged to stand aside on the Comprehensive Nuclear Test Ban Treaty in 1996 are well known. With the steps taken to address its security requirements, in May 1998, India has voluntarily announced a moratorium on further underground nuclear testing.

India has maintained that lasting non-proliferation can only be achieved through disarmament and discriminatory treaties are unstable instruments. As a responsible State committed to non-proliferation, India has declared that it shall not transfer nuclear weapons or related know-how to other countries. India maintains an effective system of export controls and shall make it more stringent where necessary to render it more effective in the context of a nuclear India.

India's nuclear policy can be summarized as:

— India's security interests require the maintenance of an effective and credible minimum deterrent. This flows from the principle of minimum sufficiency, which precludes an arms race with anyone.

— India has made a formal commitment to no first use of nuclear weapons. India maintains a unilateral moratorium on explosive nuclear tests. It is now engaged in discussions with key interlocutors on a range of issues, including the CTBT.

— India is engaged in negotiations at the Conference on Disarmament on a treaty banning production of fissile material for nuclear weapons or other nuclear explosive devices.

— India has an effective export control mechanism in place that is continuously refined and updated to prevent the unauthorised transfer of sensitive equipment, material and technologies.

— India's nuclear deterrent is based on the principle of strict political and civilian control. Such control would be exercised through appropriate scientific, technological and military management of the nuclear assets of the country to prevent unauthorised or accidental use.

— India's policy on disarmament and international security issues is predicated on certain fundamental principles that are based on a broad national consensus. These are:

— The primary factor in India's security calculus is the supreme national interest of safeguarding the sovereignty, independence and territorial integrity of the country.

— Global nuclear disarmament and elimination of nuclear weapons is an indispensable requirement for regional and global security and for genuine and durable non-proliferation.

- Disarmament and non-proliferation can only be addressed in a comprehensive, and not a piecemeal manner in artificially defined regional compartments. The all-pervading threat arising from the possession of weapons of mass destruction can only be removed with a holistic and global approach to the problem.
- International disarmament and non-proliferation treaties should be universal and non-discriminatory and must provide equal security for all.
- The clandestine and illegal transfer or receipt of sensitive materials, equipment and technology by some countries should not be overlooked or condoned for the sake of political expediency.
- There is a need for the international community to develop effective safeguards against the danger of sensitive materials and weapons of mass destruction falling into the hands of extremist and terrorist organisations by accident or by the acts of governments that support such organisations.

By ratifying the Chemical Weapons Convention (CWC) in 1993, India has demonstrated its commitment to international disarmament treaties, which are non-discriminatory in character. The implementation of all obligations assumed by India as an original state party to the Convention and related activities has proceeded satisfactorily.

India is a party to the 1972 Biological and Toxic Weapons Convention (BTWC). India actively participated in the work of the Ad Hoc Group of State Parties to the Convention in Geneva during 1999 to negotiate a Protocol to the Convention on the basis of the agreed mandate. India envisions the Fissile Material Cut-off Treaty within the overall context of its security imperatives and the broader goal of universal nuclear disarmament. A limited moratorium covering individual countries is completely unacceptable.

The proliferation of small arms to non-state actors, the qualitative improvement in the lethality of small arms, in terms of the impact of high technology and their easy availability, has drawn the attention of the international community to the problem of small arms proliferation. Apart from a deliberate transfer of small arms to parties involved in low intensity conflicts there is also a widespread clandestine movement of such arms in the international market.

The weapons recovered by Indian Forces from terrorists and insurgents in Jammu and Kashmir alone, which are enough to equip regular Army divisions, are indicative of the magnitude of the problem and the need to prevent the deliberate proliferation of such arms. The problem of curbing the indiscriminate use of anti-personnel landmines became an emotive issue with numerous countries and NGOs, calling for their total ban.

India believes that while the concerns expressed are justified on humanitarian grounds, a phased approach is desirable till such time as alternative technologies are developed. Countries plagued by landmines do not have the necessary manufacturing capability and are usually importers of such devices. The focus should thus be on restricting access coupled with increased demining activity. The use of mines should be permitted for the long-term defence of borders, perimeters and peripheries of states.

Energy Security Concerns

Energy security is particularly crucial to India for two main reasons: the country's dependence on the imports of fossil fuels and the physical proximity of the two energy rich areas of the Gulf and Central Asia, where competitive access rivalries contain inherent tendencies towards conflict involving outside powers. Inspite of improvements in indigenous production, dependence on imports of energy sources, such as crude and petroleum products, will continue. India's energy security would need to take into account some or all of the following factors:

— Mutually beneficial arrangements with India's eastern neighbours as well as Nepal for long term energy exploitation and sharing.

— Protection of the energy infrastructure within the country from disruption by terrorists and militants.

— Energy co-operation and sharing arrangements only with countries whose actions do not undermine India's security and which have demonstrated a willingness to co-operate meaningfully with India.

— International transit of energy destined for India only through stable, secure and friendly countries where there is no danger of disruption of supplies by state and non-state actors for political ends.

— Taking carefully calibrated actions to insulate India from disruption of supplies from outside by greater domestic production and recourse to nuclear and non-conventional energy sources.

— Co-operating with other interested parties in protecting the sea-lanes of communication.

— Diversification of supply routes within India.

— Focussed investments in maritime and naval assets to ensure adequate reach and endurance.

— Greater involvement in exploration projects overseas pertaining to oil and gas resources.

Peace Talks

Agra Declaration

The Prime Minister of the Republic of India and the President of the Islamic Republic of Pakistan: In keeping with the spirit of the Lahore Declaration issued on February 21, 1999;

Sharing a vision of peace and stability between their countries, and of progress and prosperity for their people;

Convinced that durable peace and development of harmonious relations and friendly cooperation will serve the vital interests of the people of the two countries, enabling them to devote their energies for a better future;

Recognising that the nuclear dimension of the security environment of the two countries adds to their responsibility for avoidance of conflict between the two countries;

Committed to the principle and purposes of the Charter of the United Nations, and the universally accepted principles of peaceful co-existence;

Reiterating the determination of both countries to implementing the Simla Agreement in letter and spirit;

Committed to the objectives of universal nuclear disarmament;

Reaffirming their agreement on Cultural Co-operation of 31 December 1988 for promoting and developing their relations and understanding in the realms of art, culture, archaeology, education, mass media and sports;

Have agreed that their respective governments:

(1) shall intensify their efforts to resolve all issues, including the issue of Jammu and Kashmir.

(2) shall remove their military forces from the disputed Siachen Glacier area and conclude an agreement making it a demilitarised zone under joint juridical control.

(3) shall refrain from intervention and interference in each other's internal affairs, and shall conclude a bilateral no-war pact.

(4) shall undertake national and co-operative measures to reduce the risk of accidental or unauthorised use of nuclear weapons under their respective control, and the risk of nuclear war, and shall conclude a bilateral agreement on nuclear risk reduction measures.

(5) shall conclude a bilateral agreement on advance notification of launches of ballistic missiles and space vehicles.

(6) shall formalise their respective unilateral moratoria on further nuclear tests by acceding to the Comprehensive Nuclear Test Ban Treaty.

(7) shall further liberalise the visa and travel regime between the two countries, and shall conclude a bilateral agreement for this purpose.

(8) shall promote academic and cultural exchanges and encourage business across the border.

(9) reaffirm their commitment to the goals and objectives of SAARC with a view to promoting the welfare of the people of South Asia.

(10) shall promote and protect all human rights and fundamental freedoms.

Treaty Between the Republic of India and the Islamic Republic of Pakistan on Measures for Nuclear Risk Reduction

The Republic of India and the Islamic Republic of Pakistan, hereinafter referred to as the Parties,

Recalling their commitments under the joint declaration at the Lahore summit on 21 February 1999,

Believing that a nuclear war cannot be won and must never be fought,

Affirming their desire to reduce and ultimately eliminate the risk of outbreak of nuclear war, which would cause immense suffering and destruction to the peoples and the environment of the two countries,

Believing that agreement on measures for reducing the risk of outbreak of nuclear war serves the interests of regional peace and security,

Recognising the need to exert every effort to avert the risk of outbreak of such a war, including measures to guard against accidental or unauthorised use of nuclear weapons,

Recognising that the geographic contiguity of the two countries puts severe limits on the time available, after receiving a warning of an attack, to ascertain whether or not the attack is real, involves nuclear weapons, is accidental, or unauthorised,

Recognising therefore the need to have sufficient time for mutual communication and consultation to avoid a hasty and disproportionate response, Have agreed as follows:

Article 1

The Republic of India and the Islamic Republic of Pakistan agree that an objective of their policies is to remove the danger of nuclear war and of the use of nuclear weapons.

Accordingly, the Parties agree that they will act in such a manner as to prevent the development of situations capable of causing a dangerous exacerbation of their relations, as to avoid military confrontations, and as to exclude the outbreak of nuclear war between them and between either of the Parties and other countries.

Article 2

The Parties commit to not deploy nuclear weapons.

Article 3

Each Party commits that as an act of non-deployment, it shall

(i)keep disassembled all nuclear weapons, with the fissile material stored separately from the high explosives

(ii) keep all disassembled components of nuclear weapons physically separated from all possible nuclear capable delivery vehicles, such as aircraft or ballistic missiles, by a distance of at least 50 kilometres;

Article 4

Each Party undertakes to maintain and to improve, as it deems necessary, its existing organisational and technical arrangements to guard against an accidental or unauthorised use of nuclear weapons under its control.

Article 5

The Parties undertake to notify each other immediately in the event of an accidental, unauthorised or any other unexplained incident involving a possible detonation of a nuclear weapon. In the event of such an incident, the party whose nuclear weapon is involved will immediately make every effort to take necessary measures to render harmless or destroy such weapon without its causing damage.

Article 6

The Parties undertake to notify each other immediately in the event of detection by missile warning systems of unidentified objects, or in the event of signs of interference with these systems or with related communications facilities, if such occurrences could create a risk of outbreak of nuclear war between the two countries.

Article 7

Each party, in other situations involving unexplained nuclear incidents, undertakes to act in such a manner as to reduce the possibility of its actions being misinterpreted by the other Party. In any such situation, each Party may inform the other Party or request information when in its view, this is warranted by the interests of averting the risk of outbreak of nuclear war. Article 8: Each Party shall establish, in its capital, a national Nuclear Risk Reduction Centre that shall operate on behalf of and under the control of its respective Government.

Article 9

The Parties shall use the Nuclear Risk Reduction Centres to transmit

(1) all information which could be useful in avoiding an unintentional or accidental outbreak of nuclear war between the Parties.

(2) notifications of all ballistic missile launches, in accordance with their Treaty on Notification of Launches of Ballistic Missiles.

Article 10

The list of notifications and communications to be transmitted through the Centres may be reviewed from time to time by agreement between the Parties. Article 11 : The Parties shall establish a special high-speed communications link between their national Nuclear Risk Reduction Centres.

Article 12

The Parties shall, by mutual agreement, employ the appropriate technologies needed to fulfil the objectives of the agreement.

Article 13

The Parties shall staff their national Nuclear Risk Reduction Centres as they deem appropriate, so as to ensure their normal functioning. The training of the staff of the Centres shall be done jointly and co-operatively.

Article 14

The Parties shall hold regular meetings between representatives of the Nuclear Risk Reduction Centres at least once each year to consider matters related to the functioning of such Centres. These meetings will consider the steps needed for the continued and improved functioning of the Centres to implement this agreement.

Article 15

If at any time relations between the Parties or between either Party and other countries appear to involve the risk of a nuclear conflict, or if relations between countries not parties to this Agreement appear to involve the risk of nuclear war between the Parties or between either Party and other countries, India and Pakistan, acting in accordance with the provisions of this Agreement, shall immediately enter into urgent consultations with each other and make every effort to avert this risk.

Article 16

This Agreement shall not affect the obligations of either Party under other agreements.

Article 17

This Agreement shall enter into force on the date of its signature.

Article 18

The duration of this Agreement shall not be limited.

Treaty Between the Reublic of India and the Islamic Republic of Pakistan on notifications of launches of Balistic Missiles and Space Vehicles

The Republic of India and the Islamic Republic of Pakistan, hereinafter referred to as the Parties:

Believing that a nuclear war cannot be won and must never be fought, Believing that agreement on measures for reducing the risk of outbreak of nuclear war serves the interests of strengthening peace and security in the region of South Asia, Recognising that the Parties possess nuclear weapons, and ballistic missiles as delivery vehicles for nuclear weapons, Recognising the similarity in the technology and physical characteristics of ballistic missiles and space vehicles, Affirming their desire to reduce and ultimately eliminate the risk of outbreak of nuclear war, in particular, as a result of misinterpretation, miscalculation, or accident, Have agreed as follows:

Article 1

Each Party shall provide the other Party notification, through the Nuclear Risk Reduction Centres of the Republic of India and the Islamic Republic of Pakistan, no less than twenty-four hours in advance, of any planned launch of a ballistic missile or space vehicle.

Article 2

A notification of a planned launch shall be valid for four days counting from the launch date indicated in such a notification. Any postponement or cancellation of the launch shall be notified.

Article 3

For launches of ballistic missiles

1. The notification shall specify the area from which the launch is planned to take place.
2. The notification shall specify the geographic co-ordinates of the planned impact area. This shall be done either by indicating the geographic co-ordinates of the boundary points of the area, or by indicating the geographic co-ordinates of the centre of a circle with a radius specified in kilometres or nautical miles. The size of the impact area shall be determined by the notifying Party at its discretion.

Article 4

For launches of space vehicles, the notification shall specify indicate the area from which the launch is planned to take place.

Article 5

The Parties undertake to hold periodic consultations, as mutually agreed, to consider questions relating to implementation of the provisions of this Agreement. Article 6 : This Agreement shall not affect the obligations of either Party under other agreements.

Article 7

This Agreement shall enter into force on the date of its signature.

No War Treaty Between The Republic of India and the Islamic Republik of Pakistan

The Republic of India and the Islamic Republic of Pakistan:

Sharing a vision of peace and stability between their countries, and of progress and prosperity for their peoples;

Convinced that durable peace and development of harmonious relations and friendly cooperation will serve the vital interests of the peoples of the two countries, enabling them to devote their energies for a better future;

Committed to the principles and purposes of the Charter of the United Nations, and the universally accepted principles of peaceful co-existence;

Reaffirming that an environment of peace and security is in the supreme national interest of both sides and that the resolution of all outstanding issues, including Jammu and Kashmir, is essential for this purpose;

Article 1

Each Party will refrain from the threat or use of force against the other Party under any circumstances.

Article 2

The Parties shall never again wage war against each other.

Article 3

For the purposes of this agreement, an act of war shall be defined as including:

(i) incursion of armed forces into the territory of the other Party,

(ii) hostile use of armed forces and implements of war against the other Party,

(iii) abetting hostile actions by armed insurrectionary groups against the other Party,

(iv) committing or helping to commit acts of sabotage and disruption of civil life in the territory of the other Party.

(v) blockading or obstructing in any way land, sea or air access routes of the other Party to the outside world.

(vi) disrupting the flow of river water to the other Party except as permitted under a bilateral agreement.

(vii) any other action mutually agreed as constituting an act of war

(viii) in case of disputes, any action may be referred to the Adjudication Commission, whose judgement will be binding.

Article 4

The Parties shall establish a permanent commission, called the "Acts of War Adjudication Commission" to adjudicate between the Parties on the acts that are deemed by either of the Parties to have been in violation of this Pact.

Article 5

The Adjudication Commission shall consist of

(1)The Chief Justice of a SAARC country to be appointed by alphabetic rotation from amongst the SAARC member countries other than the Parties to this Treaty for a term of three calendar years, who shall chair the Commission

(2)the Chief Justices of the two countries

(3)the Foreign Secretaries of the two countries

Article 6

In case the Adjudication Commission fails to arrive at a verdict in a case referred to it, the Parties will jointly take the case to the International Court of Justice, the Hague.

Article 7

The Parties undertake to develop their relations with each other and with other countries in a way consistent with the purposes of this Agreement, and shall intensify their efforts to resolve all their mutual disputes, particularly the issue of Jammu and Kashmir in accordance with the wishes of the people of Jammu and Kashmir.

Article 8

This Pact shall come into force immediately, and shall remain in force indefinitely.

Treaty Between the Republic of India and the Islamic Republlic of Pakistan on the Establishment of a Demilitarised in the Area of the Siachen Glacier

The Republic of India and the Islamic Republic of Pakistan, hereinafter referred to as the Parties,

Committed to the principle and purposes of the Charter of the United Nations, and the universally accepted principles of peaceful co-existence;

Reiterating the determination of both countries to implementing the Simla Agreement in letter and spirit;

Reaffirming the principles and spirit of the Lahore agreement;

Believing that demilitarisation of the Siachen Glacier serves the interests of regional peace and security, Have agreed as follows:

Article 1

The Parties agree to immediately withdraw all armed forces from within the Siachen Glacier area.

Article 2

For the purposes of this agreement, the area is defined as the region bounded by three lines: (1) the northern border with the Peoples Republic of China from Indira Col in the west to the Karakoram Pass in the east; (2) the line joining Indira Col to the point NJ9842 through Sia La, Bilafond La and Gyong La, and (3) the line joining the Karakoram Pass with the point NJ9842. Article 3 : The Parties declare the area to be a de-militarised zone, to remain under the joint juridical control of the Parties.

Article 4

The Parties agree to share equally the cost of environmental remediation of the area and restoring it to its natural state.

Article 5

The Parties agree to establish a Joint Commission to work out modalities for implementation of this agreement within a period of three months, to work out modalities of the joint juridical control of the area, and to, thereafter, ensure continued existence of the area as the zone of peace.

Article 6

This Agreement shall not affect the obligations of either Party under other agreements.

Article 7

The Parties shall seek a commitment from all states bordering the area to respect the statute of demilitarisation in the area.

Article 8

This agreement shall not prejudice and is subject to a final agreement on the Kashmir dispute.

Agreement between the Republic of India and the Islamic Republic of Pakistan On Easing the the Visa and Travel Restrictions

The Republic of India and the Islamic Republic of Pakistan, hereinafter referred to as the Parties, Recalling their Agreement on Cultural Co-operation of 31 December 1988 for promoting and developing their relations and understanding in the realms of art, culture, archaeology, education, mass media and sports;

Recalling the Lahore Agreement and reaffirming their commitment to further liberalise the visa and travel regime for the citizens of their two countries Have agreed to:

1. The Parties shall allow each other to open visa consulates in the following cities:

   i) Pakistan to open visa consulates in Amritsar, Mumbai, Kolkata, Chennai and Hyderabad.

   ii) India to open visa consulates in Karachi, Hyderabad, Quetta, Lahore and Peshawar.

2. The Parties shall grant visa at the port of entry to accredited

   (i) journalists,

   (ii) school, college and university teachers,

   (iii) students,

   (iv) artists,

(v) sports-persons,

(vi) senior citizens.

3. The Parties shall forthwith remove city-specific restriction from visas, and allow unrestricted travel anywhere in the country
4. The Parties shall progressively increase the frequency of road, rail and air links across the border
5. The parties shall reopen the land crossing at Khokrapar
6. The Parties shall initiate ferry services between Mumbai and Karachi
7. The Parties shall create a joint Commission to further liberalise and encourage travel between the two countries.
8. This Agreement shall enter into force on the date of its signature.

SAARC's Stand in Kashmir Issue

SAARC's greatest potential lies in its ability to provide a framework to solve the fifty-six year old Kashmir crisis between India and Pakistan, which has greatly constrained the relationship between the two nations. Since 1989, a violent separatist movement that is supported both indigenously and by foreign elements has been waged in Kashmir against the Indian government. This movement has the goal of removing Kashmir from Indian rule and is fueled by the Pakistani view that Kashmir was unfairly given to India after the subcontinent gained independence from the British government in 1947 as well as by the strong desire for autonomy by native Kashmiris.The history of the Kashmiri conflict goes all the way back to decision by the British government to leave the region.

Under the partition plan provided by the Indian Independence Act of 1947, Kashmir was free to accede to India or Pakistan. The Maharaja, Hari Singh, wanted to stay independent but eventually decided to accede to India, signing over key powers to the Indian Government - in return for military aid and a promised referendum.That referendum never occurred, and neither has a United Nations-mandated plebiscite to allow Kashmiris to determine their future independently, an event that has been blocked by India.

The battle for control of Kashmir has been waged on a grand scale between India and Pakistan twice since Independence, with wars being fought in 1947-48 and 1965, and continuous shelling and provocation from both sides.As a result of the mentioned conflicts, Kashmir is currently constituted of Indian-held Jammu- Kashmir (45%) and Pakistani-held Azad Kashmir (33%), with the remaining portion held by China.

As a result of the disastrous fighting between India and Pakistan, the economic fundamentals of both Azad Kashmir (Pakistani-held) and Jammu- Kashmir (India-held) have been ravaged, especially since the current uprising began in 1989. Although the overall Kashmiri economy has survived due to the large amounts of money being pumped into it by the Indian and Pakistani central governments,its growing dependence on the central army and government for sustenance has devastated the region's economic fundamentals (e.g. education, agriculture, capital infrastructure etc.).

The central government in Pakistan allocated Rs. 1.80 billion to spending in Azad Kashmir in 2000-2001,which is a huge drain on a government that has an overall GDP of approximately Rs. 700 billion.In India's case, Kashmir has become a bigger drain on the national government's resources than the poorest Indian state, Bihar, even though it has the potential to be one of the richest Indian states due to its indigenous tourism and textiles industries.

Kashmir takes in 4,067.14 Rs. crore from Central government, which is far greater than Bihar, which takes in only 607.45 Rs. crore in loans to meet budgetary needs. These budgets show the economic toll the Kashmir crisis has taken on the central government– an even more astounding point is that these numbers must be coupled with the huge military expenditures on nuclear and missile development in order to fully gauge the Kashmiri conflict's devastating economic impact.

By misallocating precious government funds to this crisis, the Indian and Pakistani governments have neglected to fully focus on key development issues such as: education, health care, capital infrastructure development etc. As shown above, both India and Pakistan have allocated great amounts of much-needed economic resources to building military capabilities and maintaining a military presence on the border constantly. This is a crisis that necessitates a new paradigm in South Asia that promotes regional cooperation. The SAARC structure could and would provide that new paradigm.

SAARC's role in the solution of the Kashmir crisis through the construction of an autonomous Kashmir will entail the following three key points:

— Third party enforcements provided by the United Nations on the current Kashmiri borders with India and Pakistan, respectively

— Substantial economic commitment by the world community, which will be allocated using the decentralized, bloc focused approach advocated by Mr. Arakawa

— A Kashmiri dominated legislature

The above three requirements are vital to the construction of an autonomous Kashmir and require the involvement of the world community to provide both India and Pakistan proper incentive to give up their territorial ambitions and undertake this mutually beneficial plan. Regarding the first point, third party peacekeeping troops, possibly provided by the United Nations, must be maintained at Kashmir's present borders with India and Pakistan. These troops will operate under a new cooperative framework with the SAARC bloc, much as other existing blocs collaborate. India and Pakistan will be able to greatly reduce their military expenditures with this commitment from the world community, providing both countries with enormous economic relief, as shown earlier.

But this is not enough – the world community must also commit to providing sufficient economic resources to an autonomous, SAARC-protected Kashmir. A decentralized, bloc focused approach to economic spending and trade is an extremely effective method of driving growth.

The tourism industry, Kashmir's number one cash cow, has been severely disrupted. Although the central governments of India and Pakistan have prevented economic collapse by pumping large amounts of government resources into Jammu-Kashmir and Azad Kashmir, respectively, the important economic fundamentals (education, farming, infrastructure) underlying the economy have been severely underdeveloped since 1989. This occurrence bodes poorly for the region's future, and that is why it is extremely important to have, as Mr. Arakawa espoused, third party influxes of money allocated at the state level to build up an autonomous Kashmir's economic fundamentals within SAARC's framework.

Jammu-Kashmir had a state budget of approximately Rs. 50 billion in 2001- 02, while Azad Kashmir had a state budget of Rs. 9.9 billion.By roughly combining these budgets, the absolute minimum amount of money to be provided by the world community is approximately Rs. 60 billion, or $1.2 billion. This is an extremely small amount of money, and hopefully the world community will realize that the return on this particular investment, in terms of increased global security and economic progress, will be astronomical. This minimum amount should be augmented greatly because sufficient resources must be provided in order to fuel growth in the following key areas in the new, autonomous Kashmir under the SAARC regime:

— Education

— Agriculture based industry

— Electronics

— Telecommunications

— Textiles

— Tourism

By concentrating funds in these important areas as has similarly been done in the case of Cyprus, Kashmir can take advantage of its inherent richness and provide a model for the future resolutions of long-standing, bitter and seemingly unsolvable international conflicts. In the case of Cyprus, the EU has exerted massive political and economic pressure on the warring parties in order to force them to the negotiating table, which has yielded very positive results.

A strong and proper political framework must also be provided in order to ensure the construction of a SAARC-protected, autonomous Kashmir. The most important requirement for success in this area is to ensure that the assembly body of the Kashmiri legislature is constituted of Kashmiris. Although this may seem to be an obvious point, it bears mentioning because of its importance in ensuring all parties involved that nationalistic motives to tilt the new, autonomous Kashmir towards either India or Pakistan will be mitigated, if not eliminated. This Kashmiri-constituted legislature will provide the balanced guidance needed to strengthen Kashmir economically, culturally and socially, and make it a peaceful region that spurs previously unseen cooperation between India and Pakistan and eventually throughout the entire SAARC region.

19

SAARC Law

South Asian Regional Cooperation in Law (SAARCLAW) is a regional organisation of lawyers, judges, law teachers, legal academician and legal researcher of SAARC countries. Established in 1991, it was accorded recognition as a SAARC Regional Apex Body in July, 1994. SAARCLAW Country Chapters have been formed. Nepal, India, Pakistan, Maldives, Sri Lanka, Bangladesh and Bhutan are its member country. Maldives is in the process of forming its country Chapter. It has 500 individual members. The objectives of the Association are to bring together the legal communities of the region for closer cooperation and to develop law as a source and catalyst of social change for development.

SAARCLAW has so far held nine conferences, the latest in Kathmandu in September 2000. The Conference coincided with the Meeting of the Chief Justices of SAARC Countries. Leaders of Bar Councils of SAARC Countries also met concurrently. The decisions taken by SAARCLAW relate to the formulation of a draft Regional Convention on Human Rights and the establishment of a SAARC Institute of Legal Sciences.

SAARCLAW CHARTER

WE the members of the legal communities of countries of the South Asian Association for Regional Co-operation, having gathered here in Colombo, Sri Lanka this 24th day of October Ninteen Hundred and Ninety One-

BELIEVING in the objectives of the South Asian Association for Regional Co-operation

SHARING the common aspirations of our people in the region to live in peace, freedom, social justice and economic prosperity.

CONSCIOUS that in order to realise the said objectives it is necessary to develop people to people co-operation.

AWARE of the fact that law and the legal community have a role to play in developing and building meaningful co-operation in this region which is mutually beneficial, desirable and necessary for promoting the economic social and technical co-operation for the welfare of the peoples in the region and improving their quality of life and contributing towards building national and collective self-reliance in the SAARC region.

DO HEREBY constitute and form ourselves into an Association known as SAARCLAW.

SAARCLAW conferences provide lawyers, judges and academic of the region with the opportunity to meet and network.

These conferences are given high prominence and normally inaugurated by the head of the State/the head of the government of the host country. Following countries have hosted annual conferences.

1. *Objectives:*

1.1 The objectives of the SAARCLAW shall be:

a) To bring together the legal communities within the region for closer co-operation, developing understanding, promoting exchange of ideas and dissemination of information.

b) To use and develop law as a source and an instrument towards social change for development as well as for building co-operation among the peoples of the region.

2. *Affiliated Country Chapters:*

2.1 There may be established in each SAARC country a SAARCLAW Country Chapter, the membership of which shall be open to the following categories of persons-

a) Persons professionally qualified to practise law;

b) Judges;

c) Law teachers of any University or Law college;

d) Persons possessing academic qualifications in law;

e) Any other persons who have demonstrated an interest in the law and its development in each SAARC country.

2.2 A SAARCLAW Country Chapter shall, on application made therefore to the Executive Council of SAARCLAW be affiliated to SAARCLAW provided it has a membership of not less than ten (10) members and has formulated a Constitution the objectives of which are in conformity with the objectives of SAARCLAW.

3. Membership:

3.1 The signatories to this Charter shall be members of SAARCLAW

3.2 The following shall be eligible for membership of SAARCLAW-

a) members of SAARCLAW Country Chapters established in each of the SAARC countries and affiliated to SAARCLAW in terms of Article 2 above; and

b) individual persons belonging to the categories specified in Article 2.1 above, from countries which have not established SAARCLAW Country Chapters in terms of the said paragraph

4. Subscriptions:

4.1 Every member of SAARCLAW shall pay an annual subscription of such an amount and in such manner as may be determined by the Executive Council of SAARCLAW.

4.2 Any member who shall be in arrears of subscription for a period of over two years shall be deemed to have ceased to be a member of SAARCLAW

4A. Patron

The council may invite one or more persons who have achieved eminence amongst the legal communities of the SAARC region to be a Patron or Patrons as the case may be, of SAARCLAW. Such Patron or Patrons shall be ex-officio members of the Council.

5. *Executive Council:*

5.1 There shall be an Executive Council of SAARCLAW (hereinafter referred to as the "Council") which shall consist of-

a) The Patron or Patrons, as the case may be;

b) The immediate Past President of SAARCLAW who shall be an ex-officio member;

c) Not less than twenty (20) and not more than twenty eight (28) persons equally representing, as far as possible, each of the SAARC Countries.

5.2 The members of the first Council shall be elected by the signatories to this Charter.

5.3 The members constituting every subsequent Council, other than ex-offico members, shall in compliance with 5.1 (c) above be nominated by each Country Chapter. In the event of the required minimum number of members not being nominated to the Council, the nominated persons shall, in consultation with the outgoing members of the Council, appoint such additional number of members as may be necessary to constitute the Council so however that the Council shall at all times have a minimum of twenty (20) members.

5.4 Every member of the Council shall hold office for a period of two years and shall be eligible for re-election.

5.5 In the event of any member of the Council vacating his office prior to the expiration of his term of office, the Council may fill such vacancy.

5.6 The Council shall elect the following office-bearers from among it's members:

a) President

b) Not more than seven Vice-Presidents

c) Secretary General

d) Treasurer

5.7 The Council shall have the power to determine such matters as are required to be determined in terms of the provisions hereof and to do all such things as are necessary to further the objectives of SAARCLAW and to ensure the effective and efficient functioning of the administration machinery of SAARCLAW.

5.8 Any decisions of the Council may be taken at a meeting of its members or by circulation and assent in writing.

6. Property and Assets:

6.1 The property and assets of SAARCLAW shall be vested in the Trustees to be appointed by the Council.

6.2 The Trustees shall hold the property and assets for the benefit of SAARCLAW

6.3 The funds of SAARCLAW shall be deposited in such account or accounts to be maintained at such Bank, Banks or other Institutions as may be determined by the Council. The Council shall also determine the persons, not being less than two in number, who shall be authorised to operate such account or accounts.

7. Meetings:

The Council shall meet as often as is considered necessary but not less than once in every two years.

7.2 The general membership of SAARCLAW shall meet as and when meetings shall be convened by decision of the Council or at the request of not less than two SAARCLAW Country Chapters.

7.3 The procedure to be followed at meeting of the Council or of the general membership shall be in accordancewith such rules as are formulated by the Council.

8. Amendments:

8.1 This Charter may be amended by the unanimous decision of the Council or at a general meeting of the membership by a majority of not less than two thirds of the members present and voting.

amended by the unanimous decision of Executive Council on 2nd Oct, 1997, Karachi

amended by the unanimous decision of Executive Council on 7-8 Oct, 1995, New Delhi

20

Agreement on SAARC Preferential Trading Arrangement (SAPTA)

Preamble

The Government of the People's Republic of Bangladesh, the Kingdom of Bhutan, the Republic of India, the Republic of Maldives, the Kingdom of Nepal, the Islamic Republic of Pakistan and the Democratic Socialist Republic of Sri Lanka hereinafter referred to as "Contracting States",

Motivated by the commitment to promote regional cooperation for the benefit of their peoples, in a spirit of mutual accommodation, with full respect for the principles of sovereign equality, independence and territorial integrity of all States;

Aware that the expansion of trade could act as a powerful stimulus to the development of their national economies, by expanding investment and production, thus providing greater opportunities of employment and help securing higher living standards for their population;

Convinced of the need to establish and promote regional preferential trading arrangement for strengthening intraregional economic cooperation and the development of national economies; Bearing in mind the urgent need to promote the intraregional trade which presently constitutes a negligible share in the total volume of the South Asian trade;

Recalling the direction given at the Fourth SAARC Summit meeting held in Islamabad in December 1988 that specific areas be identified where economic cooperation might be feasible immediately;

Guided by the declared commitment of the Heads of State or Government of the Member Countries at the Sixth SAARC Summit held in Colombo in December 1991 to the liberalisation of trade in the region through a step by step approach in such a manner that countries in the region share the benefits of trade expansion equitably;

Cognizant of the mandate given by the Sixth SAARC Summit in Colombo to formulate and seek agreement on an institutional framework under which specific measures for trade liberalisation among SAARC Member States could be furthered and to examine the Sri Lankan proposal to establish the SAARC Preferential Trading Arrangement (SAPTA) by 1997;

Recognising that a preferential trading arrangement is the first step towards higher levels of trade and economic cooperation in the region,

Have agreed as follows:

Article 1
Definitions

For the purpose of this Agreement:

(1) "Least Developed Country" means a country designated as such by the United Nations.

(2) "Contracting State" means any Member State of the South Asian Association for Regional Cooperation (SAARC) which has entered into this Agreement.

(3) "Serious injury" means significant damage to domestic producers, of like or similar products resulting from a substantial increase of preferential imports in situations which cause substantial losses in terms of earnings, production or employment unsustainable in the short term. The examination of the impact on the domestic industry concerned shall also include an evaluation of other relevant economic factors and indices having a bearing on the state of the domestic industry of that product.

(4) "Threat of serious injury" means a situation in which a substantial increase of preferential imports is of a nature to cause "serious injury" to domestic producers, and that such injury, although not yet existing, is clearly imminent. A determination of threat of serious injury shall be based on facts and not on mere allegation, conjecture, or remote or hypothetical possibility.

(5) "Critical circumstances" means the emergence of an exceptional situation where massive preferential imports are causing or threatening to cause "serious injury" difficult to repair and which calls for immediate action.

(6) "Sectoral basis" means agreements amongst Contracting States regarding the removal or reduction of tariff, nontariff and paratariff barriers as well as other trade promotion or cooperative measures for specified products or groups of products closely related in enduse or in production.

(7) "Direct trade measures" means measures conducive to promoting mutual trade of Contracting States such as long and mediumterm contracts containing import and supply commitments in respect of specific products, buyback arrangements, state trading operations, and government and public procurement.

(8) "Tariffs" means customs duties included in the national tariff schedules of the Contracting States.

(9) "Paratariffs" means border charges and fees, other than "tariffs", on foreign trade transactions of a tarifflike effect which are levied solely on imports, but not those indirect taxes and charges, which are levied in the same manner on like domestic products. Import charges corresponding to specific services rendered are not considered as paratariff measures.

(10) "Nontariffs" means any measure, regulation, or practice, other than "tariffs" and "paratariffs", the effect of which is to restrict imports, or to significantly distort trade.

(11) "Products" means all products including manufactures and commodities in their raw, semiprocessed and processed forms.

Article 2
Establishment and Aims

1. By the present Agreement, the Contracting States establish the SAARC Preferential Trading Arrangement (SAPTA) to promote and sustain mutual trade and the economic cooperation among the Contracting States, through exchanging concessions in accordance with this Agreement.

2. SAPTA will be governed by the provisions of this Agreement and also by the rules, regulations, decisions, understandings and protocols to be agreed upon within its framework by the Contracting States.

Article 3
Principles

SAPTA shall be governed in accordance with the following principles :

(a) SAPTA shall be based and applied on the principles of overall reciprocity and mutuality of advantages in such a way as to benefit equitably all Contracting States, taking into account their respective levels of economic and industrial development, the pattern of their external trade, trade and tariff policies and systems;

(b) SAPTA shall be negotiated step by step, improved and extended in successive stages with periodic reviews;

(c) The special needs of the Least Developed Contracting States shall be clearly recognised and concrete preferential measures in their favour should be agreed upon;

(d) SAPTA shall include all products, manufactures and commodities in their raw, semiprocessed and processed forms.

Article 4
Components

SAPTA may, *interalia,* consist of arrangements relating to:

(a) tariffs;

(b) paratariffs

(c) nontariff measures;

(d) direct trade measures.

Article 5
Negotiations

1. The Contracting States may conduct their negotiations for trade liberalisation in accordance with any or a combination of the following approaches and procedures:
   (a) Product by product basis;
   (b) Across the board tariff reductions;
   (c) Sectoral basis;
   (d) Direct trade measures.
2. Contracting States agreed to negotiate tariff preferences initially on a product-by-product basis.
3. The Contracting States shall enter into negotiations from time to time with a view to further expanding SAPTA and the fuller attainment of its aims.

Article 6
Additional Measures

1. Contracting States agree to consider, in addition to the measures set out in Article 4, the adoption of trade facilitation and other measures to support and complement SAPTA to mutual benefit.
2. Special consideration shall be given by Contracting States to requests from Least Developed Contracting States for technical assistance and cooperation arrangements designed to assist them in expanding

their trade with other Contracting States and in taking advantage of the potential benefits of SAPTA. The possible areas for such technical assistance and cooperation are listed in Annex I.

Article 7
Schedules of Concessions

The tariff, paratariff and nontariff concessions negotiated and exchanged amongst Contracting States shall be incorporated in the National Schedules of Concessions. The initial concessions agreed to by the Contracting States are attached as Annex II.

Article
Extension of Negotiated Concessions

The concessions agreed to under SAPTA, except those made exclusively to the Least Developed Contracting States in pursuance of Article 10 of this Agreement, shall be extended unconditionally to all Contracting States.

Article 9
Committee of Participants

A Committee of Participants, hereinafter referred to as the Committee, consisting of representatives of Contracting States, is hereby established. The Committee shall meet at least once a year to review the progress made in the implementation of this Agreement and to ensure that benefits of trade expansion emanating from this Agreement accrue to all Contracting States equitably. The Committee shall also accord adequate opportunities for consultation on representations made by any

Contracting State with respect to any matter affecting the implementation of the Agreement. The Committee shall adopt appropriate measures for settling such representations. The Committee shall determine its own rules of procedures.

Article 10
Special Treatment for the Least Developed Contracting States

1. In addition to other provisions of this Agreement, all Contracting States shall provide, wherever possible, special and more favourable treatment exclusively to the Least Developed Contracting States as set out in the following subparagraphs:

   (a) Duty-free access, exclusive tariff preferences or deeper tariff preferences for the export products,

   (b) The removal of nontariff barriers,

   (c) The removal, where appropriate, of paratariff barriers,

   (d) The negotiations of longterm contracts with a view to assisting Least Developed Contracting States to achieve reasonable levels of sustainable exports of their products,

   (e) Special consideration of exports from Least Developed Contracting States in the application of safeguard measures,

   (f) Greater flexibility in the introduction and continuance of quantitative or other restrictions provisionally and without discrimination in critical circumstances by the Least Developed Contracting States on imports from other Contracting States.

Article 11
Nonapplication

Notwithstanding the measures as set out in Articles 4 and 6, the provisions of this Agreement shall not apply in relation to preferences already granted or to be granted by any Contracting State to other Contracting States outside the framework of this Agreement, and to third countries through bilateral, plurilateral and multilateral trade agreements, and similar arrangements. The Contracting States shall also not be obliged to grant preferences in SAPTA which impair the concession extended under those agreements.

Article 12
Communication, Transport and Transit

Contracting States agree to undertake appropriate steps and measures for developing and improving communication system, transport infrastructure and transit facilities for accelerating the growth of trade within the region.

Article 13
Balance of Payments Measures

1. Notwithstanding the provisions of this Agreement, any Contracting State facing serious economic problems including balance of payments difficulties may suspend provisionally the concessions as to the quantity and value of merchandise permitted to be imported under the Agreement. When such action has taken place, the Contracting State which initiates such action, shall simultaneously notify the other Contracting States and the Committee.

2. Any Contracting State which takes action according to paragraph 1 of this Article shall afford, upon request from any other Contracting State, adequate opportunities for consultations with a view to preserving the stability of the concessions negotiated under the SAPTA. If no satisfactory adjustment is effected between the Contracting States concerned within 90 days of such notification, the matter may be referred to the Committee for review.

Article 14
Safeguard Measures

If any product, which is a subject of a concession with respect to a preference under this Agreement, is imparted into the territory of a Contracting State in such a manner or in such quantities as to cause or threaten to cause, serious injury in the importing Contracting State, the importing Contracting State concerned may, with prior consultations, except in critical circumstances, suspend provisionally without discrimination, the concession accorded under the Agreement. When such action has taken place the Contracting State which initiates such action shall simultaneously notify the other Contracting State(s) concerned and the Committee shall enter into consultations with the concerned Contracting State and endeavour to reach mutually acceptable agreement to remedy the situation. In the event of the failure of the Contracting States to resolve the issue within 90 days of the receipt of original notification, the Committee of Participants shall meet within 30 days to review the situation and try to settle the issue amicably. Should the consultations in the Committee of Participants fail to resolve the issue within 60 days, the parties affected by such action shall have the right to withdraw equivalent concession(s) or other obligation(s) which the Committee does not disapprove of.

Article 15
Maintenance of the Value of Concessions

Any of the concessions agreed upon under this Agreement shall not be diminished or nullified, by the application of any measures restricting trade by the Contracting States except under the provisions as spelt out in other Articles of this Agreement.

Article 16
Rules of Origin

Products contained in the National Schedules of Concessions annexed to this Agreement shall be eligible for preferential treatment if they satisfy the rules of origin, including special rules of origin, in respect of the Least Developed Contracting States, which are set out in Annex III.

Article 17
Modification and Withdrawal of Concessions

1. Any Contracting State may, after a period of three years from the day the concession was extended, notify the Committee of its intention to modify or withdraw any concession included in its appropriate schedule.

2. The Contracting State intending to withdraw or modify a concession shall enter into consultation and/ or negotiations, with a view to reaching agreement on any necessary and appropriate compensation, with Contracting States with which

such concession was initially negotiated and with any other Contracting States that have a principal or substantial supplying interest as may be determined by the Committee.

3. Should no agreement be reached between the Contracting States concerned within six months of the receipt of notification and should the notifying Contracting State proceed with its modification or withdrawal of such concessions, the affected Contracting States as determined by the Committee may withdraw or modify equivalent concessions in their appropriate schedules. Any such modification or withdrawal shall be notified to the Committee.

Article 18
Withholding or Withdrawal of Concessions

A Contracting State shall at any time be free to withhold or to withdraw in whole or in part any item in its schedule of concessions in respect of which it determines that it was initially negotiated with a State which has ceased to be a Contracting State in this Agreement. A Contracting State taking such action shall notify the Committee, and upon request, consult with Contracting States that have a substantial interest in the product concerned.

Article 19
Consultations

1. Each Contracting State shall accord sympathetic consideration to and shall afford adequate opportunity for consultations regarding such representations as may be made by another

Contracting State with respect to any matter affecting the operation of this Agreement.

2. The Committee may, at the request of a Contracting State, consult with any Contracting State in respect of any matter for which it has not been possible to find a satisfactory solution through such consultation under paragraph 1 above.

Article 20
Settlement of Disputes

Any dispute that may arise among the Contracting States regarding the interpretation and application of the provisions of this Agreement or any instrument adopted within its framework shall be amicably settled by agreement between the parties concerned. In the event of failure to settle a dispute, it may be referred to the Committee by a party to the dispute. The Committee shall review the matter and make a recommendation thereon within 120 days from the date on which the dispute was submitted to it. The Committee shall adopt appropriate rules for this purpose.

Article 21
Withdrawal from SAPTA

1. Any Contracting State may withdraw from this Agreement at any time after its entry into force. Such withdrawal shall be effective six months from the day on which written notice thereof is received by the SAARC Secretariat, the depositary of this Agreement. That Contracting State shall simultaneously inform the Committee of the action it has taken.

2. The rights and obligations of a Contracting State which has withdrawn from this Agreement shall cease to apply as of that effective date.
3. Following the withdrawal by any Contracting State, the Committee shall meet within 30 days to consider action subsequent to withdrawal.

Article 22
Entry into Force

This Agreement shall enter into force on the thirtieth day after the notification issued by the SAARC Secretariat regarding completion of the formalities by all Contracting States.

Article 23
Reservations

This Agreement may not be signed with reservations nor shall reservations be admitted at the time of notification to the SAARC Secretariat of the completion of formalities.

Article 24
Amendments

This Agreement may be modified through amendments to this Agreement. All amendments shall become effective upon acceptance by all Contracting States.

Article 25
Depositary

This Agreement shall be deposited with the Secretary General of SAARC who shall promptly furnish a certified copy thereof to each Contracting State.

IN WITNESS WHEREOF the undersigned being duly authorized thereto by their respective Governments have signed this Agreement on the SAARC Preferential Trading Arrangement.

Done at DHAKA this ELEVENTH day of APRIL One Thousand Nine Hundred Ninety Three in eight originals in the English language.

Annex I
Additional measures in favour of least developed contractiong States

(a) The identification, preparation and establishment of industrial and agricultural projects in the territories of Least Developed Contracting States which could provide the production base for the expansion of exports of Least Developed Contracting States to other Contracting States, possibly linked to cooperative financing and buyback arrangements;

(b) the setting up of manufacturing and other facilities in Least Developed Contracting States to meet intra-regional demand under cooperative arrangements;

(c) the formulation of export promotion policies and the establishment of training facilities in the field of trade to assist Least Developed Contracting States in expanding their exports and in maximising their benefits from SAPTA;

(d) the provision of support to export marketing of products of Least Developed Contracting States by enabling these countries to share existing facilities (for example, with respect to export credit insurance, access to market information) and by institutional and other positive measures to facilitate imports from Least Developed Contracting States into their own markets;

(e) bringing together of enterprises in other Contracting States with project sponsors in the Least Developed Contracting States (both public and private) with a view to promoting joint ventures in projects designed to lead to the expansion of trade;

(f) the provision of special facilities and rates in respect to shipping.

Annex II
National Schedules of Concessions

(circulated separately)

Annex III
Rules of Origin

RULE 1: Originating products - Products covered by preferential trading arrangements within the framework of the SAPTA imported into the territory of a Contracting State from another Contracting State which are consigned directly within the meaning of Rule 5 hereof, shall be eligible for preferential concessions if they conform to the origin requirement under any one of the following conditions:

(a) Products wholly produced or obtained in the exporting Contracting State as defined in Rule 2; or

(b) Products not wholly produced or obtained in the exporting Contracting State, provided that the said products are eligible under Rule 3 or Rule 4.

RULE 2: Wholly produced or obtained - Within the meaning of Rule 1 (a) the following shall be considered as wholly produced or obtained in the exporting Contracting State:

(a) raw or mineral products extracted from its soil, its water or its seabeds:[1]

(b) agricultural products harvested there;[2]

(c) animals born and raised there;

(d) products obtained from animals referred to in paragraph (c) above;

(e) products obtained by hunting or fishing conducted there;

(f) products of sea fishing and other marine products taken from the high seas by its vessels;[3/4]

(g) products processed and/or made on boards its factory ships[4/5] exclusively from products referred to in paragraph (f) above;

(h) used articles collected there, fit only for the recovery of raw materials;

(i) waste and scrap resulting from manufacturing operations conducted there;

(j) goods produced there exclusively from the products referred to in paragraph (a) to (i) above.

RULE 3 : Not wholly produced or obtained

(a) Within the meaning of Rule 1(b), products worked on or processed as a result of which the total value of the materials, parts or produce originating from non-contracting States or of undetermined origin used does not exceed 50 per cent of the f.o.b. value of the products produced or obtained and the final process of manufacture is performed within the territory of the exporting Contracting State shall be eligible for preferential concessions subject to the provisions of Rule 3(c) and Rule 4.

(b) Sectoral agreements [6]

(c) The value of the nonoriginating materials, parts or produce shall be:

   (i) The c.i.f. value at the time of importation of materials parts or produce where this can be proven: or

   (ii) The earliest ascertainable price paid for the materials, prices or produce of undetermined origin in the territory of the Contracting State where the working or processing takes place.

RULE 4: Cumulative rules of origin - Products which comply with origin requirements provided for in Rule 1 and which are used by a Contracting State as input for a finished product eligible for preferential treatment by another Contracting State shall be considered as a product originating in the territory of the Contracting State where working or processing of the finished product has taken place provided that the aggregate content originating in the territory of the Contracting State is not less than 60 percent of its f.o.b. value.[7]

RULE 5: Direct consignment - The following shall be considered as directly consigned from the exporting Contracting State to the importing Contracting State:

(a) if the products are transported without passing through the territory of any non-Contracting State:

(b) the products whose transport involves transit through one or more intermediate non-contracting States with or without transhipment or temporary storage in such countries, provided that:

(i) the transit entry is justified for geographical reason or by considerations related exclusively to transport requirements;

(ii) the products have not entered into trade or consumption there; and

(iii) the products have not undergone any operation there other than unloading and reloading or any operation required to keep them in good condition.

RULE 6: *Treatment of packing* - When determining the origin of products, packing should be considered as forming a whole with the product it contains. However, packing may be treated separately if the national legislation so required.

RULE 7: *Certificate of Origin* - Products eligible for preferential concessions shall be supported by a Certificate of Origin[8] issued by an authority designated by the government of the exporting Contracting State and notified to the other Contracting States in accordance with the Certification Procedures appearing on pages 15 and 16 of this Annex.

RULE 8:

(a) In conformity with Article 15 of the Agreement on SAPTA and national legislations, any Contracting State may prohibit importation of products containing any inputs originating from States with which it does not have economic and commercial relations.

(b) Contracting States will do their best to cooperate in order to specify origin of inputs in the Certificate of Origin.

RULE 9: Review - These Rules may be reviewed as and when necessary upon request of one-third of the Contracting States and may be open to such modifications as may be agreed upon.

RULE 10: Special criteria percentage- Products originating in Least Developed Contracting States can be allowed a favourable 10 percentage points applied to the percentage established in Rules 3 and 4. Thus, for

Rule 3, the percentage would not exceed 60 per cent, and for Rule 4, the percentage would not be less than 50 per cent.

1.Include mineral fuels, lubricants and related materials as well as mineral of metal ores.

2.Include forestry products.

3."Vessels" shall refer to fishing vessels engaged in commercial fishing, registered in a Contracting State's country and operated by a citizen orcitizens or governments of Contracting State or partnership, corporation or association, duly registered in such Contracting State's country, at cost 60 per cent of equity of which is owned by a citizen or citizens and/or government of such Contracting State or 75 percent by citizens and/or governments of the Contracting States. However, the products taken from vessels engaged in commercial fishing under bilateral agreements which provide for chartering/ leasing of such vessels and/or sharing of catch between Contracting States will also be eligible for preferential concessions.

4. In respect of vessels or factory ships operated by government agencies the requirement of flying the flag of a Contracting State does not apply.

5. For the purpose of this Agreement, the term "factory ship" means any vessels, as defined, used for processing and/or making on board products exclusively from those products referred to in paragraph (f) above.

6. In respect of products traded within the framework of sectoral agreements negotiated under SAPTA, provision may need to be made for special criteria to apply. Consideration may be given to these criteria as and when the sectoral agreements are negotiated.

7. "Partial" cumulation as implied by Rule 4 above means that only products which have acquired originating status in the territory of one Contracting State may be taken into account when used as inputs for a finished product eligible for preferential treatment in the territory of another Contracting State.

8. A standard Certificate of Origin to be used by all Contracting States is annexed and approved by the Contracting States.

ADDENDUM

Amendment to SAPTA Rules of Origin

The SAARC Council of Ministers at its Twenty-first Session held in Nuwara Eliya, Sri Lanka, on 18-19 March 1999, approved the amendments to the Rules 3(a), 4 and 10 relating to the Rules of Origin (Annex-II) of the SAARC Preferential Trading Arrangement (SAPTA) with immediate effect.

The new amended rules now read as follows:

Rule 3(a): Not wholly produced or obtained

Within the meaning of Rule 1(b), products worked on or processed as a result of which the total value of the materials, parts or produce originating from non-Contracting States or of undetermined origin used does not exceed 60 per cent of the f.o.b. value of the products produced or obtained and the final process of manufacture is performed within the territory of the exporting Contracting State shall be eligible for preferential concessions subject to the provisions of Rule 3(c) and Rule 4.

Rule 4: Cumulative rules of origin

Products which comply with origin requirements provided for in Rule 1 and which are used by a Contracting State as input for a finished product eligible for preferential treatment by another Contracting State shall be considered as a product originating in the territory of the Contracting State where working or processing of the finished product has taken place provided that the aggregate content originating in the territory of the Contracting State is not less than 50 percent of its f.o.b. value.

Rule 10: Special criteria percentage

Products originating in Least Developed Contracting States can be allowed a favourable 10 percentage points applied to the percentage established in Rules 3 and 4. Thus, for Rule 3, the percentage would not exceed 70 per cent, and for Rule 4, the percentage would not be less than 40 per cent.

21

SAARC Convention on Preventing and Combating Trafficking in Women and Children For Prostitution on the Member States

PARTIES TO THE PRESENT CONVENTION EMPHASISING that the evil of trafficking in women and children for the purpose of prostitution isincompatible with the dignity and honour of human beings and is a violation of basic human rights;

RECALLING the decision of the Ninth SAARC Summit (May, 1997) that the feasibility of a regionalConvention to combat the grave crime of trafficking in women and children for prostitution should be explored;

RECALLING ALSO the relevant international legal instruments relating to prevention of trafficking inwomen and children, including the Convention for the Suppression of Trafficking in Persons and of the Exploitationof Prostitution of Others, 1949; Convention on the Elimination of all Forms of Discrimination against

Women,1979; International Covenant on Civil and Political Rights, 1966; and the Convention on the Rights of theChild, 1989;

GIVING due regard to the implementation of the recommendations of the various pertinent InternationalBodies and Conferences including the Fourth World Conference on Women at Beijing (1995);

NOTING with concern the increasing exploitation by traffickers of women and children from SAARCcountries and their increasing use of these countries as sending, receiving and transit points;

RECOGNISING in this regard the importance of establishing effective regional cooperation forpreventing trafficking for prostitution and for investigation, detection, interdiction, prosecution and punishmentof those responsible for such trafficking;

EMPHASISING the need to strengthen cooperation in providing assistance, rehabilitation and repatriationto victims of trafficking for prostitution;

HAVE AGREED as follows:

ARTICLE I : DEFINITIONS

For the purpose of this Convention:

1) "Child" means a person who has not attained the age of 18 years;
2) "Prostitution" means the sexual exploitation or abuse of persons for commercial purposes;
3) "Trafficking" means the moving, selling or buying of women and children for prostitution within and outside a country for monetary or other

considerations with or without the consent of the person subjected to trafficking;

4) "Traffickers" means persons, agencies or institutions engaged in any form of trafficking;

5) "Persons subjected to trafficking" means women and children victimised or forced intoprostitution by the traffickers by deception, threat, coercion, kidnapping, sale, fraudulentmarriage, child marriage, or any other unlawful means;

6) "Protective home" means a home established or recognised by a Government of a MemberState for the reception, care, treatment and rehabilitation of rescued or arrested personssubjected to trafficking.

7) "Repatriation" means return to the country of origin of the person subjected to trafficking across international frontiers.

ARTICLE II : SCOPE OF THE CONVENTION

The purpose of this Convention is to promote cooperation amongst Member States so that they mayeffectively deal with the various aspects of prevention, interdiction and suppression of trafficking in women andchildren; the repatriation and rehabilitation of victims of trafficking and prevent the use of women and childrenin international prostitution networks, particularly where the countries of the SAARC region are the countries oforigin, transit and destination.

ARTICLE III : OFFENCES

1. The State Parties to the Convention shall take effective measures to ensure that trafficking in any

formis an offence under their respective criminal law and shall make such an offence punishable by appropriatepenalties which take into account its grave nature.

2. The State Parties to the Convention, in their respective territories, shall provide for punishment of anyperson who keeps, maintains or manages or knowingly finances or takes part in the financing of a place used forthe purpose of trafficking and knowingly lets or rents a building or other place or any part thereof for thepurpose of trafficking.

3. Any attempt or abetment to commit any crime mentioned in paras 1 and 2 above or their financingshall also be punishable.

ARTICLE IV : AGGRAVATING CIRCUMSTANCES

1. The State Parties to the Convention shall ensure that their courts having jurisdiction over the offencescommitted under this Convention, can take into account factual circumstances which make the commission ofsuch offences particularly grave, viz.

   a) the involvement in the offences of an organised criminal group to which the offender belongs;

   b) the involvement of the offender in other international organised criminal activities;

   c) the use of violence or arms by the offender;

   d) the fact that the offender holds a public office and that the offence is committed in misuse of that office;

   e) the victimisation or trafficking of children;

f) the fact that the offence is committed in a custodial institution or in an educational institution orsocial facility or in their immediate vicinity or in other places to which children and students visit foreducational, sports, social and cultural activities;

g) previous conviction, particularly for similar offences, whether in a Member State or any other country.

ARTICLE V : JUDICIAL PROCEEDINGS

In trying offences under this Convention, judicial authorities in Member States shall ensure that theconfidentiality of the child and women victims is maintained and that they are provided appropriate counsellingand legal assistance.

ARTICLE V : IMUTUAL LEGAL ASSISTANCE

1. The State Parties to the Convention shall grant to each other the widest measure of mutual legalassistance in respect of investigations, inquiries, trials or other proceedings in the requesting State in respect ofoffences under this Convention. Such assistance shall include:

   a) taking of evidence and obtaining of statements of persons;

   b) provision of information, documents and other records including criminal and judicial records;

   c) location of persons and objects including their identification;

d) search and seizures;

e) delivery of property including lending of exhibits;

f) making detained persons and others available to give evidence or assist investigations;

g) service of documents including documents seeking attendance of persons; andh)any other assistance consistent with the objectives of this Convention.

2. Requests for assistance shall be executed promptly in accordance with their national laws and in themanner requested by the Requesting State. In the event that the Requested State is not able to comply inwhole or in part with a request for assistance or decides to postpone execution it shall promptly inform theRequesting State and shall give reasons for the same.

ARTICLE VII : EXTRADITION OR PROSECUTION

1. The offences referred to in the present Convention shall be regarded as extraditable offences in anyextradition treaty which has been or may hereinafter be concluded, between any of the Parties to the Convention.

2. If a State Party which makes extradition conditional on the existence of a treaty, receives a request forextradition from another State Party with which it has no extradition treaty, the Requested State shall, if sopermitted by its laws, consider this Convention as the basis for extradition in respect of the offences set forthin Article III.

3. Extradition shall be granted in accordance with the laws of the State to which the request is made.

4. The State Party in whose territory the alleged offender is present shall, if it does not extradite him orher, submit, without exception whatsoever and without undue delay, the case to its competent authorities forthe purpose of prosecution in accordance with the laws of that State.

5. In States where extradition of their nationals is not permitted under their law, nationals who havecommitted offences under the present Convention shall be prosecuted and punished by their courts.

ARTICLE VIII : MEASURES TO PREVENT AND INTERDICT TRAFFICKING IN WOMEN AND CHILDREN

1. The State Parties to the Convention shall provide sufficient means, training and assistance to theirrespective authorities to enable them to effectively conduct inquiries, investigations and prosecution of offencesunder this Convention.

2. The State Parties to the Convention shall sensitize their law enforcement agencies and the judiciary inrespect of the offences under this Convention and other related factors that encourage trafficking in womenand children.

3. The State Parties to the Convention shall establish a Regional Task Force consisting of officials of theMember States to facilitate implementation of the provisions of this Convention and to undertake periodicreviews.

4. The State Parties to the Convention may also, by mutual agreement, set up bilateral mechanisms

toeffectively implement the provisions of the Convention, including appropriate mechanisms for cooperation tointerdict trafficking in women and children for prostitution.

5. The State Parties to the Convention shall exchange, on a regular basis, information in respect ofagencies, institutions and individuals who are involved in trafficking in the region and also identify methods androutes used by the traffickers through land, water or air. The information so furnished shall include informationof the offenders, their fingerprints, photographs, methods of operation, police records and records of conviction.

6. The State Parties to the Convention may consider taking necessary measures for the supervision ofemployment agencies in order to prevent trafficking in women and children under the guise of recruitment.

7. The State Parties to the Convention shall endeavour to focus preventive and development efforts onareas which are known to be source areas for trafficking.

8. The State Parties to the Convention shall promote awareness, inter-alia, through the use of the media,of the problem of trafficking in Women and Children and its underlying causes including the projection ofnegative images of women.

ARTICLE IX : CARE, TREATMENT, REHABILITATION AND REPATRIATION OF THE VICTIMS

1. The State Parties to the Convention shall work out modalities for repatriation of the victims to thecountry of origin.

2. Pending the completion of arrangements for the repatriation of victims of cross-border trafficking, theState Parties to the Convention shall make suitable provisions for their care and maintenance. The provision oflegal advice and health care facilities shall also be made available to such victims.
3. The State Parties to the Convention shall establish protective homes or shelters for rehabilitation ofvictims of trafficking. Suitable provisions shall also be made for granting legal advice, counselling, job trainingand health care facilities for the victims.
4. The State Parties to the Convention may also authorise the recognised non-governmental organisationsto establish such protective homes or shelters for providing suitable care and maintenance for the victims oftrafficking.
5. The State Parties to the Convention shall encourage recognised non-governmental organisations inefforts aimed at prevention, intervention and rehabilitation, including through the establishment of such protectivehomes or shelters for providing suitable care and maintenance for the victims of trafficking.

ARTICLE XI : IMPLEMENTATION

The State Parties to the Convention shall adopt, in accordance with their respective Constitutions, thelegislative and other measures necessary to ensure the implementation of the Convention.

ARTICLE Xl : HIGHER MEASURES

The measures provided for in the Convention are without prejudice to higher measures of enforcementand protection accorded by relevant national laws and international agreements.

ARTICLE XII : SIGNATURE AND RATIFICATION

The Convention shall be open for signature by the Member States of SAARC at the Eleventh SAARCSummit at Kathmandu and thereafter, at the SAARC Secretariat at Kathmandu. It shall be subject to ratification.The instruments of Ratification shall be deposited with the Secretary General.

ARTICLE XIII : ENTRY INTO FORCE

This Convention shall enter into force on the fifteenth day following the day of the deposit of theseventh Instrument of Ratification with the Secretary General.

ARTICLE XIV : DEPOSITORY

The Secretary-General shall be the depository of this Convention and shall notify the Member States ofsignatures to this Convention and all deposits of Instruments of Ratification. The Secretary-General shall transmitcertified copies of such instruments to each Member-State. The Secretary-General shall also inform MemberStates of the date on which this Convention will have entered into force in accordance with Article XIII.

IN WITNESS WHEREOF the undersigned, being duly authorised thereto by their respectiveGovernments, have signed this Convention.

DONE at Kathmandu on this Fifth Day of January Two Thousand and Two, in nine originals, in theEnglish Language, all texts being equally authentic.

22

SAARC Convention on Regional Arrangements for the Promotion of Child Welfare in South Asia

PREAMBLE

THE MEMBER STATES OF THE SOUTH ASIAN ASSOCIATION FOR REGIONAL COOPERATION (SAARC), PARTIES TO THE PRESENT CONVENTION

NOTING that a quarter of the world's children live in South Asia and many of them require assistance and protection to secure and fully enjoy their rights, and to develop to their full potential and lead a responsible life in family and society;

BEARING IN MIND that parents or legal guardians, as the case may be, have the primary responsibility for the upbringing and development of the child;

RECOGNIZING, therefore, that the family, as the fundamental unit of society and also as the ideal nurturing environment for the growth and well-being of children, should be afforded the necessary protection and assistance so that it can fully assume and fulfill responsibility for its children and community;

RECALLING the common proclamation of their nations in the Universal Declaration of Human Rights that childhood is entitled to special care and assistance;

REAFFIRMING their adherence to the Declaration of the World Summit for Children and their commitment to the UN Convention on the Rights of the Child;

RECOGNIZING the efforts of SAARC towards building a regional consensus on priorities, strategies and approaches to meet the changing needs of children, as embodied in Rawalpindi Resolution on Children of South Asia 1996, and noting the significant progress already made by the Member States in the field of child survival and welfare;

TAKING INTO ACCOUNT, the declaration of the years 2001-2010 as the "SAARC Decade of the Rights of the Child";

BEARING IN MIND that the development of the full potential of the South Asian child is a critical concomitant to the region's collective march towards solidarity, justice, peace and human progress;

ACKNOWLEDGING that regional solidarity and cooperation through sharing of experience, expertise, information and resources are eminently useful in galvanizing the efforts of the South Asian nations to fulfill and protect the rights of children;

REALIZING further that, together, the Member States of SAARC can move towards a comprehensive South Asian vision for the well-being of their children;

HEREBY AGREE as follows:

PART I - DEFINITIONS, PURPOSE AND GUIDING PRINCIPLES

ARTICLE I. DEFINITIONS

For the purposes of this Convention;

'Rights of the Child' shall mean the rights of children embodied in the UN Convention on the Rights of the Child.

'Child' shall mean a national of any Member State of the South Asian Association for Regional Cooperation (SAARC), below the age of eighteen years unless, under the national law, majority is attained earlier.

ARTICLE II. PURPOSES AND OBJECTIVES

The purposes and objectives of the present Convention shall be to:

1. Unite the States Parties in their determination of redeeming the promises made by them to the South Asian Child at the World Summit for Children and at various other national and international conferences and successive SAARC Summits;
2. Work together with commitment and diligence, to facilitate and help in the development and protection of the full potential of the South Asian child, with understanding of the rights, duties and responsibilities as well as that of others;
3. Set up appropriate regional arrangements to assist the Member States in facilitating, fulfilling and protecting the rights of the Child, taking into account the changing needs of the child.

ARTICLE III. GUIDING PRINCIPLES

For the establishment of regional arrangements, States Parties shall be guided by the following principles:

1. States Parties to this Convention shall consider survival, protection, development and participatory rights of the child as a vital pre-requisite for:
   a) Accelerating the process of their peoples' realization of human rights and fundamental freedoms, and
   b) Achieving economic and social development in South Asia.
2. States Parties shall reaffirm the right of the child to enjoy all rights and freedoms guaranteed by the national laws and regionally and internationally binding instruments.
3. States Parties consider the UN Convention on the Rights of the Child as a comprehensive international instrument concerning the rights and well being of the child and shall, therefore, reiterate their commitment to implement it.
4. States Parties shall uphold 'the best interests of the child' as a principle of paramount importance and shall adhere to the said principle in all actions concerning children.
5. States Parties, while recognising that the primary responsibility of looking after the well-being of the child rests with the parents and family, shall uphold the principle that the State has the right and authority to ensure the protection of the best interests of the child.

6. States Parties shall consider this Convention as a guiding force for all national laws and bilateral or multilateral agreements that are entered into in the field of child welfare.

7. States Parties shall always consider gender justice and equality as key aspirations for children, the realization of which, collectively by the governments, would enhance the progress of South Asia.

PART II - REGIONAL PRIORITIES AND ARRANGEMENTS

ARTICLE IV. REGIONAL PRIORITIES

1. Without prejudice to the indivisibility of the rights enshrined in the UN Convention on the Rights of the Child and other international and national instruments and law, States Parties shall place special emphasis on the important areas for child development and well being as regional priorities that can benefit immensely from bilateral and regional cooperation.

2. Recognising basic services such as education, health care, with special attention to the prevention of diseases and malnutrition, as the cornerstone of child survival and development, States Parties shall pursue a policy of development and a National Programme of Action that facilitate the development of the child. The policy shall focus on accelerating the progressive universalization of the child's access to the basic services and conditions.

3. States Parties shall ensure that appropriate legal and administrative mechanisms and social safety nets and defenses are always in place to:

a) Ensure that their national laws protect the child from any form of discrimination, abuse, neglect, exploitation, torture or degrading treatment, trafficking and violence.

b) Discourage entry of children into hazardous and harmful labour and ensure implementation of the Ninth SAARC Summit decision to eliminate the evil of child labour from the SAARC region. In doing so, States Parties shall adopt a multi-pronged strategy including the provision of opportunities at the primary level and supportive social safety nets for families that tend to provide child labourers.

c) Administer juvenile justice in a manner consistent with the promotion of the child's sense of dignity and worth, and with the primary objective of promoting the child's reintegration in the family and society. In doing so, States Parties shall provide special care and treatment to children in a country other than the country of domicile and expectant women and mothers who are detained along with infants or very young children, and shall promote, to the best possible extent, alternative measures to institutional correction, keeping in mind the best interest of the child.

d) States Parties shall make civil registration of births, marriages and deaths, in an official registry, compulsory in order to facilitate the effective enforcement of national laws, including the minimum age for employment and marriage.

4. Recognising the evolving capacities of the child, States Parties shall encourage and support administrative and judicial institutions to arrange for

suitable mechanisms at appropriate levels and in accordance with local customs and traditions, to provide opportunities and access for the child to:

a) Seek and receive information.

b) Express views, directly or through a representative, and receive due weight and consideration for them, in accordance with age and maturity, in all matters affecting them.

c) Participate fully and without hindrance or discrimination in the school, family and community life.

5. States Parties shall encourage the mass media to disseminate information and material of social and cultural benefit to the child. They shall also endeavour to give wide publicity to the Convention as well as other regional and international instruments having a bearing on the child.

ARTICLE V. REGIONAL ARRANGEMENTS

To ensure consistent focus on and pursuance of the regional priorities delineated above, States Parties shall promote solidarity, co-operation and collective action between and among SAARC Member States in the arena of child rights and development. States Parties view such cooperation as mutually reinforcing and capable of enhancing the quality and impact of their national efforts to create the enabling conditions and environment for full realization of child rights and attainment of the highest possible standard of child well being. In pursuance hereof, States Parties shall:

a) provide opportunities for appropriate bilateral and multilateral sharing of information, experience and expertise.

b) facilitate human resource development through planned annual schedule of SAARC Advanced Training Programmes on Child Rights and Development.

c) make special arrangements for speedy completion and disposal, on priority basis, of any judicial or administrative inquiry or proceeding involving a child who is a national of another SAARC Member State, and for the transfer of children who are nationals of SAARC countries, accused of infringing the penal code, back to their country of legal residence for trial and treatment, provided that the alleged offence has not imperiled the national security of the country where it has been allegedly committed.

d) strengthen the relevant SAARC Bodies dealing with issues of child welfare to formulate and implement regional strategies and measures for prevention of inter-country abuse and exploitation of the child, including the trafficking of children for sexual, economic and other purposes.

e) set up a South Asian nutrition initiative aimed at enhancing knowledge and promoting greater awareness, practice and attainment of higher levels of nutrition, particularly for children and women, through mass education, adequate training and ensuring food security and equitable distribution of food at the family level.

PART III - RELATIONSHIPS AND COOPERATION

ARTICLE VI. BILATERAL AND MULTILATERAL COOPERATION

States Parties shall encourage and support bilateral and multilateral agreements and cooperation that would have positive impact on regional and national efforts in facilitating, fulfilling and protecting the rights and well being of the child.

ARTICLE VII. RELATIONS WITH NATIONAL LAW AND INTERNATIONAL INSTRUMENTS

1. The States Parties to the Convention shall adopt, in accordance with their respective Constitutions, the legislative and other measures necessary to ensure the implementation of the Convention.
2. Nothing in this Convention shall affect any provisions which are more conducive to the realization of the rights of the South Asian child and which may be contained in national laws or international agreements that are in force.

ARTICLE VIII. RELATIONS WITH NON-GOVERNMENTAL BODIES

State Parties, while implementing the provisions of the Convention, may encourage and support the participation of non-Governmental bodies including community-based organisations.

ARTICLE IX. COOPERATION WITH UN AGENCIES AND OTHER INTERNATIONAL AGENCIES

Recognising their nature and scope, States Parties may encourage cooperation with UN and other international agencies.

ARTICLE X. POLITICAL COMMITMENT

States Parties shall provide the necessary political support to ensure that appropriate measures are taken, to help fulfill the provisions of this Convention. The measures, inter-alia, could include legislative reform and promulgation of appropriate new policies and legislation, trained manpower, adequately equipped institutions and adequate allocation of human and financial resources.

PART IV

ARTICLE XI. SIGNATURE AND RATIFICATION

The Convention shall be open for signature by the Member States of SAARC at the Eleventh SAARC Summit in Kathmandu, and thereafter, at the SAARC Secretariat in Kathmandu. It shall be subject to ratification. The Instruments of Ratification shall be deposited with the SAARC Secretary General.

ARTICLE XII. ENTRY INTO FORCE

The Convention shall enter into force on the fifteenth day following the date of deposit of the Seventh Instrument of Ratification with the Secretary General of the South Asian Association for Regional Cooperation (SAARC).

ARTICLE XIII. DEPOSITORY

The Secretary General shall be the Depository of this Convention and shall notify the Member States of signatures to this Convention and all deposits of instruments of ratification. The Secretary General shall transmit certified copies of such instruments to each Member State. The Secretary General shall also inform Member States of the date on which this Convention will have entered into force in accordance with Article XII.

IN WITNESS WHEREOF the undersigned, being duly authorize thereto by their respective Governments, have signed this Convention.

DONE at Kathmandu on this Fifth Day of January Two Thousand and Two, in nine originals, in the English Language, all texts being equally authentic.

23

Agreement on Establishing the SAARC Food Security Reserve

PREAMBLE

The Governments of Bangladesh, Bhutan, India, the Maldives, Nepal, Pakistan and Sri Lanka,

Recalling the Declaration on South Asian Regional Cooperation signed in New Delhi in August 1983 which called for cooperative action with a view to promoting economic and social development in South Asia;

Reaffirming their commitment to the realization of this objective by joining together in the establishment of the South Asian Association for Regional Cooperation and adopting a Charter in Dhaka in December 1985;

Recognising the importance of regional and sub-regional collective self-reliance with respect to food security as a means of combating the adverse effect of natural and man-made calamities;

Recognising further that the establishment of an emergency food security reserve by member countries of the South Asian Association for Regional Cooperation based on the principle of collective self-reliance would improve their food security;

NOW THEREFORE, in a spirit of solidarity and mutual cooperation, have agreed as follows:

Article 1
Establishment of the SAARC Food Security Reserve

1. The member countries hereby agree to establish a SAARC Food Security Reserve (hereinafter referred tee as "the Reserve") on the conditions and for the purpose described in this Agreement.
2. The Reserve shall be administered by the SAARC Food Security Reserve Board (hereinafter referred to as "the Board") provided for in Article VII.

Article II
The Reserve

1. The Reserve shall consist of wheat or rice or a combination thereof, (hereinafter referred to as "foodgrains") earmarked by the member countries exclusively for the purpose described in Article III.

   The foodgrains forming part of the Reserve shall remain the property of the member country that has earmarked them and shall be in addition to any national reserve that may be maintained by that member country.
2. Each member country undertakes to earmark as its share of the Reserve the amount of foodgrains

allocated to it in the Schedule of this Agreement. The said Schedule shall be an integral part of this Agreement.

3. The member countries shall keep the Schedule under review and may amend it in the light of operating experience in accordance with the procedure laid down in Article XI

4. A member country may, at any time, voluntarily earmark for the purpose provided for in this Agreement, foodgrains exceeding the amount allocated to it in the Schedule. In such a case the member country concerned may only withdraw the amount in excess of its allocation by giving six months' advance written notice to the Board.

5. The quality of all foodgrains earmarked by the member countries shall be at least of "fair average quality", or comply with any other quality standards laid down by the Board.

6. The member countries undertake to provide adequate storage facilities for the foodgrains that they have earmarked; to inspect the food grains periodically and to apply appropriate quality control measures, including turnover of the foodgrains, if necessary, with a view to ensuring that all times the foodgrains satisfy the required quality standards; and to replace forthwith any foodgrains that do not satisfy the said standards. In addition, the member countries agree to make every effort to comply with any guidelines on storage methods or quality control measures adopted by the Board.

Article III
Withdrawal of Foodgrains in an Emergency

Each member country shall be entitled, on the conditions and in accordance with the procedures laid down in Article IV and/or Article VI, to draw on foodgrains forming part of the Reserve in the event of an emergency. An emergency shall mean a state or condition in which a member country, having suffered a severe and unexpected natural or man-made calamity, is unable to cope with such a state or condition by using its national reserve and is unable to procure the foodgrains it requires through normal trading transactions on account of balance of payments constraints.

Article IV
Procedure for the Release of Foodgrains from the Reserve

1. The member country in need shall directly notify the other member country or countries of the emergency it is facing and the amount of foodgrains required,
2. The other member country or countries on being so requested shall take immediate steps to make necessary arrangements to ensure immediate and speedy release of the required foodgrains, subject to availability in the combination requested.
3. The prices, terms and conditions of payment in kind or otherwise in respect of the foodgrains so released shall be the subject of direct negotiations between the member countries concerned.
4. The requesting member country shall at the same time inform the Board of its request to the other member country or countries.

Article V
Replenishment of the Reserve

1. A member country that has released all or part of the foodgrains forming its share of the Reserve shall replace such foodgrains as soon as practicable and, in any event, not later than one calendar year following the date: on which the release of the foodgrains took place.

2. A member country that has released all or part of the foodgrains forming its share of the Reserve shall notify the Board of such release, of the terms and conditions on which it was effected, and the date on which the foodgrains that had been released were replaced.

Article VI
Procedure for the withdrawal of Foodgrains by a Member Country from its Own Share of the Reserve

1. A member country in need shall be entitled to withdraw foodgrains from its own share of the Reserve.

2. In doing so it shall inform the member countries and the Board of such withdrawal.

3. It shall replace such foodgrains as soon as practicable and in any event not later than two calendar years following the date on which the release of the foodgrains took place.

Article VII
The SAARC Food Security Board

1. There shall be a Board of which each member country shall be a member.
2. Decisions of the Board shall be taken on the basis of unanimity.
3. The Board shall elect a Chairman and Vice-Chairman based on the principle of rotation among member countries whose terms of office shall be two years. Rules of Procedure for the meetings of the board shall be the same as for other SAARC meetings.
4. The Board shall meet at the same place and time as the Standing Committee, preceding the annual Summit.

Article VIII
Functions of the Board

The function of the Board shall include:

1. Undertaking a periodic review and assessment of the food situation and prospects in the region including factors such as production, consumption, trade, prices, quality and stocks of foodgrains. The periodic assessment reports shall be disseminated to all member countries.
2. Examining immediate, short term and long term policy actions as may be considered necessary to ensure adequate supplies of basic food commodities in the region and to submit, on the basis of such examination, recommendations for appropriate action to the Council of Ministers.

3. Reviewing implementation of the provisions of the agreement, calling for such information from member countries as may be necessary for the effective administration of the Reserve ad issuing of guidelines of technical matters such as maintenance of stocks, storage conditions and quality control.
4. Keeping the Schedule to this Agreement under review.
5. Suggesting amendment to the Agreement, as and when considered necessary, in accordance with the procedure specified in article XI.

Article IX
Secretariat

The Board shall be assisted by the SAARC Secretariat. The Secretariat's responsibilities shall include monitoring all matters relating to the release of foodgrains from the Reserve and convening and servicing meetings of the Board.

Article X
Entry into Force

This Agreement shall enter into force on a date to be determined by the Council of Ministers provided that the member countries have collectively earmarked at least one hundred and twenty-five thousand metric tons of foodgrains on that date for the purpose of this Agreement.

Article XI
Amendment

1. A member country may propose any amendment to this Agreement by submitting the proposed amendment to the Board through SAARC Secretariat.

2. The board may enclose the proposed amendment and submit it to the Council of Ministers for approval. Unless otherwise specifies, amendments shall enter into force as from the date of their approval by the Council of Ministers.

Article XII
Depositary

1. An original of this Agreement shall be deposited in the SAARC Secretariat.

2. The Secretary-General shall be the depositary of this Agreement and amendments thereto.

IN WITNESS WHEREOF, the undersigned plenipotentiaries being duty authosized thereto have signed this Agreement.

Signed at Kathmandu on the Fourth Day of November One Thousand Nine Hundred and Eighty Seven in Eight originals in the English language.

24

SAARC Convention on Narcotic Drugs and Psychotropic Substances

MINDFUL of the principles of cooperation enshrined in the SAARC Charter;

RECALLING that at the Islamabad Summit on December 29-31, 1988, Heads of State or Government of the Member States of SAARC expressed grave concern over the growing magnitude and the serious effect of drug abuse and drug trafficking and recognised the need for urgent and effective measures to eradicate this problem including the possibility of concluding a Regional Convention on Drug Control;

RECOGNISING that a regional Convention on Narcotic Drugs and Psychotropic Substances would be a step forward in augmenting SAARC efforts to eliminate drug trafficking;

ALSO RECOGNISING the need to re-enforce and supplement, at the regional level, the measure provided in the Single Convention on Narcotic Drugs, 1961, as amended by the Protocol of 1972, the Convention

Psychotropic Substances, 1971, the United Nations Convention against Illicit Traffic in Narcotic

Drugs rind Psychotropic Substances, 1988, taking into account concerns which are specific to the SAARC region,

DESIRING to eliminate the root causes of the problem of abuse of Narcotic drugs and psychotropic substances, including the illicit demand for such drugs and substances and the enormous profits derived from illicit traffic;

TAKING COGNIZANCE of the links between illicit drug trafficking and other related organised criminal activities, which undermine the economies and threaten the stability, security and sovereignty of States;

CONVINCED of the importance of strengthening and enhancing effective legal means for regional cooperation in criminal matters for suppressing international criminal activities of illicit traffic in narcotic drugs and psychotropic substances;

HAVE AGREED as follows:

Article I
DEFINITIONS

Except where otherwise expressly indicated or where the context otherwise requires, the following definitions shall apply throughout this Convention:

(a) "Cannabis plant" means any plant of the genus Cannabis;

(b) "Coca Bush" means the plant of any species of the genus Erythroxylon; ,

(c) "Confiscation" which includes forfeiture where applicable; means the permanent deprivation of property by order of a court or other competent authority;

(d) "Controlled delivery" means the technique of allowing illicit or suspect consignments of narcotic drugs, psychotropic substances, substances listed in Table I and Table 11 annexed to the 1988 U.N. Convention, or substances substituted for them, to pass out of; through or into the territory of one or more countries, with the knowledge and under the supervision of their competent authorities, with a view to identifying persons involved in the commission of offences established in accordance with Article 3, paragraph I of this Convention;

(e) "1961 Convention" means the Single Convention on Narcotic Drugs, 1961;

(f) "1961 Convention as amended" means the Single Convention on Narcotic Drugs, 1961 as amended by the 1972 Protocol amending the Single Convention on Narcotic Drugs, 1961;

(g) "1971 Convention" means the Convention on Psychotropic Substances, 1971;

(h) "1988 U.N Convention" means the United Nations Convention against Illicit Traffic in Narcotic Drugs and Psychotropic Substances, 1988;

(i) "Freeze" or "Seize" means to temporarily prohibit the transfer, conversion, disposition or movement of property or temporarily assuming custody or control of properly on the basis of an order issued by a court or a competent authority;

(j) Illicit traffic" means the offences set forth in Article 3, of this Convention;

(k) "Narcotic Drug" means any or the substances, natural or synthetic, listed in Schedules I and II of the 1961 Convention and the 1961 Convention as amended;

(I) "Opium poppy" means the plant of the species Papaver Somniferum;

(m) "Proceeds" means any property derived from or obtained, directly or indirectly, through the commission or an offence established in accordance with Article 3, paragraph 1 of this convention;

(n) "Property" means assets of every kind, whether corporeal or incorporeal, movable or immovable, tangible or intangible, and legal documents or instruments evidencing little to, or interest in, such assets;

(o) "Psychotropic Substance" means any substance natural or synthetic, or any natural material listed in Schedules I, II, III and IV of the 1971 Convention;

(p) "Secretary General" means the Secretary General of the South Asian Association for Regional Cooperation (SAARC).

Article 2
SCOPE OF THE CONVENTION

1. The purpose of this Convention is to promote cooperation among Member States, so that they may address more effectively the various aspects of prevention and control of drug abuse and the

suppression of illicit traffic in narcotic drugs and psychotropic substances, which are specific to the SAARC region,

2. Member States in carrying out their obligations under this Convention shall take necessary measures, including legislative and administrative measures, in conformity with the fundamental provisions of their respective domestic legislative systems.

3. Member States shall carry out their obligations under this Convention in a manner consistent with the principles of sovereign equality and territorial integrity of States and that of non-intervention in the domestic affairs of other States

4. A Member State shall not undertake in the territory of another Member State, the exercise of jurisdiction and performance of functions, which are exclusively, reserved for the authorities of that other State by its domestic law.

Article 3
OFFENCES

1. Each Member State shall adopt such measures as may be necessary to establish as criminal offences tinder its domestic law, when committed intentionally:

   (a) the production, manufacture, extraction, preparation, offering, offering for sale, distribution, sale, delivery on any terms whatsoever, brokerage, dispatch, dispatch in transit, transport, importation or exportation of any narcotic drug or any psychotropic substance contrary to the provisions of the 1961 Convention,

The 1961 Convention as amended or the 1971 Convention;

(b) the cultivation of opium poppy, coca bush or cannabis plant for the production of narcotic drugs contrary to the provisions of the 1961 Convention and the 1961 Convention as amended;

(c) the possession or purchase of any narcotic drug or psychotropic substance for the purpose of any of the activities enumerated in (a) above;

(d) manufacture transport or distribution of equipment of materials, or of substances as listed in Table I and Table II of the 1988 UN Convention, knowing that they are being or are to be used in or for the illicit cultivation, production or manufacture of narcotic drugs or psychotropic substances;

(e) the organisation, management or financing or any of the offences enumerated in (a), (b), (c) or (d) above;

(f) the conversion or transfer of property, knowing that such property is derived from the proceeds from any offence or offences established in accordance with sub-paragraph (a), (b), (c), (d) or (e) of this paragraph, or from an act of participation in such offence or offences, for the purpose of concealing or disguising the illicit origin of The properly or of assisting any person who is involved in the commission of such an offence or offences to evade the legal consequences of his actions;

(g) the concealment or disguise of the true nature, source, location, disposition, movement, rights with respect to, or ownership of property, knowing that such property is derived from an offence or offences established in accordance with sub-paragraph (a), (b), (c), (d) or (e) of this paragraph or from an act of participation in such an offence or offences;

(h) the acquisition, possession or use of property, knowing, at the time of receipt, that such property was derived from an offence or offences established in accordance with subparagraph (a), (b), (c), (d) or (e) of this paragraph or from an act of participation in such offence or offences;

(i) the possession of equipment or materials, or of substances listed in Table I and Table 11, of the 1988 U.N. Convention knowing that they are being or are to be used in or for the illicit cultivation, production or manufacture of narcotic drugs or psychotropic substances;

(j) publicly inciting or inducing others, by any means, to commit any of the offences established in accordance with this Article or to use narcotic drugs or psychotropic substances illicitly;

(k) participation in, association or conspiracy to commit, attempts to commit and aiding, abetting, facilitating and counselling the commission of any of the offences established in accordance with this Article.

2. Subject to its constitutional principles and the basic concepts of its legal system, each Member State shall adopt such measures as may be necessary to establish as a criminal offence under its domestic law, when committed intentionally, the possession, purchase or

cultivation of narcotic drugs or psychotropic substances for personal consumption contrary to the provisions of the 1961 Convention, the 1961 Convention as amended or the 1971 Convention.

Article 4
SANCTIONS

1. Each Member State shall make the commission or the offences established in accordance with Article 3 punishable by appropriate penalties, which take into account their grave nature.
2. The Member States may provide in addition to conviction or punishment for an offence established in accordance with Article 3, paragraph 1 that the offender shall undergo measures such as treatment, education, after care, rehabilitation or social re-integration.
3. Notwithstanding anything contained in the preceding paragraphs, in appropriate cases of a minor nature, the Member States may provide, as alternatives to conviction or punishment, measures such as education, rehabilitation or social re-integration, as well as, when the offender is a drug abuser, treatment and aftercare.
4. The Member States shall ensure that their courts and other competent authorities having jurisdiction can take into account factual circumstances which make the commission of the offences established in accordance with Article 3, paragraph particularly serious, such as:

(a) the involvement in the offence of an organised criminal group to which the offender belongs;

(b) the involvement of the offender in other international organised criminal activities;

(c) the involvement of the offender in other illegal activities facilitated by commission of the offence;

(d) the use of violence or arms by the offender;

(e) the fact that the offender holds a public office and that the offence is connected with the office in question;

(f) the victimisation or use of minors;

(g) the fact that the offence is committed in a penal institution or in an educational institution or social service facility or in their immediate vicinity or in other places to which school children and students resort for educational, sports and social activities;

(h) prior conviction, particularly for similar offences, whether foreign or domestic, to the extent permitted under the domestic law of a Member State.

5. The Member States shall also ensure that their courts or other competent authorities bear in mind the serious nature of the offences established in accordance with Article 3, paragraph I or the circumstances enumerated in paragraph 4 of this Article, when considering the eventuality of early release or parole of persons convicted for such offences.

Article 5
JURISDICTION

1. Each Member State shall take such measures as may be necessary to establish its jurisdiction over the offences established in accordance with Article 3, paragraph I when:

   (a) the offence is committed in its territory;

   (b) the offence is committed on board a vessel flying its flag or an aircraft, which is registered under its laws at the time the offence, is committed;

   (c) the offence is committed by one of its nationals or by a person who has his habitual residence in that territory;

   (d) the offence is one of those established in accordance with Article 3, paragraph 1(k) and is committed outside its territory with a view to the commission, within its territory, of an offence established in accordance with Article 3,. paragraph I.

2. Each Member State may likewise take such measures as nay be necessary to establish its jurisdiction over the offences established in accordance with Article 3, paragraph I, in cases where the alleged offender is present in its territory and it does not extradite him to another Member State.

3. This Convention does not exclude the exercise or any criminal jurisdiction established by a Member State in accordance with domestic law.

Article 6
PROVISION OF INFORMATION

1. The Member State in which any or the offences established in accordance with Article 3, paragraph 1, has been committed shall, if it has reason to believe that, an alleged offender had fled from its territory, communicate to all other States concerned all the pertinent facts regarding the offence committed and all available information regarding the identity of the alleged offender.

2. Upon being satisfied that the circumstances so warrant, the Member State in whose territory the alleged offender is present shall take appropriate measures under its domestic law so as to ensure his presence for the purpose of prosecution or extradition. Such measures shall be notified, without delay to:

   (a) the State where the offence was committed, and

   (b) the State or States of which the alleged offender is a national or if he is a stateless person in whose territory he permanently resides,

Article 7
PROSECUTION

The Member State in whose territory the alleged offender is present shall, if it does not extradite him, submit, without exception whatsoever and without undue delay, the case to its competent authorities for the purpose of prosecution through proceedings in accordance with the laws of that State.

Article 8
EXTRADITION

1. To the extent that the offences established in accordance with Article 3, paragraph I, are not listed as extraditable offences in any Extradition Treaty existing between Member States, they shall be deemed to be included as such therein.
2. Member States undertake to include the offences established in accordance with Article 3, paragraph I, as extraditable offences m every future Extradition Treaty to be concluded between them.
3. If a Member State which makes extradition conditional on the existence of a Treaty receives a request for extradition from another Member State with which it has no Extradition Treaty, the requested State may, at its option, consider this Convention as the basis for extradition in respect of the offences established in accordance with Article 3, paragraph I.
4. Member States which do not make extradition conditional on the existence of a Treaty, shall recognise the offences established in accordance with Article 3, paragraph I, as extraditable offences between themselves.
5. Extradition shall be subject to the law of the requested Stale

Article 9
NON-FISCAL AND NON-POLITICAL OFFENCES

The offences established in accordance with Article 3, paragraph shall not be regarded as fiscal offences or as political offences or as offences connected with a political offence or as offences inspired by political motives, without prejudice to the constitutional limitations and the fundamental domestic law of the Member States.

Article 10
CONFISCATION

1. Each Member State shall adopt such measures as may be necessary to enable the confiscation of:
   (a) Proceeds derived from offences established in accordance with Article 3, paragraph 1, or property the value of which corresponds to that of such proceeds;
   (b) Narcotic drugs and psychotropic substances, materials and equipment or other instrumentalities used in or intended for use in any manner in offences established in accordance with Article 3
2. Each Member State shall also adopt such measures as may be necessary to enable its competent authorities to identify, trace and freeze or seize proceeds, property, instrumentalities Or any other things referred to in paragraph I or this Article for the purpose of eventual confiscation.

Article 11
MUTUAL LEGAL ASSISTANCE

1. The Member States shall afford one another pursuant to this Article, the widest measures of mutual legal assistance in investigations prosecutions arid judicial

proceedings in relation to criminal offences established in accordance with Article 3, paragraph I.

2. Mutual legal assistance to be afforded in accordance with this Article may be requested for all or any of the following purposes:

   (a) Taking evidence or statements from persons;

   (b) Effective service of judicial documents;

   (c) Executing searches and seizures;

   (d) Examining objects arid sites;

   (e) Providing information and evidentiary items;

   (f) Providing originals or certified copies of relevant documents and records, including bank, financial, corporate or business records;

   (g) Identifying or tracing proceeds, property, instrumentalities or other things for evidentiary purposes

3. The Member States may afford one another any other forms of mutual legal assistance allowed by the domestic law of the requested State.

4. Upon request, the Member States shall facilitate or encourage, to the extent consistent with their domestic law and practice, the presence or availability of persons, including persons in custody, who consent to assist in investigations or participate in proceedings

5. A Member State shall not decline to render mutual legal assistance under this Article on the ground of bank secrecy.

6. The provisions of this Article shall not affect the obligations under any other treaty, bilateral or multilateral, which governs or will govern, in whole or in part, mutual legal assistance in criminal matters

7. The Member States shall designate an authority, or when necessary authorities, which shall have the responsibility and power to execute requests for mutual legal assistance or to transmit them to the competent authorities for execution the authority or the authorities designated for this purpose shall be notified directly to each Member State and to the Secretary General. Transmission or requests for mutual legal assistance and any communication related thereto shall be effected between the authorities designated by the States; this requirement shall be without prejudice to the right of a State to require that such requests and communications be addressed to it through diplomatic channels and, in urgent circumstances, where the States agree, through channels of the International Criminal Police Organisation, if possible.

8. Requests for mutual legal assistance shall be made in writing. In urgent circumstances, and where agreed to by the States, requests may be made orally, which shall he confirmed in writing forthwith.

   (a) The identity of the authority making the request;

   (b) The subject matter and nature of the investigation prosecution or proceeding to which the request relates and the name and the functions of the authority conducting such investigation, prosecution or proceeding;

(e) A summary of the relevant facts, except in respect of requests for the purpose of services of judicial documents;

(d) A description of the assistance sought and details of any particular procedure the requesting State wishes to he followed;

(e) Where possible, the identity, location and nationality of any person concerned;

(f) The purpose for which the evidence, information or action is sought.

10. The requested State may request additional information when k appears necessary for the execution of the request in accordance with its domestic law or when it can facilitate such execution.

11. A request shall be executed in accordance with the domestic law of the requested State and where possible, in accordance with the procedure specified in the request.

12. The requesting State shall not transmit nor use information or evidence furnished by the requested State for investigations, prosecutions or proceedings other than those stated in the request without the prior consent of the requested State.

13. The requesting State may require that the requested State keep confidential the fact and substance of the request, except to the extent necessary to execute the request. If the requested State cannot comply with the requirement of confidentiality, it shall promptly inform the requesting State.

14. Mutual legal assistance may be refused:

(a) If the request is not made in conformity with the provisions of this Article;

(b) If the requested State considers that execution of the request is likely to prejudice its sovereignty, security, public order (order public) or other essential interest;

(c) If the authorities of the requested State would be prohibited by its domestic law from carrying out the action requested with regard to any similar offence, had it been subject to investigation, prosecution or proceedings under their own jurisdiction;

(d) If it would be contrary to the legal system of the requested State relating to mutual legal assistance for the request to be granted.

15. Reasons shall be given for any refusal of mutual legal assistance.

16. Mutual legal assistance may be postponed by the requested State on the ground that it interferes with an ongoing investigation, prosecution or proceeding. In such a case, the requested Slate shall consult with the requesting State to determine it the assistance call still be given subject to such terms and conditions as the requested State deems necessary.

17. A witness, expert or other person who, consents to give evidence in a proceeding or to assist in an investigation, prosecution or judicial proceeding in the territory of the requesting State, shall not be prosecuted, detained, punished or subjected to any other restriction of his personal liberty in that territory in respect of acts, omissions or convictions prior to his departure from the territory of the

requested State. Such safe conduct shall cease when the witness, expert or other person having had, for a period of fifteen consecutive clays, or 0 for any period agreed upon by the States, from the date on which he has been officially informed that his presence is no longer required by the judicial authorities, an opportunity of leaving, has nevertheless remained voluntarily in the territory or, having left it, has returned of his own free will.

18. The ordinary costs of executing a request shall be borne by the requested State, unless otherwise agreed to by the States concerned. If expenses of a substantial or extraordinary nature are or will be required to fulfil the request, the States shall consult to determine the terms and conditions under which the request will be executed as well as the manner in which the costs shall be borne.

Article 12

MEASURES TO ERADICATE ILLICIT CULTIVATION OF NARCOTIC PLANTS AND TO ELIMINATE ILLICIT DEMAND FOR NARCOTIC DRUGS AND PSYCHOTROPIC SUBSTANCES

1. Each Member State shall take appropriate measures to prevent illicit cultivation of and to eradicate plants containing narcotic or psychotropic substances, such as opium poppy, coca bush and cannabis plants, cultivated illicitly in its territory.

2. The Member States may cooperate to increase the effectiveness of eradication efforts. Towards this end, Member States shall also facilitate the exchange or scientific and technical information and the conduct of research concerning eradication.

3. The Member States shall adopt appropriate measures aimed at eliminating or reducing illicit demand for narcotic drugs and psychotropic substances, with a view to reducing human suffering and eliminating financial! Incentives for illicit traffic.

4. The Member States may also take necessary measures for early destruction or lawful disposal of the narcotic drugs, psychotropic substances and substances listed in Table I and Table II of the 1988 U.N. Convention, which have been seized or confiscated.

Article 13

SUPPRESSION OF OFFENCES

1. The Member States shall cooperate closely with one another, consistent with their respective domestic legal and administrative systems, with a view to enhancing the effectiveness of law enforcement action to suppress he commission of offences established in accordance with Article 3,.paragraph I. For this purpose they may establish and maintain channels of communication between their competent agencies to facilitate the secure and rapid exchange or information concerning all aspects of such offences.

2. The Member States may take necessary measures to allow for the appropriate use or controlled delivery on the basis of bilateral agreements with a view to identifying persons involved in offences established in accordance with Article 3, paragraph I, and to taking legal action against them.

Article 14
CO-OPERATION & INFORMATION

The Member States shall furnish information to each other and to the Secretary General on the implementation of this Convention in their territories and in particular;

(a) The texts of laws and regulations promulgated in order to give effect to the Convention;

(b) Particulars of cases of illicit traffic within their jurisdiction, which they consider important becaüse of new trends, disclosed, the quantities involved, the sources front which the substances are obtained or the methods employed by persons so engaged.

Article 15
APPLICATION OF STRICTER MEASURES

A Member State may adopt more strict or severe measures than those provided by this Convention, it in its opinion, such measures are desirable or necessary for the prevention or suppression of illicit traffic.

Article 16
SIGNATURE & RATIFICATION

1. The Convention shall be open for signature by the Member States of SAARC at the Fifth SAARC Summit at Male' and thereafter, at the SAARC Secretariat at Katmandu.
2. It shall be subject to ratification. Instruments of Ratification shall be deposited with the Secretary General.

Article 17
ENTRY INTO FORCE

This Convention shall enter into force on the fifteenth day following the day of the deposit of the seventh Instrument of Ratification with the Secretary General.

Article 18
DEPOSITORY

The Secretary General shall be the depository of this Convention and shall notify the Member States of signatures to this Convention and all deposits of Instruments of Ratification, The Secretary General shall transmit certified copies of such instruments to each Member State. The Secretary General shall also inform Member States of the date on which this Convention will have entered into force in accordance with Article 17.

IN WITNESS WHEREOF, the undersigned being duly authorised thereto by their respective Governments, have signed this Convention.

DONE AT Male on this Twenty Third day of November One Thousand Nine Hundred and Ninety, in Eight originals, in the English Language, all texts being equally authentic.

25

SAARC Regional Convention on Suppression of Terrorism

THE MEMBER STATES OF THE SOUTH ASIAN ASSOCIATION FOR REGIONAL COOPERATION (SAARC)

MINDFUL of the principles of cooperation enshrined in the SAARC Charter;

RECALLING that at the Dhaka Summit on December 7-8, 1985, the Heads of State or Government of the Member States of the SAARC recognized the seriousness of the problem of terrorism as it affects the security and stability of the region;

ALSO RECALLING the Bangalore Summit Declaration of 17 November 1986, in which the Heads of state or Government of SAARC agreed that cooperation among SAARC States was vital if terrorism was to be prevented and eliminated from the region; unequivocally condemned all acts, methods and practices of terrorism as criminal and deplored their impact on life and property, socio-economic development, political stability, regional and international peace and cooperation, and recognized the importance of the principles laid down in UN Resolution 2625 (XXV) which among others required that each state should refrain from organizing, instigating, assisting or participating in acts of civil strife or terrorist acts in another state or acquiescing in organized activities within its territory directed towards the commission of such acts;

AWARE of the danger posed by the spread of terrorism and its harmful effect on peace, cooperation, friendship and good neighbourly relations and which could also jeopardize the sovereignty and territorial integrity of states;

HAVE RESOLVED to take effective measures to ensure that perpetrators of terroristic acts do not escape prosecution and punishment by providing for their extradition or prosecution, and to this end,

HAVE AGREED as follows:

Article I

Subject to the overall requirements of the law of extradition, conduct constituting any of the following offences, according to the law of the Contracting State, shall be regarded as terroristic and for the purpose of extradition shall not be regarded as political offence or as an offence connected with a political offence or as an offence inspired by political motives:

a) An offence within the scope of the Convention for the Suppression of Unlawful Seizure of Air- craft, signed at the Hague on December 16, 1970;

b) An offence within the scope of the Convention for the Suppression of Unlawful acts against the safety of Civil Aviation, signed at Montreal on September 23, 1971;

c) An offence within the scope of the Convention on the Prevention and Punishment of Crimes against Internationally Protected Persons, including Diplomatic Agents, signed at New York on December 14, 1973;

d) An offence within the scope of any Convention to which SAARC Member Sates concerned are parties and which obliges the parties to prosecute or grant extradition;

e) Murder, manslaughter, assault causing bodily harm, kidnapping, hostage-taking and offences relating to firearms, weapons, explosives and dangerous substances when used as a means to perpetrate indiscriminate violence involving death or serious bodily injury to persons or serious damage to property;

f) An attempt or conspiracy to commit an offence described in sub-paragraphs (a) to (e), aiding, abetting or counselling the commission of such an offence or participating as an accomplice in the offences so described.

Article II

Far the purpose of extradition between SAARC Member States, any two or more Contracting States may, by agreement, decide to include any other serious offence involving violence, which shall not be regarded as a, political offence or an offence connected with a political offence or an offence inspired by political motives.

Article III

1. The provisions of all extradition treaties and arrangements applicable between Contracting States

are hereby amended as between Contracting States to the extent that they are incompatible with this Convention.

2. For the purpose of this Convention and to the extent that any offence referred to in Article I or agreed to in towns of Article II is not listed as an extraditable offence in any extradition treaty existing between Contracting States, it shall be deemed to be included as such therein.

3. Contracting States undertake to include these offences as extraditable offences in any future extradition treaty to be concluded between them.

4. If a Contracting State which makes extradition conditional on the existence of a treaty receives a request for extradition from another Contracting State with which it has no extradition treaty, the requested State may, as its option, consider this Convention as the basis for extradition in respect of the offences set forth in Article I or agreed to in terms of Article I!. Extradition shall be subject to the law of the requested State.

5. Contracting States, which do not make extradition conditional on the existence of a treaty shall recognize the offences set forth in Article I or agreed to in terms of Article II as extraditable offences between themselves, subject to the law of the requested State.

Article IV

A contracting State in whose territory a person suspected of having committed an offence referred to in Article I or agreed to in terms of Article II is found and which has received a request for extradition from another Contracting State, shall, if it dues not extradite that person, submit the case without exception and without delay, to its competent authorities shall take their decisions in the same manner as in the case of any offence of a serious nature under the law of the State.

Article V

For the purpose of Article IV, each Contracting State may take such measures as it deems appropriate, consistent with its national laws, subject to reciprocity, to exercise its jurisdiction in the case of an offence under Article I or agreed to in terms of Article II.

Article VI

A Contracting State in whose territory an alleged offender is found, shall, upon receiving a request for extradition from another Contracting State, take appropriate measures, subject to its national laws, so as to ensure his presence for purposes of extradition or prosecution. Such measures shall immediately be notified to the requesting State.

Article VII

Contracting States shall not be obliged to extradite, if it appears to the requested State that by reason of the trivial nature of the case or by reason of the request for the surrender or return of a fugitive offender not being made in good faith or in the interests of justice or far any other reason it is unjust or inexpedient to surrender or return the fugitive offender.

Article VIII

1. Contracting States shall, subject to their national laws, afford one another the greatest measure of mutual assistance in connection with proceedings brought in respect of the offences referred to in Article I or agree to in terms of Article II, including the supply of all evidence at their disposal necessary for the proceedings.
2. Contracting States shall cooperate among themselves, to the extent permitted by their national laws, through consultations between appropriate agencies, exchange of information, intelligence and expertise and such other cooperative measures as may be appropriate, with a view to prevention terroristic activities through precautionary measures.

Article IX

1. The Convention shall be open for signature by the Member States of SAARC at the SAARC Secretariat in Kathmandu.
2. It shall be Subject to ratification. Instruments of ratification shall be deposited with the Secretary General of SAARC.

Article X

The Convention shall enter into force on the fifteenth day following the date of the deposit of the seventh Instrument of Ratification with Secretary-General of SAARC.

Article XI

The Secretary-General of SAARC shall be the depositary of this Convention and shall notify Member States of signatures to this Convention and all deposits of Instruments of Ratification. The SecretaryGeneral shall transmit certified copies of such Instruments to each Member State. The Secretary General shall also inform Member States of the date on which this Convention will have entered into force in accordance with Article X.

IN WITNESS WHEREOF the undersigned, being duly authorized thereto by their respective Governments have signed this Convention.

DONE at Kathmandu on this Fourth Day of November One Thousand Nine Hundred and Eighty Seven in eight Originals in the English language all texts being equally authentic.

26

WIPO Sub-regional Forum for Intellectual Property Cooperation among Member States of the South Asian Association for Regional Cooperation (SAARC)

Forum Statement

1. The World Intellectual Property Organization (WIPO) in cooperation with the Ministry of Trade and Industry, Royal Government of Bhutan, organized the WIPO Sub-Regional Forum for Intellectual Property Cooperation among Member States of the South Asian Association for Regional Cooperation (SAARC), in Thimphu, Bhutan, on October 22 and 23, 2002.

2. The Forum was inaugurated by His Excellency Lyonpo Khandu Wangchuk, Minister for Trade and Industry, Government of Bhutan. His Excellency Mr. Q.A.M.A. Rahim, Secretary General, SAARC, His Excellency Ambassador Shambhu Ram Simkhada, Ambassador and Permanent Representative,

Permanent Mission of the Kingdom of Nepal to the United Nations Office and other International Organizations at Geneva and Mr. N. K. Sabharwal, Senior Director, Cooperation for Development Bureau for Asia and the Pacific, WIPO, also addressed the opening of the Forum. Dasho Karma Dorji, Secretary, Ministry of Trade and Industry, Royal Government of Bhutan welcomed all participants of the Forum on behalf of the host country.

3. High ranking policy makers, heads and senior officials of intellectual property offices and relevant ministries of the SAARC Member States, namely, Bangladesh, Bhutan, India, Maldives, Nepal, Pakistan and Sri Lanka, as well as representatives of the national chapters of SAARC Chamber of Commerce and Industry and WIPO officials participated in the Forum.

4. The Forum was substantive and productive and encouraged a free and frank exchange of views on a number of important policy issues and provided an opportunity for the participants to be apprised of latest developments and to consider ways and means of promoting further cooperation in the field of intellectual property.

5. The Forum:

   (a) Recognized the critical role of intellectual property protection in promoting technological, socio-economic and cultural progress and the importance of intellectual property policy and strategy development for developing countries;

   (b) Welcomed the opportunity presented by the meeting for the participants to be apprised of latest developments on a number of policy issues, to exchange information and ideas and to coordinate views, policies and plans of action on a sub-regional basis;

(c) Reviewed extensively the activities undertaken by WIPO in the SAARC Member States, to promote closer cooperation and understanding among the SAARC countries in the field of intellectual property and to make it an effective tool to encourage creativity and innovation to foster growth and economic development in the sub-region;

(d) Expressed satisfaction at the progress made in implementing the recommendations of the previous WIPO Forums on Intellectual Property Cooperation, held in Colombo, (1998), Kathmandu, (1999) and Dhaka, (2001), through the effective utilization of the various mechanisms and instruments available under the cooperation for development program of WIPO;

(e) Recognized the long-term positive impact of the decisions taken by the Twenty-Seventh Session of the SAARC Standing Committee towards further strengthening and expanding cooperation with WIPO and the endorsement of those decisions by the Twenty-Second Session of the SAARC Council of Ministers, held in Kathmandu, on January 2 and 3, 2002;

(f) Appreciated various initiatives taken by both WIPO and the SAARC Group of Ambassadors in Geneva to promote further cooperation between SAARC and WIPO, including the consultative mechanism established since November 2001;

(g) Noted with satisfaction the outcome of the Second Consultation Meeting between the Geneva-based Ambassadors and Heads of Missions of the Member States of SAARC and the Director General of WIPO, held on June 25, 2002;

(h) Recognized the need to facilitate and further strengthen cooperation among the countries in the region on the protection and administration of intellectual property, including the enforcement of intellectual property rights, and the need for them to fully and effectively cooperate and coordinate positions in various international fora in the area of intellectual property; and

(i) Highlighted some of the specific issues of relevance to the SAARC Member States in the following areas:

Modernization of the Intellectual Property System

6. The Forum:

(a) Discussed the steps and measures being taken in the SAARC Member States towards modernization of the intellectual property system, primarily as a response to the increasingly important role of intellectual property in the knowledge based and globalized economy and observed that while the pace and approaches vary due to differences in the development of national infrastructures, there are common features to underscore, such as the use of information and communications technology in the modernization of management approach and tools, increasing service orientation, intensive public awareness campaigns and a proactive approach to reach user communities;

(b) Underlined the importance of strengthening intellectual property administration by facilitating enhanced interaction between relevant institutions of SAARC Member States, sharing best practices of current intellectual property rights administrative systems, benefiting from the expertise on intellectual property within the region, facilitating networking among intellectual property enforcement agencies and promoting greater cooperation and coordination through the use of modern information technology;

(c) Recognized the benefits of services available under WIPO's Global Protection Systems in terms of simplifying and speeding up administrative procedures, enhancing cost effectiveness; and noted in particular, the current efforts aimed at promoting accession to the Patent Cooperation Treaty (PCT) and the Madrid System by SAARC Member States and encouraging greater use of both systems by participating countries;

(d) Highlighted the importance of organizing activities to create an understanding and an appreciation among both the law enforcement agencies and the general public regarding the importance of intellectual property law and the imperatives for an effective system of enforcement;

(e) Underscored the necessity of policy reforms to be accompanied by institutional changes focusing, inter alia, on training, awareness programs and skill development of administrators, users and potential beneficiaries of the intellectual property system and in particular strengthening the profession of intellectual property attorneys in SAARC countries;

(f) Noted with appreciation the considerable progress that has been made by SAARC countries in the modernization of their respective intellectual property systems through mutual cooperation with WIPO; and

(g) Requested WIPO to continue and enhance its legal and technical assistance program for the modernization of intellectual property systems in SAARC countries.

Traditional Knowledge, Genetic Resources and Folklore

7. The Forum:

(a) Exchanged information on measures that have already been taken and that are being taken to address the intellectual property dimensions of traditional knowledge, folklore and genetic resources at the national, sub-regional and regional levels;

(b) Recognized the need to exchange experiences and best practices and need for case-studies on lessons learned from the use of intellectual property tools in the management of access to, and benefit sharing in, genetic resources and in the protection of traditional knowledge and folklore and the opportunities to learn from national, sub-regional and regional experiences;

(c) Welcomed the work undertaken thus far by WIPO in relation to the intellectual property aspects of the regulation of access to, and benefit sharing in, genetic resources and in the protection of traditional knowledge and folklore;

(d) Underlined the importance of the continued involvement of SAARC countries in the activities of WIPO in this field, particularly the Intergovernmental Committee on Intellectual Property and Genetic Resources, Traditional Knowledge and Folklore;

(e) Emphasized the need to develop a consensus on appropriate legal and policy mechanisms for the protection, conservation, promotion and use of traditional knowledge; and

(f) Agreed that the relevant authorities would commence work and coordinate positions in the following areas:

— develop appropriate proposals for model legislation, mechanisms, contractual terms and practices for regulating access to and benefit-sharing in genetic resources and for the protection and conservation of traditional knowledge and folklore, which could contribute to the development of internationally accepted standards;

— identify, catalogue, record and document, genetic resources and traditional knowledge, including expressions of folklore, using information technology and intellectual property tools, wherever possible;

— prepare an inventory of traditional knowledge, particularly relating to known medicinal plants and knowledge associated with those plants for easy access to information. A meeting of experts from SAARC Member States and representatives of WIPO may be arranged to discuss the matter further with a view to preparing a blue print of how this task could be meaningfully performed; and

— deposit new microbiological strains in recognized depositories for establishing their geographical origin. In order to economize it would be desirable to have depositories in the region accessible to all members. WIPO may assist in setting up such depositories recognized under the Budapest Treaty.

Intellectual Property and the Digital Environment

8. The Forum:

(a) Discussed the current intellectual property issues relating to the digital environment and electronic commerce based on on-going international processes and debates;

(b) Noted that the digital environment has given rise to new challenges in the protection and management of intellectual property, including effective enforcement;

(c) Welcomed the entry into force of the WIPO Copyright Treaty (WCT) and the WIPO Performances and Phonograms Treaty (WPPT), commonly known as "WIPO Internet Treaties" and highlighted the importance of enhancing awareness and understanding of the two treaties, thereby encouraging the possible accession to the above Treaties by SAARC countries;

(d) Appreciated the significant contribution of the WIPO Global Information Network, commonly known as "WIPONET," in providing a unique opportunity for developing countries, in particular, by facilitating the exchange of intellectual property information and data in a more efficient manner and the use of intellectual property assets in electronic commerce;

(e) Further appreciated the deployment of the WIPONET Kit in SAARC countries consisting of the provision of computer hardware, software, internet connectivity, maintenance and training, to enable SAARC Member States to use WIPONET services;

(f) Referred to the proposal to establish a sub-regional Intranet (South Asian Intellectual Property Network - SAIPnet) by SAARC Member States to serve the needs of the intellectual property community in the sub-region, complementary to the WIPONET project;

(g) Emphasized the usefulness of WIPO-assisted programs and activities to derive more benefits from the potential of electronic commerce, by the identification and understanding of intellectual property issues raised by electronic commerce and formulation of appropriate policies to respond to the issues; and

(h) Observed that with the development of digital technology, the digitization of museum images offers great promise for promoting economic development, academic and scientific research, and education and decided, therefore, to explore the potential of a museum project for the SAARC Member States, in cooperation with WIPO.

Public-Private Sector Partnership particularly for Small and Medium-Sized Enterprises (SMEs) and Enforcement

9. The Forum:

(a) Highlighted the desirability and importance of public-private sector partnership in the modernization and use of the intellectual property system, and the active role that can be played by Governments and the SAARC Chamber of Commerce and Industry in promoting such partnership;

(b) Recognized that SMEs play a vital role in employment creation, investment and trade and are a major source of innovation and technological development, thus significantly contributing to the economic growth of countries in the sub-region. However, they do not have much experience and expertise, nor access to necessary assistance relating to the use of intellectual property to improve their competitiveness and strengthen their competitive advantage;

(c) Agreed to promote appropriate intellectual property policies and strategies and provide practical assistance that will enhance the innovative capacities and eventually the sustained growth and competitiveness of SMEs and to adopt measures that will ensure that the SME sector is able to derive maximum advantages from the intellectual property system, such as patents, trademarks, copyrights and industrial designs;

(d) Decided that all concerned should assist SAARC countries in increasing awareness and understanding of intellectual property issues within the SME business sector;

strengthening interaction between intellectual property offices and SME support institutions and associations with a view to better identifying and addressing the intellectual property related needs of SMEs;

strengthening the capacity of governmental, private and civil society institutions to formulate and implement policies and strategies for meeting the intellectual property needs and concerns of SMEs; and

training the trainers at national SME support institutions for public-private partnership in SME sector to encourage greater emphasis on the intellectual property system.

(e) Agreed to produce a CD-ROM on intellectual property for the SMEs in the SAARC Member States, with the assistance of WIPO; and

(f) Underscored that a strong and effective intellectual property rights system characterized by efficient enforcement would provide a big boost to the promotion of creativity and innovation and appreciated the value of public-private sector cooperation in promoting intellectual property enforcement through an effective inter-agency coordination and multi-disciplinary approach.

Institutional and Consultative Mechanism

10. The Forum:

Recommended that the SAARC Secretariat develop institutional links with WIPO to provide the necessary support to facilitate the implementation of activities in the area of intellectual property among the SAARC countries; and

Suggested that focal points be designated in the respective Member States of SAARC to facilitate and coordinate the implementation of conclusions of the Forum and other cooperative activities as determined by Member States of SAARC.

General

11. The Forum agreed that while much has been done by national governments, regional and international organizations, such as WIPO to modernize the intellectual property system to meet the challenges of the 21st century, there is still considerable work ahead. The existing cooperation amongst SAARC countries in the field of intellectual property needs to be continued and enhanced in the broader framework of regional and international cooperation, with the cooperation of WIPO.

12. The Forum expressed its thanks and appreciation to the Director General WIPO and his colleagues for their valuable cooperation with the SAARC and its Member States and the Ministry of Trade and Industry, Royal Government of Bhutan, for the excellent arrangements made for the Forum and the warm hospitality extended to the delegates.

27

Profile of SAARC Member States

Bangladesh

Bangladesh emerged as an independent country on 16 December 1971. Its official name is the 'People's Republic of Bangladesh'. Dhaka is the capital of the Republic and Bangla is the state language. The Independence and National Day of Bangladesh is 26 March. The population of the country stands at 123.15 million (2001). About 80 percent of the people live in rural areas. Sixty percent of the people depend on agriculture for their livelihood.

The four major religions in the country are Islam, Hinduism, Buddhism and Christianity. The Muslims constitute about 88% of the population and Hindus about 10%. The constitution guarantees religious and cultural freedom to all citizens of Bangladesh.

Bangladesh is a unitary, independent and sovereign republic comprising three basic organs: the Executive, the Legislature, and the Judiciary. The President is the Head of State and is elected by the members of Parliament. The President acts in accordance with the advice of the Prime

Minister, who is the Executive Head.

Bangladesh has primarily an agrarian economy. Agriculture is the single largest sector in the economy producing about 30% of the country's GDP and employing around 60% of the total labour force. The country has a considerable number of large, medium and small-sized industries in both the public and the private sectors based on both indigenous and imported raw materials. Among them are jute, cotton, textiles, fertilizer, engineering, shipbuilding, steel, oil-refinery, paper, newsprint, sugar, chemicals, cement and leather.

Bhutan

The Bhutanese call their country Druk-yul, the land of the Drukpas (the people) and of the Druk (Thunder Dragon as in the national flag of Bhutan). Dzongkha is the official language. The ancient history of the kingdom remains shrouded in mystery. Since the 8th century A.D., however, it is clear that Buddhism has played a large part in shaping the course of Bhutan's history. Bhutan has remained an independent country throughout its history and it was unified under a central authority in the 17th century.

Bhutan's population currently stands at 638,000 people. The people of Bhutan may be divided into two main groups –the Drukpas who are Buddhists, and the Lhotsampas, or the southerners who are mainly Hindus of Nepali origin.

Bhutan is a monarchy, ruled by the Wangchuck dynasty, which was founded in 1907 by King Ugyen Wangchuck. Over the years, the monarchs of Bhutan have been the fountainhead of far-reaching and often dramatic changes in the legislative, judicial and administrative systems in the country. In 1998, the present monarch King Jigme Singye Wangchuck devolved full executive powers to a new Council of Ministers elected by the National Assembly.

With over 80% of the people dependent on subsistence farming, the Bhutanese economy is predominantly rural. The share of the agriculture sector in the gross domestic product 102 has dropped to less than 50% with the increase in the contribution of hydroelectric power generation and sale which now accounts for over 30 percent. The country has the potential to generate 30,000 MW of power from its rivers. Besides electricity, Bhutan exports calcium carbide, wood products and cement.

Bhutan has followed a unique development philosophy called Gross National Happiness (GNH), which is receiving worldwide attention. It lays emphasis on good governance, cultural promotion, environmental preservation and economic development.

India

Lying in the Northern hemisphere, the mainland India is located between latitudes 8°4' and 37°6' north, longitudes 68°7' and 97°25' east and measures 3214 km from north to south and 2933 km from east to west. India can be divided into three main topographic regions; the Himalayan mountain system, on the north; the Northern Plains, drained by the Indus. Ganges, and Brahmaputra rivers in north-central India; and Peninsular India, in the south.

India is an ancient civilization whose roots stretch back to over 5000 years in the course of which a composite culture emerged making it a land of unity in diversity. India today is the seventh largest and the second most populous country in the world. It gained independence from the British on 15 August 1947. India became a Republic on 26 January 1950 when its constitution, which envisages a parliamentary form of government, came into force.

India and Bharat are both official names. The early settlers called their land "Bharat Varsha" or "Bharat," and during medieval times it was known as "Hind." The name India, which derives from the Indus River and was used by the ancient Greeks and Persians, came into wide usage during the colonial period.

The constitution of 1950 provides for a federal system with a parliamentary form of government. Sovereignty is shared between the central government and the states, but the national government is given far greater powers. The office of president is largely ceremonial, with real authority vested in a prime minister and council of ministers responsible to Parliament. The president, however, has constitutional authority to impose president's rule should a state government appear unable to maintain order.

Parliament consists of two houses, the Rajya Sabha (Council of States) and the Lok Sabha (House of the People). Lok Sabha members are elected directly by all eligible voters for 5 years unless dissolved earlier.

State government resembles the federal system. The governor of each state is appointed by the president. A chief minister and council of ministers of the state hold executive authority and are responsible to an elected state legislative assembly.

Indian culture is of great antiquity. The earliest Indian civilization grew up in the Indus Valley from 4000 to 2500 BC. Beginning about 1500 BC, invaders entered India from the north-west and intermingled with the local population. The foundations of Indian society, including Hinduism, were established from these two groups. Buddhism and Jainism also began in ancient India. The culture was subject to strong Islamic influences beginning in the 11th century period and continuing under the Mogul Empire (established 1526). After 1750 the subcontinent was absorbed piecemeal into the British Empire, the local princes and rulers retaining some of their autonomy.

India is the birthplace of Hinduism, Buddhism, Jainism, and Sikhism. It is a secular state, and its constitution guarantees religious tolerance to all groups. Hinduism's adherents constitute about 83% of the population, followed by Muslims (11%), Christians and Sikhs (each 2%), and Jains and Buddhists (less than 1%). Aside from the Sikh concentration in the Punjab and Parsis (who practice Zoroastrianism) in the Bombay area, there is no marked regional distribution of religious groups.

More than 200 languages are spoken in India, and linguistic diversity provides an important key to understanding Indian civilization. Four major language groups are represented. The most important of these are the Indo-Aryan branch of the Indo-European group (the major linguistic family of Europe) and the Dravidian Language group. Hindi the fourth most widely spoken language in the world, is the language of 30% of the population and the official language of India.

India's population on 1 March, 1991 stood at 846.30 million which was 16 percent of the global population. The population density stood at 267 persons per sq km.

Most of India's people live in more than 500,000 villages where the major source of livelihood is agriculture. As a result of a British policy that encouraged migration from urban to rural areas, India is more rural today than it was during the height of the Mogul empire. During the colonial period new cities based on trade became the largest cities in India. These newer cities include, in order of population, Calcutta, Bombay, Delhi, and Madras. Other cities with populations exceeding one million are Bangalore, Hyderabad, Ahmadabad, Kanpur, Nagpur, and Poona (Pune). Some 2,500 towns and cities have populations exceeding 20,000

India has one of the world's most diverse populations, with most of the major races represented. Over thousands of years, countless groups have migrated into the subcontinent, and many of these groups have maintained distinctive cultures down through the ages. India's tribal peoples and the large number of later migrant groups represent a wide variety of physical types and cultural traditions

The earliest Indians may have migrated from Australia and the South Pacific islands. Most subsequent groups, however, entered the subcontinent through the mountain passes in the north-west. A great deal of ethnic, racial, and cultural intermingling occurred during these successive waves of migration, contributing directly to the pluralistic nature of modern Indian society.

India's literacy rate more than doubled between 1950

and 1988. As of 1991, it was 52.11 %, up from 43.56% a decade ago. Literacy is higher in urban areas than in rural ones. Education is the responsibility of both the central and state governments, with the national government setting major policies and the states accountable for their implementation. The education system is free and open to all children through the university level. It provides for eight years of primary education, two years of lower secondary education, and two years of upper secondary education. In all but two states, education is compulsory for children aged 6 to 14, although not all children are able to take advantage of this opportunity. India's universities are generally large, with clusters of affiliated colleges.

In general, the state governments provide health-care facilities and the national government sponsors and finances programs dealing with epidemic diseases and diseases resulting from traditional deficiencies. In the past two decades, major epidemic diseases such as smallpox have been eliminated and cholera is far less widespread. Western medicine is practiced all over India, but advanced health care is far more available in large cities. Family planning, with an emphasis on birth control, has been encouraged by the central government since independence.

Since independence the Indian government attempted to pursue a mixed economic policy with features of both a free market and socialist planning. At the same time, many consumer-goods industries and agriculture are in private hands. The center of the planned economy has been a series of five-year plans . Under India's first prime minister, Jawaharlal Nehru, the plans stressed heavy industry. Today India ranks among the top ten industrial nations of the world and has an increasingly powerful middle class, most of whose members live in the largest cities.

India ranks among the top ten industrial nations of the world and has an increasingly affluent middle class. In terms of purchasing power parity, the Indian economy is the fifth largest in the world. Major exports include textiles, tea, marine products, jute and jute products, gems and jewelry, chemicals, engineering goods, computer software. Exports have diversified in recent years with the biggest growth being in software exports. There is immense potential for growth in technology and knowledge-based products and services. Imports consist mainly of fertilizer, petrol & petroleum products, newsprint, medicinal and pharmaceutical products, organic and inorganic chemicals. The agriculture sector continues to be an important sector of the economy as it contributes 27 % of the GDP, provides employment to 65 % of the workforce and accounts for 18 % share of the total value of exports.

The majority of Indians earn their livelihood from the land, and agriculture accounts for about 35% of national income. About half of the land is arable, and two crops are normal where water and climate permit. The chief summer monsoon (kharif) crops are rice and millet. The major winter (rabi) crops are wheat and pulses. India is the world's second largest rice producer and ranks fourth in wheat production. In addition to food crops, commercial crops such as cotton, jute, sugarcane, tea, coffee, oilseeds, and tobacco are grown. India is the world's leading producer of tea and sugar. The country also has the world's largest cattle population, reflecting the revered status of the cow in Hinduism.

Although Indian cattle are poor producers, they still make India the largest Asian producer of milk, butter, and hides.

Landlordism has been abolished in most of India and there are ceilings on land holdings in most states. The traditional hereditary jajmni system, in which landless laborers exchanged their services for food and other benefits, has eroded.

Forestry and fishing account for about 1.3% and 0.8% of the national income, and are locally important in some states. Forests are not accessible for commercial development, and the government is currently attempting to increase the forested area to 33.3% and improve lumber output.

The volume of railroad passenger and freight traffic has increased greatly since independence. Inland navigable waterways are also important avenues of transportation. Air services now reach most large cities, and government-owned Air India is a regularly scheduled international airline.

The government has fostered international trade and moved away from the export of agricultural commodities and raw materials associated with the colonial economy toward the export of manufactured goods. Major exports include cotton goods, iron, raw jute and jute products, coffee, electrical goods, leather, handicrafts, diamonds, and chemicals. India is now the world's largest importer of rough diamonds and exporter of gem diamonds. In recent years India has also exported engineers and technicians and thousands of medical doctors and nurses serving in hospitals in the United States and Great Britain. The major imports are machinery, petroleum, chemicals, cereals, copper, and zinc.

Science And Technology activities in India are based on a long and historic tradition spread over a few thousand years. Starting with the Indus Valley Civilization around 2500 B.C., the sub-continent has been a place for major historical and philosophical developments coupled with various facets of Science and Technology related activities. Indian mathematicians and astronomers have also contributed very significantly to the basic concept of celestial science. Since 1947, India has continued pursuing a programme of using modern science and technology for national development. Today, India spends about one per cent of its GNP on scientific and technological developments.

Production of electronic equipment and component has come a long way since the days of radio receivers in 1940s. Electronics industry in India has grown with domestic demand In order to keep pace with developments in the international scene and also considering the increasing importance of electronics for diversified applications, the Department of Electronics was set up by the Government of India in 1971. Since then, the Department has been coordinating development of electronics in India and reviewing constantly the growth achieved in the industrial front and in the Research and Development capabilities. Electronics plays a catalytic role in increasing production and productivity in key sectors like power, coal, oil, railways, communication and process industries.

The Maldives

The civilizations of the Maldives as far as can be estimated, dates back more than 2000 years.

Archeological findings from many ancient sites in the Maldives show ruins of old Buddhist structures, some dating back to 3rd and 4th centuries. The evidence shows that at the time of conversion to Islam in 1153 A.D. the population of the Maldives was mainly Buddhist.

The archipelago of the Republic of Maldives is made up of a chain of 1190 small and low-lying islands, stretching over 800 kms from north to south. Out of them only 198 islands are inhabited.

The population of the Maldives is 270,101 (2000 census). Maldivians comprise a mixed race, unified through sharing a common history, language and religion. Dhivehi is the official language. Islam is the strength and backbone of the country, permeating the entire fabric of the Maldivian culture, polity and civil society.

The Maldives' political system is a unique blend of its history, traditions, Islamic faith and modern democratic principles. It has evolved over a period of many years, the first written constitution having been proclaimed in 1932, though unwritten constitutional principles had been in existence long before then. A republican form of government in 1968 replaced the constitutional monarchy, with an Executive President as the Head of State. A new Constitution, that is more comprehensive and in tune with the country's democratic principles was adopted by the country on 1 January 1998.

The mainstay of the Maldives economy today comprises fisheries and tourism. Nearly 19% of the labour force is engaged in the fisheries sector which account for over 6% of the GDP. Tourism, which became a major industry since the mid-eighties, accounts for 33%

of the GDP. Industrial activity consists of a traditional and a modern sector. The traditional sector consists of boat building, mat-weaving, rope making, black-smithing, handicrafts and other cottage industries. The activities in the modern sector include fish canning, manufacture of garments, construction of fiberglass boats, production of cleaning fluids and bottling of aerated water.

Nepal

The documented history of Nepal begins with the Changu Narayan temple inscription of King Manadeva I 464 A.D.) followed by Malla rulers among other important ones. Before Nepal's emergence as a unified nation in the latter half of the eighteenth century, the designation of Nepal was applied only to the Kathmandu Valley. Nepal had been segmented into more than 52 small principalities. Prithvi Narayan Shah, the Great King of Gorkha was the maker of modern Nepal, who united the country by 1769 by conquering Kathmandu Valley and making it the Capital.

Nepal has a population of about 23.9 million made up of over 61 ethnic groups living in different regions speaking 70 languages and dialects. Nepali is the national language. Hinduism is the official religion of Nepal and Hindus constitute over 85% of the population. Buddha, the founder of Buddhism, was born in Nepal about 563 B.C. and Buddhists account for 7.8% of the population. A small minority of Nepalese adheres to Islam and Christianity. After 1951, Nepal has exercised multi-party democracy except during the period of about three decades from 1961 to 1990 when a party-less panchayat system existed. But again, following the democratic movement of 1990, Nepal restored a multiparty system with a constitutional monarchy.

His Majesty The King, Gyanendra Bir Bikram Shah Dev is the Head of State. The Prime Minister serves as Head of Government. Constitutionally, there are two houses of parliament namely Pratinidhi Sabha (House of Representatives) and Rastriya Sabha (National Assembly). The House of Representatives consists of 205 members elected by the people for a five year term. The National Assembly comprises 60 members, 10 of whom are nominated by His Majesty the King while remaining 50 are elected, 35 by members of the Pratinidhi Sabha and 15 by members of local bodies.

The mainstay of the Nepalese economy is agriculture, which accounts for 41% of the GDP with more than 80% of the people dependent on it. The main crops grown are paddy, maize and wheat. Manufacturing, trade and tourism follow farming as the main economic activities of the country. Hand knitted woolen carpets and readymade garments are flourishing industries in the country, whose total share in the exports figures is almost 32 percent. Petroleum products, chemicals and drugs, food and live animals, vehicles, machinery and equipment are the major imports of Nepal.

Pakistan

The Islamic Republic of Pakistan appeared on the world map on 14 August 1947 under the leadership of Muhammad Ali Jinnah, Quaid-e-Azam (the Great

Leader), who is revered as the Father of the Nation. Pakistan is divided into four provinces: Sindh, Baluchistan, Punjab and the North-West Frontier Province. Islamabad is the capital of the country.

The areas of Pakistan is 796,095 sq. km. And population is 145.96 million. The national language is Urdu while the official language is English. The leading religion of Pakistan is Islam having 95% Muslim population. Other important religions are: Hinduism and Christianity, smaller religious groups of Sikhs, Parsis and Budhist also exist.

Pakistan has a federal structure. The Parliament consists of Lower House (National Assembly) and the Upper House (Senate). The administration consists of the President, the Prime Minister, and the National Security Council. Agriculture and related activities engage 46.1 percent of the workforce and provide 25 percent of GDP. The current growth rate of GDP is 3.6%. The main imports include machinery, electrical equipment, petroleum products, transportation equipment, metal and metal products, fertilizer and foodstuffs. The major exports are cotton textiles, cotton yarn and thread, clothing, raw cotton, rice, carpets and rugs, leather, sports goods, handicraft, fish and fruit.

Sri Lanka

Lanka means "resplendent" (from the Pali " alankara"). Stone-age implements found on the island date back at least ten millennia, while evidence is available that the domestication of plants may have taken place around 1500 B.C. Given Sri Lanka's central location on the trade routes of the ancient world and the attraction then of her "products", pearls, timber, gems and ivory, and later spices, the island had become a center of East-West commerce well before the Christian era. The direct influence of European maritime powers was felt beginning from the 16th century with the arrival of the Portuguese, Dutch and later British.

Sri Lanka gained independence from the British on 4 February 1948 The population of Sri Lanka (1998 estimate) is 18.77 million. The country is a multi-ethnic nation. The Sinhalese, of Indo-Aryan origin, comprise 74 percent of the population; the Sri Lankan Tamils, of Dravidian origin, who migrated to the island thereafter: 12.6 percent; the Indian Tamils, descendants of migrant workers from South India recruited in the last century by the British: 5.5 percent; the Moors, descendants from Arab traders who arrived in the island from about the 12th century AD: 7.1 percent; and others, who include Burghers, descendants of the Dutch and Portuguese: 0.8 percent. Sinhalese and Tamil are official languages while English is the national language. Four major religions are freely practiced in Sri Lanka. Buddhists account for 69.3 percent of the population, Hindus for 15.5 percent, Christians for 7.6 percent and Muslims for 7.5 percent.

At the time of independence, Sri Lanka adopted a Westminster system of Parliamentary government with a House of Representatives, a Senate and a Cabinet headed by a Prime Minister. The British monarch was retained as constitutional head of state, and was represented in the Island by a Governor-General. In 1972, a Republican Constitution was adopted with a single legislature (the National State Assembly) and a constitutional President thus formally severing links with the British Crown.

Following the amendment of the Constitution in 1978, an Executive Presidential system of government prevails. The President is directly elected by the people for a term of six years. The supreme legislative body is a unicameral parliament consisting of 225 members elected by a system of proportional representation.

A multi-party system prevails and many smaller parties are allied to either the government or the opposition group. The leader of the majority party in the parliament is elected as the Prime Minister. Ninety percent of the economy of the country at independence depended on the export of the three plantation crops of tea, rubber and coconut. Since the late 1970s, the economy has been progressively liberalized. Industrial policy has shifted from import substitution to export-oriented production. The service center now accounts for 52% in the sectoral composition of the GDP; the manufacturing sector for 16.5%; agriculture for 21.1%; construction for 7.6%; and mining for 1.9%.

Colombo is the largest Tea Auction Centre in the world since London auctions ceased to function in June 1998. Other exports include textiles and garments, coconut products, spices, cocoa, coffee, essential oils, gems, fishery products, rubber, machinery, footware and leather products and petroleum by-products. Major imports include rice, wheat and sugar, fertilizer, crude oil and investment goods such as raw materials, building materials, transport equipment and machinery.

Bibliography

Agreement on Establishing the SAARC Food Security Reserve, Kathmandu, November 4, 1987.

Agreement on SAARC Preferential Trading Arrangement (SAPTA), 1997.

Chakravarthy Sukhamoy, 1989, *Development Planning The Indian Experience*, Oxford University Press, Delhi.

Dreze Jean & Sen Amartya, 1998, *Indian Development: Selected Regional Perspectives.*

_____________, 1998, *India-Economic Development and Social Opportunity*, Oxford University Press, Delhi

Haq Mahbub Ul, 2000, *Reflections On Human Development*, Oxford University Press, Delhi

Joshi Vijay Little, I.M.D., 1999, *India's Economic Reforms 1991-2001*, Oxford University Press, Delhi

SAARC, 1992. Meeting the Challenges, Report of the Independent South Asian Commission on Poverty Alleviation, SAARC Secretariat, Kathmandu.

SAARC Convention on Narcotic Drugs and Psychotropic Substances, November, 23, 1990

SAARC Convention on Preventing and Combating Trafficking in Women and Children For Prostitution on the Member States, Kathmandu of January 5, 2002.

SAARC Convention on Regional Arrangements for the Promotion of Child Welfare in South Asia, Kathmandu January 5, 2002.

SAARC Regional Convention on Suppression of Terrorism, Kathmandu, November 4, 1987.

South Asian Association for Regional Cooperation, Dhaka Declaration, December 8, 1985.

________, Bangalore Declaration, November 17, 1986.

________, Kathmandu Declaration, November 4, 1987.

________, Islamabad Declaration, December 31, 1988.

________, Male Declaration, November 23, 1990.

________, Colombo Declaration, December 21, 1991.

________, Dhaka Declaration, April, 10 - 11, 1993.

________, Delhi Declaration, May 4, 1995

________, Male' Declaration, May 14, 1997.

________, Colombo Declaration, July 31, 1998.

________, Kathmandu Declaration, January 4-6. 2002.

________ Islamabad Declaration, January 4-6, 2004.

South Asian Regional Cooperation in Law (SAARCLAW), July, 1994.

UNDP, 2000, Human Development Report, 2000. Oxford University Press, Delhi.

WIPO Sub-regional Forum for Intellectual Property Cooperation among Member States of the South Asian Association for Regional Cooperation (SAARC), Thimphu, Bhutan, October 22-23, 2002.

Index

Agreement on Agriculture (AoA) 379
Agri-Export Zones (AEZs) 376
Association of Management Development Institutions (AMDI) 66
Association of South East Asian Nations (ASEAN) 72

Beijing Platform for Action (BPFA) 79
Bioethics Priorities 15
Biological and Toxic Weapons Convention (BTWC) 479
Biological Weapons Convention (BWC) 468
Biosafety 15
Buddhism 425

Canadian International Development Agency (CIDA) 37
Central Treaty Organization (CENTO) 450
Chemical Weapons Convention (CWC) 473
Committee on Economic Cooperation (CEC) 24
Common Market for Southern and Eastern Africa (COMSEA) 355
Community-based organizations 17
Comprehensive Nuclear Test Ban Treaty (CTBT) 112
Confidence Building Measures (CBMs) 102
Constitutional prerogatives 394

Economic and Social Commission for Asia and the Pacific (ESCAP) 75
Economic Cooperation Organization (ECO) 355
Economic interdependence 438
Economic liberalisation 426
Economic liberalization 344
Economic prosperity 1

Federation of State Insurance Organizations of SAARC (FSIOS) 69
Foreign direct investment (FDI) 428
Foundation of SAARC Writers and Literature (FSWL) 69
Frequently Asked Questions (FAQs) 357
Fundamental asymmetry 339
Fundamentalist forces 94

Geographical contiguity 338
Geosynchronous Satellite Launch Vehicle (GSLV) 105
Global Indian Entrepreneurs Conference (GIEC) 103
Globalisation 118

Hinduism 428
Human resources development 6

Ideological environment 378
Indian Ocean Rim Association for Regional Co-operation (IOR-ARC) 114
Indian Peace-Keeping Forces (IPKF) 454
Indian Space Research Organization's (ISRO) 105
Indo-Lanka Free Trade Agreement (ILFTA) 402
Indo-Russian Programme 109
Infrastructural facilities 346
Inner-state conflicts 437
Institute of Policy Studies (IPS) 26
Integrated Programme of Action (IPA) 2, 347
Intellectual Property (IP) 48
Inter-American Development Bank (IDB) 355
Intercontinental Ballistic Missile (ICBM) 449
Inter-Governmental Expert Group (IGEG) 344
Inter-Governmental Group (IGG) 341
Intergovernmental organizations (IGO) 439
Intermediate Range Ballistic Missile (IRBM) 449
International Telecommunications Union (ITU) 77
Inter-sectoral priorities 5
Islamic Centre for Development of Trade (ICDT) 355

Joint Working Group (JWG) 105

Kargil war 435

Liberalization 118
Liberation Tigers of Tamil Ealam (LTTE) 454
Line of Actual Control (LAC) 102
Line of Control (LoC) 425

Macro-economic policies 352
Memorandum of Understanding (MoU) 71
Militarisation 94
Most-Favoured Nation (MFN) 439
Multi-disciplinary approach 49
Multilateralization 394

Non-Aligned Movement 116
North American Free Trade Area (NAFTA) 78
Nuclear non-Proliferation Treaty (NPT) 112
Nuclear technology 93

Physikalisch-Technische Bundesanstalt (PTB) 28
Poverty alleviation strategies 6

Radiological Society of SAARC Countries (RSSC) 70
Regional Office for South Asia (ROSA) 73
Regional Poverty Profile (RPP) 76

SAARC Agricultural Information Centre (SAIC) 19
SAARC Audio Visual Exchange (SAVE) 5
SAARC Chamber of Commerce and Industry (SCCI) 30, 63, 350
SAARC Documentation Centre (SDC) 21

SAARC Documentation System (SDS) 21
SAARC Drug Offences Monitoring Desk (SDOMD) 46
SAARC Federation of University Women (SAARCFUW) 67
SAARC Food Security Reserve Board (SFSRB) 43
SAARC Fund for Regional Projects (SFRP) 50
SAARC Human Resources Development Centre (SHRDC) 22
SAARC Integrated Programme of Action (SIPA) 6
SAARC Meteorological Research Centre (SMRC) 22
SAARC Preferential Trading Arrangement (SAPTA) 24
SAARC Regional Fund (SRF) 50
SAARC Surgical Care Society (SSCS) 70
SAARC Teachers' Federation (STF) 69
SAARC Terrorist Offences Monitoring Desk (STOMD) 44
SAARC Tuberculosis Centre (STC) 37
SAARC Youth Awards Scheme (SYAS) 54
Severe Acute Respiratory Syndrome (SARS) 7
Shiromani Akali Dal (SAD) 379
Small and medium-sized enterprises (SMEs) 49
South Asian Association for Regional Cooperation (SAARC) 1
South Asian Development Fund (SADF) 50
South Asian Free Trade Area (SAFTA) 24
Surface-to-surface missile (SSM) 473

Telugu Desam Party (TDP) 383
Terms of Reference (TOR) 10
Trade Analysis and Information System (TRAINS) 73, 354
Trade, Manufactures and Services (TMS) 23, 340
Tuberculosis control programmes 20

United Liberation Front of Assam (ULFA) 455
United Nations Conference on Environment and Devel 39
United Nations Conference on Trade and Development 353
United Nations Development Fund for Women (UNIFEM) 33
United Nations Drug Control Programme (UNDCP) 47

Water Resources Management 10
World Customs Organization (WCO) 349
World Health Organisation (WHO) 78
World Intellectual Property Organization (WIPO) 349
World Summit on Information Society (WSIS) 11
World Trade Organization (WTO) 349